From Reliable Sources

FROM RELIABLE SOURCES

An Introduction to Historical Methods

MARTHA HOWELL AND
WALTER PREVENIER

Cornell University Press

ITHACA AND LONDON

First published 2001 by Cornell University Press
First printing, Cornell Paperbacks, 2001

Printed in the United States of America

Library of Congress Cataloging-in-Publication Data

Howell, Martha C.
    From reliable sources : an introduction to historical methods /
Martha Howell and Walter Prevenier.
        p. cm.
    Includes bibliographical references and index.
    ISBN 0-8014-3573-0 (alk. paper) ISBN 0-8014-8560-6 (pbk.)
    1. History—Methodology. 2. History—Research. 3. Historiography.
4. History—Philosophy.   I. Prevenier, Walter. II. Title.
D16 .H713 2001
907'.2—dc21   00-012624

Cornell University Press strives to use environmentally responsible suppliers
and materials to the fullest extent possible in the publishing of its books.
Such materials include vegetable-based, low-VOC inks, and acid-free papers that
are recycled, totally chlorine-free, or partly composed of nonwood fibers. Books
that bear the logo of the FSC (Forest Stewardship Council) use paper taken from
forests that have been inspected and certified as meeting the highest standards for
environmental and social responsibility. For further information, visit our website at
www.cornellpress.cornell.edu.

1 3 5 7 9   Cloth printing   10 8 6 4 2
    5 7 9   Paperback printing 10 8 6 4

Contents

Research Bibliography

Acknowledgments

This book is based on *Uit goede bron* by Walter Prevenier, which was first published in 1992.[1] Although its title is a direct translation of the Dutch original, *From Reliable Sources* itself is not a translation. It is an adaptation and expansion of the Dutch text for American students, whose needs are in some ways significantly different from those of Belgian and Dutch history students.

Each of us necessarily played distinct roles in translating, revising, and adding new material to the Dutch original, but we worked so closely together on all aspects of the project that it is impossible to distinguish one contribution from the other. *From Reliable Sources* is, thus, a fully collaborative effort, a jointly authored book in the most literal sense. We did not, however, work alone, for we could not have completed it without the advice and help of many other scholars and students. It is a great pleasure to be able formally to thank them for their assistance.

Marc Boone of the Department of History at the State University of Ghent provided valuable suggestions and corrections to the entire text. Jean Bourgeois of the Department of Archaeology, also at Ghent, assisted us with the sections on archaeological techniques; Melody Eble of Janssen Pharmaceuticals in Titusville, N.J., helped us gain information about the

1. The 1992 version was a revision and expansion of a handbook first issued in 1969 [Walter Prevenier, *Een overzicht van de geschiedkundige kritiek. Nota's bij de cursus* (Seminarie Geschiedenis: Ghent, 1969)] and republished every year until 1992. *Uit goede bron* was recently reissued in a revised seventh edition, coauthored by Walter Prevenier, Marc Boone, and Martha Howell (Garant: Leuven-Apeldoorn, 2000).

Levamisole story we relate in chapter 3; and Jack Matlock of the Institute for Advanced Study, Princeton, provided crucial details about President Reagan's actions during the Cold War. A group of graduate students in history at Columbia University read the manuscript in draft and offered excellent suggestions concerning presentation of our material and the book's organization. For this help, we thank Eric Barry, Mary Doyno, Abigail Dyer, Christopher Ebert, Anna Maslakovic, Dominique Reil, and Ramzi Roughi; we hope they recognize their contributions to this version. John Ackerman, our editor at Cornell, was a wise and patient supporter at every stage in the process; to him and to the fine readers he selected for the Press, our grateful thanks.

In preparing the reference bibliography, we relied heavily on the expertise of many scholars. Volker Berghahn and Adam Kosto of Columbia University's History Department provided key references, as did Luc François of the Department of History at Ghent. At Columbia, Michael Stoller, Director of the Humanities and History Collection in Butler Library, and Eileen McIlvaine, Head of Reference Services in Butler, along with their staff, made extensive suggestions about organization and content at an early, critical stage of preparation. Martine De Reu of the Department of Manuscripts in the library of the State University of Ghent added valuable material to our lists. Marcia Tucker, librarian in the School of History at the Institute for Advanced Study in Princeton, also generously assisted our work, as did Don Skemer, librarian in the Department of Manuscripts at Princeton University's Firestone Library. Finally, Connie Kearns McCarthy, Dean of University Libraries at the College of William and Mary's Swemm Library, provided much-appreciated research help. Nadia Zonis and Dominique Reil of Columbia's graduate history program assisted with editorial matters.

We owe deep thanks as well to the many students who began historical studies with us in years past. Their questions about historical method, its own history, and its future are the genesis of this book; we hope to have provided as useful a response as they deserve.

MARTHA HOWELL *and* WALTER PREVENIER

New York City and Ghent

From Reliable Sources

Introduction

All cultures, all peoples, tell stories about themselves, and it is these stories that help provide the meanings that make a culture. In its most basic sense, this is what history is: the stories we tell about our prior selves or that others tell about us. In writing these stories, however, historians do not discover a past as much as they create it; they choose the events and people that they think constitute the past, and they decide what about them is important to know. Sometimes historians think they need to know about an event because it seems to have had a direct role in making the present; sometimes historians choose their object of study simply because it seems central to a past that is important today. But historians always create a past by writing it. History is not just there, awaiting the researcher's discovery. Unlike a forgotten poem, the ruins of a cathedral, or a lost law code that might be uncovered, history has no existence before it is written.

Yet it is exactly these kinds of artifacts that historians use to interpret the past, exactly such materials that constitute the *sources* with which historians build meanings. It is no wonder then that at least since the nineteenth century, when history writing in the West was firmly located in the academy and professionalized, when it became what some still call "scientific," historians have paid careful attention to how sources are chosen and interpreted. They have developed sophisticated techniques for judging a source's authenticity, its representativeness, and its relevance. They have constructed typologies of sources, dividing them into genres that lend themselves to systematic comparative analyses, and they have invented ingenious strategies for decoding and interpreting sources. This technical work has long been considered the backbone of history writing in the West, and historians have traditionally judged the quality of their own or their colleagues' work in terms of its mastery of these skills. Seen from this point of view, the historian's basic task is to choose *reliable* sources, to read them *reliably*, and to put them together in ways that provide *reliable* narratives about the past.

One purpose of this book is to introduce beginning researchers to the techniques historians deploy in that task. Although readers will soon discover that reliability is a stubbornly elusive goal, our text is nevertheless based on the premise that critical analysis of sources is the basis of good historical scholarship. Thus, the body of this book begins at the beginning, with sources. Chapter 1 first asks what materials count as sources and then considers such questions as how sources can be categorized according to their forms, the kinds of information they can provide, and the ways historians have typically used them. Chapter 2 opens the historian's tool box, introducing and cataloging techniques that have been developed for decoding particular kinds of sources, marshaling their strengths and exposing their weaknesses.

It will have become apparent, however, that no source, and no interpretation of it, is perfectly *reliable*, if by that one means that it provides certain knowledge about the past. The remainder of our book works to demonstrate the limitations of a historical method aiming at such certainty and discusses the strategies historians have devised to cope with these limitations. It does so in two ways. First, in chapter 3, we consider the fallibility of sources themselves, that is, their inherent inability to provide anything but a partial, incomplete, and necessarily biased view of the events they ostensibly report, and the difficulties any historian faces in trying to adjust for that partiality. We also discuss how the historian's distance from the culture under study makes full appreciation of a source's limitations impossible. Second, in chapter 4, we consider how historians come to mine sources for certain kinds of information at the expense of others, how they come to ask the questions they ask and select the issues on which they concentrate. Here, too, we examine the historiographical theory and practice that has particularly influenced the last two generations of historians in the West. Chapter 5 considers the way historians in the past and those of today have thought about change and causality— once considered the central questions of historical inquiry and still today on every historian's agenda, if only implicitly. The book ends with a discussion of history's uses, both in a past that was less skeptical about the possibilities for absolute knowledge and in a present where such matters seem considerably less certain.

From Reliable Sources is not, then, intended as a handbook explaining how to research and write history correctly.[1] To be sure, it offers a guide to the most useful of the techniques historians in the West have devised for analyzing sources, and it preserves the profession's central tenet that a critical engagement with the records of the past can produce useful knowledge about that past. But it also attempts to unseat easy assumptions about the certainty of our knowledge about the past, and to make clear that the uncertainty lies not just in the stubborn opacity of sources but in our inherent inability to get beyond sources themselves. Thus it exposes the central paradox of our profession: historians are prisoners of sources that can never be made fully reliable, but if they are skilled readers of sources and always mindful of their captivity, they can make their sources yield meaningful stories about a past and our relationship to it.

\(\textit{\large ❧}\)

This book was written by historians trained in European and American traditions of scholarship and representing a small branch of that profession, the medieval and early modern history of northern Europe, particularly the Low Countries. Its progenitor was a text first written over thirty years ago at the University of Ghent, Belgium, in connection with an introductory course in a Master's and Ph.D. program. That text has had a long life, in many subsequent editions, throughout the Dutch-speaking Low Countries. Although this English-language version of the text has evolved very far from those beginnings, it still bears the marks of its origin, in a seminar on historical methodology taught in Europe.

Inevitably, then, this is not only a Eurocentric book, written from the point of view of European historiography; it is also to some extent a specialist's text, emphasizing techniques of particular use to medieval and Renaissance scholars. We intend this book, however, for a much larger readership, hoping that beginning researchers working in other periods and specializing in different regions, not only outside Europe but also outside the West, will find it helpful. Any history written by Westerners today, whether focused on the West or not, is the heir of the tradition described in this book, and any such scholarly account of the past is written with the aid of these techniques. Even scholars from non-Western coun-

---

1. Readers interested in such a guide might consult Gordon B. Davis and Clyde A. Parker, *Writing the Doctoral Dissertation: A Systematic Approach* (Hauppauge, N.Y., 2nd ed., 1997).

tries are indebted to these practices, for they are members of an international intellectual community that includes the West; moreover, many write and teach at universities modeled on Western institutions, and some have studied in the West. The historical method described in this book has had, then, an effect far beyond the borders of Europe, and certainly far beyond the temporal and geographic boundaries set by the medieval and early modern Low Countries.

These traditions of historical scholarship have a long and complicated history, extending to Greek and Roman culture, the Jewish and Christian tradition, and Islamic civilization. Together they fashioned for western Europe a set of scholarly and critical skills for studying the past and for seeing the past as profoundly related to the present. To be sure, today we write history differently than the Ancients did, and we refuse many of the methodologies they developed, but we are nevertheless their heirs. In the chapters that follow we will return to certain features of this historiography, emphasizing the elements of lasting influence as well as the moments of rupture and of rapid change. As we will also point out, this historiography has a political past as complicated as its methodological one. This is necessarily so, for methodological choices are inevitably political choices in the sense that they dictate the particular sources examined, the evidence deployed, the events studied, the importance assigned to any event, source, or piece of evidence. Previous ages were frequently quite self-conscious about the politics of history, forthright in their claims about its appropriate uses. Historians today are sometimes less forthcoming, but they are no less bound by notions about what kind of history counts and what methodological standards should be imposed in making that judgment.

History writing proper, as the West has conceived it, is usually considered to have begun with the Greek Herodotus (ca. 485–425 B.C.E.), for he made, as his contemporaries generally did not, an effort to distinguish a verifiable past from what counted as myth, that is, from stories that could not be substantiated according to rules of evidence. He also sought to differentiate the essential from the incidental, to make connections and locate cause. He had many distinguished successors, including Thucydides (ca. 455–400 B.C.E.) and Polybius (200–120 B.C.E.), who tried to construct narratives which related the peoples of the past to the present. Thucydides himself relied heavily on dramatists such as Euripides for his psychological portraits of characters and his use of a dialectic to describe and explain historical change. Polybius is perhaps best remembered for his cyclical model of periodization patterned after the human life cycle of growth, maturity, and decay, a model that was later deployed by such historians as Ibn Khaldun, Machiavelli, Montesquieu, and Arnold Toynbee.

For long centuries after Polybius, history was conceived of as a series of studies in practical morality. Sallust (ca. 86–35 B.C.E.), for example, attacked the aristocracy of his time for moral decay, attributing the Roman state's weakness to its elite's failure to uphold the standards of their predecessors. Plutarch (46–119) and Suetonius (69–122) compiled massive biographical sketches to illustrate good and bad behavior, to display men honored for their integrity, bravery, probity, or wisdom—or dishonored for their dishonesty, cowardice, vulgarity, or stupidity. The genre is still with us; as schoolchildren, all of us read the lives of men such as George Washington, Winston Churchill or Charles de Gaulle, who were presented as paragons of virtue, farsightedness, courage, and intelligence. While professional historians and biographers do not today usually write such uncritical biographies, many do still look to the past for lessons about the present—negative or positive. Consider, for example, Daniel Goldhagen's *Hitler's Willing Executioners* (1996), which offers contemporary Germans a lesson about their past national character, a critique of present-day politics, and, implicitly, a cautionary tale about the future.

Early Jewish and Christian scholars tended to shift the focus away from practical morality, seeking instead to make connections between the divine and the earthly narrative. For them, religion was part of human history, a sacred story that unrolled in earthly time and space. Christian writers thus treated Christ as the visible manifestation of God on earth, part of the human story of salvation. In order to render the Bible intelligible and increase its verisimilitude, historians from Eusebius of Caesarea (fourth century) forward also struggled to locate every event and each person from the Old and New Testaments in what was then the dominant narrative of secular history, the Roman. Augustine's (354–430) *City of God*, surely the best example of the genre, portrayed human history as an enactment of God's plan, a pilgrimage toward the final judgment.

During the Middle Ages, history was even more emphatically merged with religion, to the point that miracle stories became history, that is, they were understood and reported as though they had occurred in the same way a flood, famine, or battle might have occurred. And reports of such happenings were accepted without the degree of critical scrutiny now associated with history writing, for the chroniclers to whom such events were reported were less interested in verifying the event than they were in the *story* of the event. To be sure, some miracles were meticulously documented, in efforts to "prove" their authenticity, and modern-day scholars have shown that the naïveté of these chroniclers was often more apparent than real, for medieval chroniclers were able to judge evidence more critically than their narratives sometimes suggest. In fact, many such accounts were explicitly written as propaganda, tales to convince readers of the power of a bishop, the sanctity of a local holy person, the justice of a cause—just as modern-day agents promote the virtues of this tourist attraction, the magnificence of that mogul's home, the sufferings caused by that accident, the evil of this or that politician. For Guibert of Nogent, a very Christian author, for example, the purpose was to paint Mohammed in the worse possible light; there was no story about this man that was too terrible to report, no deed too heinous to relate. The last thing Guibert was concerned with was whether the tales he told were *true*; he cared only if they helped his case. While it is easy to mock such chroniclers, we should remember that our own age tells such stories as well. Think, for example, of Ronald Reagan's polemics about the "evil empire" of the Soviet Union. Although this kind of history writing is very far from what we would call serious history today, it did attempt something few classical authors had thought necessary—to reach a broad public. Medieval chroniclers were not writing exclusively for a state or ecclesiastical elite; their stories were meant to be told to—meant to create a history for—more ordinary people as well.

Although medieval historiography was designed to serve Christianity, it never lost its interest in and respect for antiquity, an affinity that was especially apparent during the celebrated "medieval Renaissances" of the ninth and twelfth centuries. In the Carolingian Renaissance, for instance, Einhard imitated and shamelessly plagiarized Suetonius's *Vitae Caesarum* (*Lives of the Roman Emperors*) when writing his own *Life of Charlemagne*. During the richer twelfth-century Renaissance, Christian scholars studiously examined and adapted Roman law, and Christian copyists transcribed hundreds of Greek and Roman manuscripts, including works of Caesar and Livy. It is to this copying project that we owe most of the copies of these texts that we possess today.

It was not, however, Christians alone who studied and preserved classical culture, for pride of place in this enterprise easily goes to Jewish and, above all, Islamic scholars. In certain cities where the three cultures lived side by side, such as medieval Toledo, scholars read, exchanged ideas about, and debated new interpretations of the ancient scientists. In thirteenth-century Perpignan (now in southern France), Jewish scholars collaborated with Christian teachers at the university. The most important center of cultural exchange was, however, medieval Islamic Andalusia. The great Jewish scholar Maimonides (1135–1204), who lived in Cordoba, Fez, and Cairo, was one of several who introduced the Greek philosopher Aristotle to Islamic science and directly influenced the work of Christian scholars such as Thomas Aquinas. The Islamic historian Ibn Khaldun (1332–1406), who lived in Tunis, Granada, and Cairo, was a student of Greek historiography and was well known in Christian Europe by way of Mozarabic Spain.

By the later Middle Ages, historians had entered the service of the secular elites—lords, monarchs, and the state. Medieval aristocrats patronized historians who created for them noble, glorious pasts, sometimes entirely fabricating the evidence but more often simply selecting evidence that made the case and interpreting it in a way that gave legitimacy to the elite to whom it was offered. Some of these histories had even more profound effects. Villehardouin's thirteenth-century narratives, which celebrated the Burgundian aristocracy's valor and religious faith, inspired many of the exploits of the Crusades. In the fourteenth and fifteenth centuries, Froissart and other chroniclers of the Burgundian court gave this aristocracy a past which helped make the splendor of that court possible. After the emergence of an urban middle class, that class too found its historians.

The Renaissance of the fourteenth to sixteenth century (the "great" Renaissance) marks, however, the first clear break with medieval historiography. The Italian intellectuals who gave birth to this Renaissance, and the northern Europeans who followed, were to explore classical literature and philosophy more deeply than their medieval predecessors had done. Yet the distinguishing feature of Renaissance learning was not so much its return to classical learning; that had occurred during previous "Renaissances" in medieval Europe. The decisive features of the Italian Renaissance were, first, its break with the narrow provincialism of medieval European culture and, second, its destruction of the church's monopoly on learning.

There are, nonetheless, two paradoxes involved here. The first is that, however much historiography may have been freed from exclusive service to the Latin church, which sought to impart a universal Christian doctrine, it did not become a secular project. On the contrary: it was co-opted by both sides in the religious conflicts of the sixteenth century. That century of reform produced, in fact, some of the most partisan, apologetic historiography western Europe has known. In Protestant circles there was, for example, Matthias Flacius Illyricus, who edited the *Historia ecclesiastica* (1559–74), the chief purpose of which was to demonstrate that the Roman church's claim to be the direct heir of first-century Christianity had no historical basis. The Catholics answered with Cesar Baronius's *Annales ecclesiastici* (1588–93), which argued, in conformity with decisions of the Council of Trent, that the line of descent was in fact direct and pure.

The second paradox is that these debates helped produce a critical historiography, for each of the sides challenged the other by showing that the opponent had misused evidence, suppressed relevant information, reasoned illogically, and so on. They also advanced the techniques of source criticism, furthering work done in the fifteenth century by such luminaries as Lorenzo Valla, who famously uncovered some medieval forgeries by showing the anachronisms in their content. Seventeenth-century critics went further, learning to identify fraud by studying the formal properties of documents—structure, paleography, vocabulary, and the like. The Bollandists (a Jesuit order located in the Spanish Netherlands) played an important role in this evolution, by establishing editorial standards for the saints' lives they began publishing in 1643. Dom Jean Mabillon's *De re diplomatica* of 1681, the first manual of diplomatics, was the product of a similar effort by the Maurists (a Benedictine order from St. Germain des Près near Paris). Thus, a "rational" historiography was born, as it became no longer possible to authenticate a document simply by making claims about its authorship or its provenance.

The Enlightenment of the eighteenth century added a certain cosmopolitanism to history writing, for this was the century when European intellectuals began to revise their view of themselves and their culture as they confronted the rest of the world and were compelled to conclude that the Christian West was not its center. Scholars such as Voltaire (1694–1778) argued, for example, in his *Essai sur les moeurs et l'esprit des nations* of 1756 (translated as *The General History and State of Europe*), that the Indian, American, and Chinese civilizations were in many ways superior to the European. It was in this period as well that the concept of "civilization" entered the historian's vocabulary, a term that would be central in the work of later scholars such as Jacob Burckhardt and Johan Huizinga. Obviously, this cosmopolitanism was born in the explorations that had started in the late fifteenth century with the Portuguese, and it was the encounters with the peoples of the rest of the globe that inspired the optimism that characterized the histories of so many of the eighteenth-century philosophers and historians. Reason and nature replaced god; possibility replaced determinism. Giovanni Battista Vico's *Scienza nuova* (*New Science*) of 1725 perhaps best expresses this spirit.

Some, however, were not made optimistic by the encounters with the New World. Montesquieu (1689–1755) drew upon Polybius's more pessimistic cyclical theories of history in his *Considérations sur les causes de la grandeur et de la décadence des Romains* (*Considerations on the Causes of the Greatness of the Romans and Their Decline*) of 1754. His ideas were taken up by Edward Gibbon in his famous *History of the Decline and Fall of the Roman Empire*, which appeared in 1776–88. He saw the fall of Rome as the result of a conflict between two civilizations, the Roman on one hand, and the Christian on the other. In his eyes, however, the Christian was contaminated by the influences of the pagan barbarians (about whom Gibbon knew almost nothing). In the collision, Rome fell and Christianity, which was in part barbarian, triumphed.

Romanticism, a reaction to the abstraction and rationalism of Enlightenment thought, dominated the first half of the nineteenth century. For these intellectuals, culture and feeling were paramount, an approach perhaps best represented by Johann Gottfried von Herder's *Ideen zur Philosophie der Geschichte der Menschheit* (*Reflections on the Philosophy of the History of Mankind*) of 1784–91. Although Herder was in fact a man of the Enlightenment—cosmopolitan, liberal, optimistic—he transformed Enlightenment historiography with his concept of the "Volksgeist" (the soul of the people). This rather vague notion refers to a sort of genius considered unique to each culture and comprising the economic, social, political, and spiritual traditions of the people. While Herder himself was a complex intellectual whose own attitudes were very far from the racism later associated (under Hitler) with the notion of "Volksgeist," this idea caught the imagination of many romantics who would help transform it into an apology for aggressive nationalism. The romantic movement also bred the cult of the individual and, in historiography, a passionate interest in individuals and the heroism of their stories. Thomas Carlyle's *On Heroes, Hero-Worship, and the Heroic in History* of 1841, is exemplary, and his *Frederick the Great* of 1858 is a song of praise to that leader's power. Romanticism also, and most famously, took up the task of celebrating the liberal state—the creation of the French Revolution—with Jules Michelet's *Histoire de France* (1833), which celebrated the realization of the French "Volksgeist" in the popular movements that fueled that revolution.

In the nationalist tradition of history writing that reached an apogee in the later nineteenth century, historians became water carriers for a kind of political nationalism that celebrated the national character and treated the particular culture being celebrated as the end point of a long development toward which some vaguely defined historical forces were striving. Such narratives have, of course, a long and distinguished history. The ancient Greeks wrote histories of the Greek nation, and Roman historians, as chroniclers of the Roman state, bequeathed a profoundly nationalist historiography, dedicated to the purposes of state. In his history of the Gallic Wars, for example, Julius Caesar (100–44 B.C.E.) celebrated the military power of the Romans, along with his own formidable talents as military leader. Livy (59 B.C.E.–17 C.E.) fed Roman chauvinism with a history that celebrated eight proud centuries of the Roman past.

For centuries thereafter western Europeans imagined their civilization as the pure form of civilization, thus very early formulating the kind of narratives that we today call Eurocentric. The Dutch, as one of the first self-conscious nations, were early contributors to this genre. In the late sixteenth century, just as the economic and cultural separation of northern Europe from the south was taking form, we see the first flourishing of histories centered on the Dutch nation (then called the United Provinces), which had led the way in northern Europe's expansion. Emmanuel van Meteren's *Historien der Nederlanden* (translated as *A true discourse historicall of the succeeding governours of the Netherlands*), from 1599, and Pieter Corneliszoon Hooft's *Nederlandsche Historien* (History of the Netherlands) of 1642 were among the first; these studies privileged not just the Dutch state, but the province of Holland (which contains Amsterdam) to the exclusion of the rest of the country, particularly its eastern and southern regions.

The nationalist revolutions of the nineteenth century obviously helped fuel this kind of historiography. It is from this period that we have Jules Michelet's *Histoire de France*, already mentioned. Also in this tradition is the first volume of Henri Pirenne's *Histoire de Belgique* (1900; History of Belgium), for it sought to give the newly formed Belgian state a past in the rich medieval history of the region. Thomas Macaulay's *History of England* (5 volumes, 1849–61) represents a characteristically English brand of such nationalistic romanticism, what is known as Whig historiography. His work, an account of the English revolution of 1688 and its aftermath, is a panegyric to the virtues of those (especially the Whigs) who brought the revolution about. The effects of this book on generations of English people and on their historiography were profound, for it provided a smug sense of English superiority and gave the English license to export their version of bourgeois culture to the rest of the world.

Nationalist histories, even in benign forms, served to reify and celebrate the state by creating exclusionary stories about the past, stories that erased oppressions, obscured certain historical actors, and exaggerated the triumphs and talents of the winners. In Germany after 1870, much nationalist historiography took the form of praise for the Bismarckian state. Gustav Schmoller's (1838–1917) influential school of historical economy and Friedrich Meinecke's pre-1914 political histories characterize the genre. Later in Germany, and in other European countries as well, nationalistic historiography took even more ominous turns, abandoning any attempt at "objectivity" as a "Blut und Boden" ("blood and soil") history was deployed to create a national past that supported newly racist ideologies and politics.

There have, of course, always been resisters to this kind of nationalist historiography. During the eighteenth century, Vico, Voltaire, and Montesquieu were among the many who argued that people of different cultures shared more than they did not share, that cultural practices and beliefs were learned, not innate, and that they were almost infinitely variable. In the course of the twentieth century, nationalist historiography has taken a new, more productive, turn. In The Netherlands, the traditional Hollandocentric narrative was ended when Pieter Geyl published his *Geschiedenis van de Nederlandsche stam* (1930–37; History of the Netherlands race). Reacting against the historiography of the past, Geyl took a wider area as his subject, the whole of the Low Countries, excluding French-speaking Wallonia. His use of the word "stam" (race) was unfortunate and seemed to ally him with the right-wing movements then taking hold throughout Europe, although Geyl was himself an ardent antifascist. In fact, he stubbornly refused ethnicity as the basis of cultural coherence, insisting instead on language and culture, which united the peoples who shared topography and social history. For him, the Dutch state (formed in 1648 at the end of the eighty years' war) was a result of rather capricious military and political factors, not an inevitable or even productive occurrence.

Although few academic historians today write nationalist histories in the nineteenth-century vein, there are, even so, varieties of nationalist historiography still in fashion. During the 1980s in France, for example, a new form of the genre was developed, most famously by one of the great twentieth-century masters, Fernand Braudel. His three-volume *L'identité de la France* (1986; *The Identity of France*) did, indeed, begin with a ringing statement recalling past historiography: "J'aime la France avec la même passion, exigeante et compliquée, que Jules Michelet" ("I love France with the same insistent and complicated passion as Jules Michelet did"). Nevertheless, Braudel is very far away from Michelet in spirit, for he locates "la France" in demography, social infrastructure, and formal institutions, not in the soul. In the same period another French "nationalist" surge was begun by Pierre Nora. His 1984 *Les lieux de mémoire* (*Realms of Memory*), written with the flair typical of the *Annales* school, provides an inventory of "places of memory" that are national symbols (monuments, sites), texts, or even abstract notions (lineage, generation), which together constitute France.[2] Braudel, Nora, and their colleagues have thus given us a richer, more complex, and more generous vision of what it is to be French.

The past is thus open territory for historians and their readers, available for various uses, to fill different needs. Before the eighteenth century, we have seen, historians tended to treat the past as a storehouse of examples from which to construct lessons for the present. For them the past was a close-by, accessible place, not a distant time. Thereafter, historians came to treat the past as a far-away and alien culture. Still, even for these historians, the past had relevance for the present. Romantics saw it as the birthplace of the *Volk*, the womb in which the authentic culture of a people was nurtured and from which it could somehow be reborn. Nationalists tended to search through the past for the threads that connected it to their vision of the present. Nostalgia for the past, for a time when things were better—more peaceful, beautiful, or mysterious—infects many histories, probably none more so than medieval histories. But not all nostalgia respects the past. Some of today's projects to build or venerate historical monuments are often driven by contradictory motives, some to honor, some to question. Think, for example, of the Vietnam War Memorial in Washington, D.C., or the S.S. cemetery in Bitburg, Germany, so famously visited by Ronald Reagan during his presidency.[3]

Although the nationalist historiography so readily associated with the nineteenth century has thus not entirely disappeared today, the century is perhaps best remembered for the men who professionalized history writing and joined forces with the great social theorists of the age. In the wake of this scholarship, the discipline of history was forever changed. Leopold von Ranke (1795–1886), to whom we will frequently refer, is credited with the founding of "scientific method" in history writing, and it is from this moment that the discipline proceeded to become what it is today. In Ranke's view, history was a learned craft, the science of "telling things as they actually occurred," of insisting that "if it is not in the documents, it did not exist." His (anti)theoretical stance gave birth to what is called <u>historicism</u> (in this sense, the notion that the past must be understood simply on its own terms—and that such understanding is available only through carefully analyzed sources), and, in the nineteenth-century intellectual climate where it originated, historicist method served as a useful corrective to a kind of imaginative storytelling that had dominated much

2. For the *Annales* school, see chapter 4.
3. On the Bitburg cemetery and President Reagan's visit to it, see Alan B. Spitzer, *Historical Truth and Lies about the Past* (Chapel Hill, N.C.—London, 1996), pp. 97–115.

of romantic historiography. Ranke was, however, hardly free of ideology or theory. He was, emphatically, a nineteenth-century liberal, and his works, especially his famous *History of the Popes* (1901; orig., *Die Römischen Papste, ihre Kirche und ihr Staat im XVIII. Jahrhundert,* 1834–36), betray all the anticlericalism of that ideology and, along with so many of his contemporaries, a deep commitment to the national state.

Positivism—the notion that objective knowledge about cause and effect is attainable via objectively analyzed data—was closely associated with Rankean method, but it owes its theory to the work of the century's social theorists. Auguste Comte is credited with positivism's fullest formulation, which was presented in his *Cours de philosophie positive,* published between 1830 and 1842 (translated in abridged form as *The Positive Philosophy,* 1853). His specific argument, that the cultural was determined by socioeconomic factors that underlay and were thus more fundamental than the cultural, would dominate social thought during the rest of the century. For historians, positivism posed essential questions about causality and determinism—was man the "agent" of his own history or captive of forces larger than he? For Christian thinkers, "free will" on earth had been a given; for Comte the concept of free will had no meaning. Alongside this pessimism about individual agency, however, positivism brought optimism about the future. Because humankind was subject to laws outside itself, it was also knowable because those laws were knowable. And the human condition could be improved, even perfected, once those laws were perfectly understood. Its promise and its premises influenced almost every historian who followed—from Hippolyte Taine (1828–95), one of the great liberal scholars, to Karl Marx, the greatest of the socialist theorists.

Marx has many intellectual debts, of course, positivism being only one of them. But he did share with positivists the assumption that a kind of objective knowledge about the past was achievable and that historical change turned, fundamentally, on socioeconomic change. In this regard, he influenced scholars such as Karl Lamprecht (1856–1915) and his Belgian student Henri Pirenne (1862–1935), two of the century's greatest socioeconomic historians, for they too emphasized the role of socioeconomic structure, although neither could be called marxist. Lamprecht, a liberal from a bourgeois German family, shifted Marx's emphasis from class and class conflict to the role of the entrepreneur in capitalist development—a predilection starkly visible in Pirenne's work and in a vigorous tradition of liberal socioeconomic history that has followed.

Whatever its naïveté about its biases, "scientific historiography" (in both its historicist and its positivist forms) did encourage the development of new methods and exchange with other disciplines. It was in this period that historians discovered archaeology and that archival science was born (the famous Ecole des Chartes in Paris was established in 1821). It was also during this period that the history seminar, focusing on research with primary sources, emerged as the centerpiece of graduate training throughout the West, first in Germany in the middle of the nineteenth century, then in France and the United States.[4]

The twentieth century was as creative as its predecessor, although it is fair to say that much of the creativity was deployed to unseat nineteenth-century historicism and positivism. Later in this book we will return to the innovations of the "new" histories of various sorts, with their taste for new territories and new methodologies. The "new social history," we shall see, has radically expanded the range of subjects available for historical study. What the French call "marginals"—the poor, the sick, the insane, the lame and halt, the criminal—have become a central focus of many such historians, as have social institutions and social groups that previous historians had all but ignored—the family, the school, the prison, the hospital, women, homosexuals, children, African Americans, immigrants, people of color. Social history has rewritten political history as well, shifting emphasis from great men and their deeds to the institutions and networks that make politics possible—clans, clientage and patronage systems, voting blocks, political parties, and so on. And social historians of the past century have recast Marx, sometimes by debating the implications of his writings, sometimes by preserving only part of the marxian apparatus and turning to new questions. In the Soviet bloc, of course, marxism had evolved differently, into a rigidly orthodox way of writing history that allowed no deviation from officially sanctioned marxist doctrine. Since 1989, however, that historiography has been superseded. Although many of the scholars trained in those traditions have found integration into the new academy difficult, a new generation of historians from both the Soviet and Western blocs is now rewriting the history of that area.

The "new cultural history" represents a perhaps sharper break with the past, although there were important prewar progenitors. Huizinga, for example, with his *Herfsttij der Middeleeuwen* of 1919 (most recent English ver-

---

4. The first efforts to adopt the German method in the United States were made at Harvard and Columbia, in 1857; thereafter, the seminar method was firmly institutionalized at Johns Hopkins under Herbert Baxter Adams. In the 1880s, John W. Burgess made it the center of graduate training in history at Columbia. This history is recounted in Bryce D. Lyon, *Henri Pirenne* (Ghent, 1974), pp. 42–44; also see Harry E. Barnes, *A History of Historical Writing*, 2nd ed. (New York, 1962), pp. 259–66.

sion, *The Waning of the Middle Ages,* 1999) approached late medieval Burgundian aristocratic society as though it were a work of art, a stylistic creation that expressed the sociopolitical system, the moral values, the religious longings, the mentalité, of the culture. That the culture he studied had lost its material underpinnings—that the world of knights and ladies, chivalry, honor, and God which it imagined no longer existed (perhaps had never really existed)—was, for Huizinga, unimportant. Or, perhaps, it was exactly the point; culture, the meanings that humans impose on their actions, Huizinga argued, has a life and an agency of its own. It is not, as generations of social histories had assumed, reducible to or a reflection of a more fundamental reality. Huizinga's method was, then, to pay more attention to performance than to structure, to the aesthetics (the "poetics," to use a modern-day cultural studies term) of a society than to its social systems, its political apparatus, or even its learning. Huizinga himself was indebted for this approach to another, even older, scholar, the Swiss Jacob Burckhardt, whose *Kultur der Renaissance in Italien* of 1860 (*The Civilization of the Renaissance in Italy*) practically invented Renaissance studies. Their notions that each culture has a mentalité, a way of understanding, imagining, and presenting the world, bears close affinities to much of what the most modern cultural histories see as the object of their study.

The truly "new" cultural history is, however, usually considered to have emerged after the 1970s, in the wake of the scholarly transformations wrought by the many varieties of social history of the middle third of the twentieth century. Much of that explosion was fueled by what is generally called the "linguistic turn," the new attention to language and textual form generated by poststructuralist literary and cultural analysis. In chapters 4 and 5 of this book we return to these developments, discussing their origins and implications for historical studies in greater detail. As we shall see, they challenge many of the assumption on which professional history writing is based, for they call into question the very terms of our craft—our search for "reliable sources." They do not, however—we will insist—render critical historical method obsolete.

❦

Remnants of past historiography, whether in its nationalist or its moralizing mode, whether positivist or historicist in its search for truth, survive today among professional historians in the contemporary West. Still, historians today rarely write as their predecessors did. The dominant mood today is considerably less celebratory, more self-reflective, and more revisionist than it was a century, two centuries, or ten centuries ago. It is also

equal measure, and it is the historian's job to supplement the raw material available in the source itself.

Both relics and testimonies were usually created for the specific purposes of the age in which they were made. What are called relics were, typically, objects of practical use in daily life and only later, in the ages that followed, came to be treated as historical sources. The same is true of most testimonies, whether oral or written. They were composed to provide contemporaries proof of an act or of a right, or in order to inform them about a fact. Only rarely were they designed for the use of posterity, although that sometimes occurred. In contrast to a relic, the content of a testimony is thus usually more important than its form. Still, the form of such a report often tells the alert historian a great deal; to this point we will later return. It is perhaps unnecessary to point out that one of the historian's principal tasks is to uncover the original purpose or function of the relics or testimonies that have come down to posterity, to divine what use they were intended to serve and what purposes they actually served at the time they were created.

Testimonies and artifacts, whether oral or written, may have been intentionally created, perhaps to serve as records, or they might have been created for some other purpose entirely. Scholars sometimes think of the first as having had an "intention," the second as being "unintentional." In fact, however, the distinction is not as clear at it may at first seem, for a source designed for one purpose may come to have very different uses for historians. For example, a film taken to record one event but which inadvertently captured another might well be "unintentional" in conception, as was the film of President John F. Kennedy's assassination taken by a bystander who meant only to record the parade for his private enjoyment. That film's role in history and in historical interpretation has, however, been profoundly more important. A memoir written to explain a life, a legal brief designed to prove a case in court, and a portrait commissioned by a noblewoman obviously are not innocent of design and motive, for they were produced with specific purposes in mind. To distinguish an "intentional" source from an "unintentional" is not to argue that one is more transparent, more reliable than another. Unintentional sources are unintentional only in the sense that they were not produced with the historian's questions in mind; they are not, however, otherwise "innocent." Conversely, intentional sources contain features not under the control of their authors and have lives beyond their original intentions. A memoir intended to justify the choices its author made during her life may, in fact, inadvertently reveal the uncertainties and untruths that she sought to conceal. It may, moreover, have been received in totally unexpected ways, therefore affecting the future in ways the author would never have intended.

Historians must thus always consider the conditions under which a source was produced—the intentions that motivated it—but they must not assume that such knowledge tells them all they need to know about its "reliability." They must also consider the historical context in which it was produced—the events that preceded it, and those that followed, for the significance of any event recorded depends as much on what comes after as it does on what comes before. Had the Boston Tea Party of 1773 not been followed by the American Revolution, it would have had considerably less significance than historians have since given it, and the very same newspaper report of the uprising, in the very same archive, would have had a very different status from the one it actually acquired. Thus, historians are never in a position—and should never imagine themselves as being in a position—to read a source without attention to both the historical and the historiographical contexts that give it meaning. This, of course, is the heart of historical interpretation.

Sources are thus those materials from which historians construct meanings. Put another way, a source is an object from the past or testimony concerning the past on which historians depend in order to create their own depiction of that past. A historical work or interpretation is thus the result of this depiction. The relationship between the two can be illustrated by an example: The diary left by a midwife who lived in colonial New England constitutes a source. On the basis of such a source, Laurel Thatcher Ulrich created a prize-winning historical study, *A Midwife's Tale* (1990). A source provides us evidence about the existence of an event; a historical interpretation is an argument about the event.

Although when we use the term "source" we have in mind these primary sources, such sources can themselves be direct or indirect. A direct source might be the letters or chronicles that come to us from eighteenth-century businessmen, a law code written in 846, or a poem penned just yesterday. An indirect source might be an eighteenth-century inventory listing the letters and books found in an educated woman's study, from which scholars could deduce something about the kind of training she had received and her intellectual interests; or, to pursue the examples given here, it might be an eleventh-century register cataloging the contents of a princely archive that named the ninth-century code; or it could be a computer printout of sales of poetry volumes from the Barnes and Noble at Broadway and 82nd in Manhattan.

The boundaries between a source (whether direct or indirect) and a historical study are not always, however, so clear. Although an ancient weapon—a spear or a catapult, for instance—or a deed transferring ownership of a piece of land is, obviously, a source in the usual sense, certain documents have an ambiguous and shifting status. Herodotus and Thucydides, for example, each of whom provided accounts of events in their own days, can be considered both historians of their ages—creators of historical interpretations—and authors of sources in that they provide modern-day historians evidence both about these events and about the intellectual culture of the ages in which they wrote. In many cases, moreover, the sources that former historians used to compile their own accounts are lost to the present, so the historical interpretation they constructed serves present-day historians also as a "source of sources," their only route to lost evidence. The church history left by Eusebius of Caesarea (ca. 265—340 C.E.), for example, mentions countless texts that are now lost; his work thus serves not only as a historical interpretation concerning the first Christian centuries, but also as an indirect source about this era.

It is thus one of the primary responsibilities of the historian to distinguish carefully for readers between information that comes literally out of the source itself (in footnotes or by some other means) and that which is a personal interpretation of the material. For the literal content of a citation—what is transcribed from the source itself—historians have no ethical responsibility; for the meaning they impart to that material, of course, they are entirely responsible.

B. Source Typologies, Their Evolution and Complementarity

Written sources are usually categorized according to a tripartite scheme: as narrative or "literary," as diplomatic/juridical, or as social documents. Although these categories are arbitrary and, as we shall see, can distort as much as clarify the status of the evidence a particular source can provide, it is important to recognize that sources do, in fact, have generic qualities. One kind of source can not be read exactly like another, and each should be analyzed in terms of its formal properties as well as in terms of content.

Sources traditionally classified as *narrative or literary* include chronicles or tracts presented in narrative form, written in order to impart a particular message. The motives for their composition vary widely. A scientific tract is typically composed in order to inform contemporaries or succeeding generations; a newspaper article might be intended to shape opinion; the so-called ego document or personal narrative such as a diary or memoir might be composed in order to persuade readers of the justice of the author's actions; a novel or film might be made to entertain, to deliver a moral teaching, or to further a religious cause; a biography might be written in praise of the subject's worth and achievements (a panegyric or hagiography). Such sources thus take many different forms, which are highly dependent upon the conventions of the age in which they were written. The category of "narrative source" is therefore considerably broader than what we usually consider "fiction." Novels and poetry—the archtypical fictions—are, nevertheless, a subset of this category, a kind of source, although they were not composed with the purpose of informing successors about the time in which they were written.

Questions of intentionality, discussed above, become especially important in the case of "ego documents." Diaries, for example, can almost never treated as reliable reports about an event, but must be read in terms of the very individual perspective from which they were written, as an index of what the author (that is, the "intellectual author," a term we will define later) considers his truth.[1] Memoirs are similarly selective accounts, always highly edited versions of the life being recorded, almost always highly teleological in structure (in that they are written to explain the outcome of a life, not to record its process). In general, then, ego documents record the author's perception of events, perhaps even his memory of how he experienced them, and they can often tell us a great deal about the writer's political intentions and his tactics, as well as his ideology and the culture of the age.

Diplomatic sources are understood to be those which document an existing legal situation or create a new one, and it is these kinds of sources that professional historians once treated as the purest, the "best" source. The classic diplomatic source is the charter, a "legal instrument," what Germans call the *Urkunde*, the French the *charte* or *diplôme*. This is a document, usually sealed or authenticated in some other way, intended to provide evidence of the completion of a legal transaction or proof of the existence of juristic fact and which could serve as evidence in a judicial proceeding in the event of dispute. Scholars differentiate those legal instruments issued by public authorities (such as kings or popes, the New York Court of Appeals or the U.S. Congress) from those involving only private parties (such as a will or a mortgage agreement).

The form of any particular legal instrument is fixed. It possesses specific formal properties (external, such as the hand or print style, the ink,

1. "Truth" is, to be sure, a slippery notion for the individual recounting an event. See, for further discussion, Donald P. Spence, *Narrative Truth and Historical Truth: Meaning and Interpretation in Psychoanalysis* (New York, 1982).

the seal; internal, such as particular rhetorical devices and images) which are determined by the norms of law and by tradition. Such characteristics thus vary in time (each generation has its own norms) and according to provenance (each bureaucracy has its own traditions—the emperor's has one style, the pope's another, the United States House of Representatives' still another).

Technically, a diplomatic source is composed of three parts. The first is the "protocol," which is generally quite stereotypical; it includes the names of the author or issuer and of the recipient, a standard opening or salutation, and an appeal to some higher authority that legitimates the legal act—perhaps a god ("in the name of the Father . . ."), a secular lord ("by the power invested in me . . ."), or a principle of justice ("we hold these truths to be self-evident . . ."). The second is the content itself, the recitation of the case and its determination. Here the form is variable, being determined largely by the purpose of the document. The third is the closing (the *eschatocol*); again, the form is stereotypical, containing various authenticating formulas, witnesses, dates, and so on.

These charters can also be categorized according to function. Some are law-giving (ordinances, declarations of law, statutes, etc.). Others are juridical (judgments of courts and of other legal authorities); still others record voluntary agreements between individuals authenticated by public notaries, by officials of bishops, or by aldermen of cities. They deal with contracts, wills, marriage licenses, and all other forms of social agreements.

What historians often refer to as *social documents* are the products of record-keeping by bureaucracies such as state ministries, charitable organizations, foundations, churches, and schools. Containing information of economic, social, political, or judicial import, these documents provide accounts of particular charges or agencies (ambassadors' reports, municipal accounts, the findings of a particular commission), of meetings (parliamentary debates), of business policy. Or they give a survey of an administrative structure (the property registers of a monastery), of a fiscal structure (tax rolls), of a social structure (registers of births, marriages, and deaths, lists of citizenship registrations), or of a political administration (lists of rulers, cabinet officers, legislators).

Written sources of these kinds, although certainly essential to most historians' work and although sometimes imagined to be the exclusive suppliers of historical data, are by no means the only kind of historical source. Unwritten sources, both material and oral, are as essential elements of the historian's arsenal. Like written sources, they are of different types, or genres.

Archaeological evidence, whether articles from daily life, artistic creations such as jewelry or vases, dwellings, graves, roads, churches, or fortifications, counts as one of the most important categories of unwritten evidence. Such artifacts can tell historians a great deal about the culture of the area, the ways of life, the artistic ambitions of the people who lived there. If the objects unearthed in one place can be identified as having been made in another, they can also reveal a great deal about the commercial and sociocultural interconnections of the age.

Sometimes the archaeological object is little more than the trace of a former settlement, a scar left on a landscape. Even relics as apparently insignificant as the charred beams of a burned house, especially if they have been left untouched through time, can provide the historian valuable information. Archaeological sites of interest to historians are sometimes buried under present-day structures and first unearthed during excavations undertaken in the course of building a modern construction such as a subway or sewer line. For example, in 1993, Native American burial grounds were discovered in New York City during excavations for new subway construction.

Coin hoards, and sometimes hoards of paper currencies, have similarly provided historians with valuable information about the institutions of government, about economic conditions, about trade relations, about fiscal policy. In addition, historians rely heavily on visual representations, whether handmade or hand-finished, such as paintings, etchings, and drawings, or machine-produced, such as films and photographs.

Oral evidence is also an important source for historians. Much comes from the very distant past, in the form of tales and the sagas of ancient peoples, or from the premodern period of Western history in the form of folk songs or popular rituals. Such evidence also comes, however, from our own day, in the form, for example, of protest songs or other kinds of artistic performances. The interview is another of the major forms of oral evidence produced in our age. In their original form, all these sources were purely oral (or visual), and few were recorded in permanent ways. Hence, they are lost to scholars today. But some were preserved in one way or another, and it is thanks to those preservations, often accidental, that historians can still have access to them. In the present age of film and radio, a great many oral or otherwise ephemeral sources have thus been rendered "written," so that in some ways historians are today even more likely to use "oral" sources.

The degree to which any historian uses oral or material evidence depends, to a large extent, on the period being studied or on the particular subject under investigation. Historians' knowledge about prehistoric times—that is, the age before written records—is necessarily based entirely on the material or, indirectly, on the oral record. Beginning about

3000 B.C.E., writing was invented in Mesopotamia, thus inaugurating the "historical" age in human history. Thereafter, Greeks and Romans developed writing to an art, to a highly sophisticated form of communication, and it is for that reason that scholars have so much deeper and more nuanced knowledge of these ancient societies than of others. This is also the explanation for the profound influence these cultures have had on our own. During the early Middle Ages, however, oral communication became relatively more important, and it was only around the twelfth century that written communication achieved dominance even in elite circles in medieval Europe. With the invention of the printing press at the end of the fifteenth century, western European history came to be based principally on written sources. The press permitted exact reproduction, in quantity, of documents of all kinds—news reports, statutes, letters, fictions, poetry, drawings—thus assuring their long survival and wide circulation. The introduction of writing and printing had an enormous influence on intellectual history as well, for they gave scholars more extensive and more accurate access to the thoughts of their predecessors.

Nevertheless, historians do not rely entirely on written sources for their knowledge even of those ages in which the printed text existed. Moreover, the boundaries between written and oral, or for that matter between verbal and material, are arbitrary. Although historians have traditionally categorized material and oral sources apart from written, thereby calling attention to the generic differences among them and the dangers of treating them the same, skilled researchers know not to assume the differences, but to consider them critically. Today most scholars are use a mixture of oral, written, and other material sources as the situation requires.

What scholars know, for example, about the people of the "Ancien Régime" (the term used in much of France and western Europe to refer to the period from the late Middle Ages to about 1800)—about their actions, ideas, beliefs, and fantasies—comes to them through a wide variety of sources, some originally written, some written only after the fact, some never written. Folk songs, monuments, stories and tales, miniatures, drawings and other visual representations (vanity alone saw to it that we have countless portraits from the age) take their places alongside newspapers and diplomatic documents to provide the material on which historians have based extraordinarily rich accounts.

Technical innovations of the nineteenth and twentieth centuries have yielded new kinds of sources that continue to blur the boundaries between written, oral, and "material." To a certain extent, such innovation involved simply an improvement in quality: the photograph and, above all, the film provide representations that are in some ways more realistic than the painted or drawn image. The years between 1802, when Thomas Wedgwood invented the photogramm on silver nitrate paper, and 1888, when Kodak introduced the film roll, were the decisive decades in the history of the still photograph. The period between 1832, when Joseph Plateau began experiments with moving film, and 1893, when Thomas Edison perfected techniques, was the crucial age for the development of technology for moving pictures. It was only around 1950, however, that the technology became available to preserve films adequately, and it is still more recently that efforts have been made to copy and thus preserve films made before that period. Until 1900, most films were what we call "documentaries," reports of current events or of natural phenomena. Dramatic films were made after that date, although it was not until after 1927 that we had "talkies."

Sound recordings date from the late nineteenth century, at least from Thomas Edison's creation of 1877. The gramophone recording followed, and since the 1980s we have had the compact disk. The collection of oral information on a grand scale began, however, with the tape recording, first made (out of metal) in 1931, and around 1940 produced synthetically.

The radio began in 1896 and was publicly available after 1902; regular transmission began in the United States after 1920. Television saw the first experiments in 1927; in 1936 it was made publicly available in London, in 1941 in New York. Ten years later it came to most of the European countries. This medium did not, however, constitute a true source, at least not in its early years, for the transmissions via television were mostly live, and were rarely recorded or saved. In contrast, tape or celluloid film recording events had a much greater chance of being saved, but it was only between about 1940 and 1970 that these media were widely used. These tapes do not, however, constitute a secure source. Typically, they have not lasted, and as they have deteriorated, information has been lost. Even the saved information is sometimes inaccessible. The French TV system, to cite just one example, has over 500,000 documentaries on tape—but has no way to make them easily accessible to researchers. Television's potential as a historical source has, then, some distance to go.

Similar problems beset the computer files on which a huge quantity of recent decades' social documents are stored. Many are at risk of erasure or inaccessibility; an even greater problem is posed by the rapid changes in hardware and software, for a record made today may be unreadable with the technology of tomorrow. In 1983, for example, it was discovered that a huge portion of the fiscal records kept by the United States government were inaccessible, because the Japanese company which had supplied the original technology for reading these records was no longer making it. The problem here is not so much technical as organizational; what is needed is a political and financial commitment to maintaining the accessibility of these materials.

All these sources, although different from one another, are in many ways complementary. Oral records obviously can complement the written, a realization that was for too long lost on most professional historians. One of the first to recognize the relation of oral traditions to written texts was Jan Vansina, a Flemish historian who is now teaching in the United States.[2] A student of West African culture, he established that the stories handed down from one generation to another in that culture were as stable and reliable accounts of their past as were the written chronicles and personal narratives that have survived from the western European past, that in fact they were of the same genre.

Vansina's argument was, in essence, methodological, for he was not saying that all oral accounts achieve this level of reliability; they do so only if they meet several tests. Vansina's tests concerned both matters external to the text (is the narrator [or witness] a member of the group that controls the transmission of the narrative? does the narrative come to the researcher via a social institution or via a closed caste?) and those internal (is the narrative stylistically coherent, that is, does the witness's or reporter's tale conform to the linguistic, stylistic, ritualistic, and juridical norms of the period and the place from which his tale is told [or pretends to originate]?). Vansina's contribution to historical methodology was significant, for historians had by and large not understood that in many societies (including Europe of the tenth and eleventh centuries), social relations were sustained through oral acts, and that the most important legal transactions achieved their authenticity by means of oral witnessing and the like. Oral communication thus rarely indicates arbitrary action and social anarchy; it can, in fact, be the mark of a complex and well-ordered sociopolitical system.

Still, historians can place trust in oral sources only to the extent that they can be verified by means of external evidence of another kind, such as archaeological, linguistic, or cultural. In one case, for example, researchers studying travelers' reports from sixteenth-century Africa were able to make sense of attitudes and practices described in those reports by comparing them to similar behaviors characteristic of modern, better-understood cultures and by analysis of the archaeological record. Thus, in this case historians were able to use the present to understand the past. It would, however, be a mistake to conclude from this instance that such

2. J. Vansina, *De la tradition orale. Essai de méthode historique* (Tervuren, 1961); in English as *Oral Tradition as History* (Madison, Wis., 1985).

comparisons will always be fruitful. Human cultures do not remain unchanged over time. Even before the period of colonial rule in Africa, we know, sociocultural upheavals of enormous importance took place on that continent; thus, neither there nor anywhere else dare we assume that the social codes and cultural patterns are in any sense "eternal." Indeed, the anthropologist's impulse, to look for basic—and somehow unchanging—patterns, should be complemented by the historian's bias—to expect and look for change.

It is not only premodern cultures that produce oral sources of use to the historians. All cultures do so, and in certain instances oral reports can provide critically important evidence. In times of social upheaval (during wars, revolts, and strikes, for example), witnesses are not inclined to write down their experiences—resisters have to fear their occupiers, strikers their bosses and the law. For that reason, interviews can sometimes substitute for the personal account that cannot be written. Al Santoli's oral history of the Vietnam War provides one revealing example of the value of such techniques. Santoli interviewed thirty-three veterans of the conflict who reported events that never made it into the official documents constituting the military archives. The men interviewed told of their initial optimism and bravado and then how the realities of combat—the body bags, carnage on the battlefield, terror, shock, and loss—destroyed morale and humanity among them.[3]

Interviewing—or the kind of interviewing that can serve the careful historian—is, however, no simple art. The questions asked must be carefully designed, in accordance with an overall plan about the kind of information sought and about the tests of reliability to which it will be subjected; at the same time, however, the interviewer must be flexible, able to shift the terms of the interview to pursue unexpected avenues and avoid dead ends. In general, "hard" interviews can be distinguished from "soft." In the first—the kind of real value to historians—the interviewer has worked hard to reconstruct the historical situation in which the informant lived in order to get beyond the simple narrative about what did or did not happen. A good interview is one in which the story becomes richer, more nuanced, more understandable in the telling, not one in which guilt or innocence is proved, a cause is vindicated, a person found out. Thus, even an interview constructed as though it were a "fact-finding" expedition is something much more; it is in itself an interpretation, a source that must be analyzed with extreme care.

3. Al Santoli, *Everything We Had: An Oral History of the Vietnam War by Thirty-three American Soldiers Who Fought It* (New York, 1981); see also Mark Baker, *Nam: The Vietnam War in the Words of Men and Women Who Fought It* (New York, 1981).

C. The Impact of Communication and Information Technology on the Production of Sources

Although historians make choices among the materials left by the past, treating one object or text as a source and rejecting another or relegating it to secondary status in the hierarchy of evidence, they must choose from what is available. Only certain kinds of potential evidence was produced in any given age, only some of that was preserved, and only a portion of that is accessible to any given historian. If they are to make wise choices among potential sources, historians must thus consider the ways a given source was created, why and how it was preserved, and why it has been stored in an archive, museum, library, or any such research site.

The availability of sources is, in general, very much determined by technology, that is by the conditions under which a given culture received and collected information. The mechanisms of communication and the speed at which information circulated are both elements of this technological history of sources. This history can be divided into three periods.

In the first, information was transmitted by people who walked or ran with the news, at a rate probably never exceeding six miles per hour. The medium of transmission was thus the messenger himself. Sometimes messages were also sent by visual signal (flags) or by sound (drums), and thus news traveled faster, but in none of these cases could a complex message be delivered with great precision, and in all of them geographic or climatic conditions could radically limit the range and speed of transmission. Today, such methods are of course rarely used, but some conventions have survived—the custom, for example, of flying flags at half mast to mark a death or the practice of ringing sirens to sound an alarm.

In the second phase, information was transported using pack animals. This phase began about 2000 B.C.E. in central Asia, about 1000 B.C.E. in the Mediterranean area, and sometime during the sixteenth century among the Incas in Peru, and is still used in some parts of South America and Africa. Average speeds using this form of transportation were at least double, often triple, those in areas where information was carried by people.

Other technical developments further improved this mode of transmission. By 3000 B.C.E., Mesopotamians were using clay tablets to record information; around 1000 B.C.E. the Phoenicians developed an alphabet, which made writing much more efficient. Persian kings created the courier system of transport, in which messages were handcarried by specially designated agents, a method later used both in Byzantium and in Rome. By the thirteenth century an elaborate system for delivering the

mail had been worked out to connect the Florentine banking and merchant houses to the trade fairs in Champagne (France); the system was
adopted by the pope in the following century. By the end of the fifteenth
century Europe had a net of postal connections that had been developed
by the Milanese firm of Thurn and Taxis; in 1505 the firm was granted a
monopoly for the Spanish post.

In 1436, a trip between London and Venice took 23 to 51 days, and in
1442, a journey from Genoa to Bruges lasted 22 to 25 days. Thus, distance traveled daily averaged 30 to about 50 miles. Between the fifteenth
and the nineteenth century, this rate of travel was to double, thanks to the
long-distance routes that were constructed during this period.

Three categories of information were transported in this period, each
of which required a slightly different technology of literacy. The first included secret correspondence ("litterae clausae") of various kinds (economic or business, diplomatic, military) which had to be written in code.
The second was general correspondence ("litterae patentes") which, in
time, was taken over by the newspaper, the third category. The forerun-
ners in the production of this genre were the Venetians, who regularly
penned commentaries (called *avvisi*) to accompany the business correspondence they sent all over Europe; they were followed by the German
trade cities like Nuremberg and Wittenberg, which produced what they
still call *Zeitungen* (newspapers). True, printed newspapers with a regular
periodicity appeared first in Strasbourg (1609) and Antwerp (1629). It
was only later that a distinction was made between simple newssheets
(which had no explicit editorial content) and "newspapers of opinion."

The third phase of communication is, of course, defined by mechanical media. In 1830, the train increased the speed at which information
could be transmitted to 30 to 35 miles per hour. With the invention of
the telegraph in 1844, information transmission became almost instantaneous. By 1896 it required only seven minutes to transmit a message
from one place on the globe to another. The more recent innovations
such as telephone, fax, radio, television, and satellite have made information transmission truly instantaneous and practically universal. Accompa-
nying this technological revolution were organizational changes in the
way information was gathered and delivered. The nineteenth century saw
the emergence of huge wire services such as Reuters and U.P.I, which
provide news services to thousands of small clients; most newspapers rely
entirely on these services for information from beyond their own locality
and thus have no independent sources by which they can verify the data
they receive.

It is evident that the speed at which a piece of information can be transmitted, along with its ubiquitousness, directly affects its influence. Today's media (CNN, for example) make the world a "global village," and that is in some sense a cheerful thought, for it means that people today increasingly have access to exactly the same information at the same time and often react similarly. But it also means that an incident such as the Cuban Missile Crisis of 1962 elicits an immediate reaction, in Moscow and Washington alike, with all the risks that such speed entails.[4] Still, there are real advantages to the speed of communication possible today. Consider, for example, that when the harvest failed in fifteenth-century England or the Low Countries, it took two months before grain could be purchased in the Baltic area and another two months before it arrived where needed— far too late for a huge portion of the population.

The power of modern-day communications, with their steady stream of fashion changes and technical innovations, depends, however, not just on the speed at which messages travel but also on the quality of the carrier and of the distribution system. It also depends on the readiness of the audience to accept the innovation. It is, for example, no accident that the first mechanical clocks were developed in Italy in the fourteenth century and were first imitated and distributed in Flanders and England, where Italy had good commercial relations and where the commercial infrastructure and socioeconomic system were similar.

The material qualities of the message itself affect its influence as well. When, in the human past, messages were first written and then printed, their survivability and distribution potential increased enormously, but with the advent of radio and TV, messages have in some ways become more ephemeral. In general, one can say that the quality and accuracy of messages increased when letters and manuscripts replaced oral transmissions and then, later, printed materials replaced handwritten. Marshall McLuhan has famously argued, in fact, that the "medium is the message," that the form in which information comes is often more significant than the message itself. The centuries-long domination of the written word implicitly privileged—and developed capacities for—abstract thinking; TV and film, in contrast, emphasize the visual, the concrete.

Mass communications can also create collective memories. By this, we mean that when information about an event, or series of events, is broadcast widely and simultaneously, the event becomes part of a shared experience, part of historical memory. The Vietnam War in the late sixties and early seventies provides a perfect example: the daily news reports about

---

4. See, on the Cuban missile crisis, E. R. May and P. D. Zelikow, *The Kennedy Tapes: Inside the White House during the Cuban Missile Crisis* (Cambridge, Mass., 1997).

the war created for a great many Americans, especially young Americans, a single experience, an experience that galvanized political resistance to the war. The lesson, it should be noted, was not lost on the American military. Media coverage of the Gulf War (1990–91) was much more restricted, and if a collective memory survives of that war, it will surely be of the way it was covered rather than the conflict itself. The Velvet Revolution in Prague, the fall of the Berlin Wall and Tiananmen Square, all in 1989, similarly joined the West's collective memory, largely as a result of the mass media.

Mass media and the technology that makes it possible have thus utterly changed the character of news reporting and its relationship to scholarship. Very early in the history of the press, however, even in the days of the sixteenth-century *avvisi* written strictly for Italian businessmen, the mass potential of the press was recognized, and with that development came political control. Even then, governments sought to limit the press's potentially subversive character by requiring that such newspapers obtain official licenses to publish. In the nineteenth century, western European governments often imposed onerous taxes on newspapers, a practice which restricted their ability to collect, publish, and circulate news; it was only under the pressure of public opinion that such taxes were abolished, in Belgium in 1848, for example, England in 1855, and France in 1881.

Today, most newspapers in the West depend for their financial support on governments (the former Soviet Union's *Pravda*, for example), private interest groups (*L'Osservatore Romano*) or private firms (*Stampa*, in Italy, is owned by Fiat). Thus, most are subject to political and ideological pressures of various kinds. Sometimes it is subtle, delivered implicitly; sometimes it is more direct. Dictatorial regimes have gone even further, often even prescribing what is to be published. An early highpoint (or lowpoint) in government control of the press was reached by Hitler's minister for propaganda, Joseph Goebbels, with his Ministerium für Volksaufklärung und Propaganda. The historical consequences of this ominous move are well known.

In contrast, some presses are relatively "free," in that they function independently of political affiliation or other direct control. The London *Times* was for years the archetypal newspaper of this genre; on the continent, France's *Le Monde* and Germany's *Frankfurter Allgemeine Zeitung* represent the tradition. In the United States, a handful of nationally circulated newspapers such as the *New York Times* and the *Washington Post* provide critical coverage of politics and are powerfully able to mobilize public opinion. The rapid technological developments of recent years— those making CNN or the Internet possible, for example—are often considered part of this tradition of press "freedom." Although the growth of these media is driven by commercial motives, it is frequently argued that they provide such easy access, both for the public and for newsmakers, that they help preserve the "freedom of the press."

The press, then, including the nonprint press, is considerably more than a purveyor of news; it can play a decisive role in political processes themselves. Consider, for example, the importance of the *Washington Post*'s coverage of Watergate; or more recently of the *New York Times*'s April 13, 1995, report that Serbian President Slobodan Milosevic was directly associated with the Bosnian concentration camps run by Serb paramilitaries and the systematic extermination of Muslim populations in the territory. Ted Turner's CNN goes a step further, providing uniform, 24-hour per day TV coverage around the world. In Turner's hands, the news becomes a purely commercial, uniform product, and simultaneously an important vehicle by which politicians and governments seek to influence world events. In 1991, a pan-Arab channel (MBC) was begun (out of London), and in 1993, the Europeans launched their own competitor (Euronews). In the same year, the United Kingdom's BBC went global.

No matter the medium in which it is delivered and no matter the care with which editorial freedom is protected, however, every news report is in some sense selective and therefore "biased." The journalist who composes it—or the team of journalists and editors who put it together—is choosing among the thousands and thousands of pieces of information available, on the basis of what might interest or please the "public," the owner, the state, one or another interest group, or a certain ideological position. One journalist may decide that, having been told of one instance of a development—let us say the first heart transplant—the public does not need to know about subsequent operations of the same type; another journalist, in contrast, may decide that the successful repetition of the operation is the important point, and she will thus continue to "follow the story." In fact, she is not "following" the story; she is creating it. The point is not, however, that one journalist is right and another wrong. The point is that journalists are always affecting the news, making one story "important," and another "unimportant," making "news" on one hand and "not-news" on the other.

Of course, no matter what story he or she is choosing to tell, the journalist is responsible for verifying sources, for making sure that the bits of information used are accurate. Recent scandals in the U.S. press have demonstrated how easily such responsibility can be abdicated. In the rush to "scoop," to keep up with the competition, journalists have sometimes been exposed for making up facts or, in the case of a recent erroneous CNN-*Time* story about the U.S. government's use of nerve gases in the Gulf War, have been shown to have done sloppy investigations of their sources.

Let us close this discussion of the press's functions with a few comments for the scholar who would use the press—whether the premodern *avvisi* or the modern Internet flash—as a source. To employ these sources usefully, the historian must consider not just the content of the text, but its author and issuer, the publisher and its institutional location, the audience, and the immediate (political, social, economic) context of its original publication. It is surely true that sensational or tendentious reports can have a bigger effect on public opinion than a sober, careful report, and it may be that the historian will have to take the first more seriously than the second, for it was the first that had the greater impact. In addition, the historian must remember that the emission of a report itself can affect the events being reported, that there is no clear separation between the event and the report of the event. Normally, we imagine, a report of an event is *about* the event, not part of it. But sometimes this relationship is distorted, as when participants in a protest listen to reports about their actions as they go to the streets (a common event during the student revolts in the United States and Europe in the late 1960s and early 1970s), when voters have news of early returns in an election, or when reports of polls influence the next poll—or the vote itself.

Finally, the careful scholar will be attentive to what we might call "short-circuiting" of information flows, the distortion that occurs as information passes from hand to hand. Scholars using sources from oral cultures—folktales, for example—are very sensitive to such risks, for tales told orally can easily change in the telling, but even those historians using printed sources or the reports from electronic media are not free of these problems of interpretation. A message delivered electronically can be literally distorted, just as can a line of print or a story passed by mouth from generation to generation. The listener or reader can misinterpret what is reported, simply because he or she does not understand the linguistic or cultural code in which the message was written, or does not grasp the context of the message. Let us illustrate with a very simple example: what would a foreigner with very little ability in the English language make of an exchange between two Americans being formally introduced?—one offers her hand and says, "How do you do?"; the other replies in kind. Only someone deep in the culture can "read" that text!

D. Storing and Delivering Information

The archive is often considered the historian's principal source of information. The term has two meanings. In the most general sense, an archive is the collection of documents held by a natural or a legal person (for example, a government agency), and possibly also the copies of documents sent by these bodies to others. They are kept, of course, for practical reasons—to have a record of previous actions, both to assure administrative stability and to preserve useful ways of doing things and to preserve evidence for possible future legal proceedings. In a more technical sense, however, the term "archive" means the place or the institution itself that holds and manages the collection. In principle, diplomatic sources and social documents are kept in archives, narrative sources in libraries. But of course there are exceptions. By chance, as a result of gifts made to special institutions or the like, we sometimes find the reverse.

So long as an archive is growing and acquiring new material because the owner or the institution for which it is the repository is still active, it is considered a "living archive." When a collection, in part or in whole, is separated from the living archive, perhaps because it is considered of no value for ongoing operations, perhaps because the firm or the operation no longer exists, it is considered "old" or "historical." In that case the documents have lost their official or juridical status.

Until the end of the eighteenth century in the West, almost all archival material was held by its original owners or by the institution that produced the documents. Churches, monasteries, cities, and noble families kept their own papers and treasured objects themselves, usually in a special room or storage chest. Princes typically made their castles their depositories, and the archives traveled with them as they changed the seat of their operations. The medieval Council of Flanders, the highest court of the count of Flanders, kept its archive successively in Lille, Audenarde, Ghent, Ypres, then again, as of 1498, in Ghent.

The French Revolution brought a reversal of practice. The new state confiscated much of the property of the monasteries and lordships, along with their archives, and simultaneously demolished most of the administrative apparatus of the old regime; the result was a huge and sudden influx of documents to the new central state. In response, the new government created a central state archive, which was public; most other European lands soon followed suit.

The original structure of the new central archive was as follows: each constituted region of the country (in France, each *département*; elsewhere the region might be the province, or even the county) established a depository to which were sent all documents originating in institutions that had once been at least partially subject to the rulers of this region. Thus, the collections of the Council of Flanders finally ended up the state archive in Ghent, capital city of East Flanders. Similarly, the archives of confiscated ecclesiastical institutions, of noble families, of the notaries who had worked in the district, and of the cities and parishes located in a French département found their way to the regional archive in the capital city of this département. Typically, the national capital (Paris, The Hague, Berlin, etc.) served as depository both for the region and for the nation, in the latter capacity holding the documents emanating from the central government.

Some local archives, particularly those of big cities, escaped this confiscation and today retain their own collections. In some parts of Europe, particularly in England, France, Belgium and The Netherlands, a great many additional local institutions have similarly kept their archives—parishes, monasteries, bishoprics, and private institutions. And everywhere there are some government agencies whose archives remain their own, just as there are still a few ordinary people (to be sure, people of some influence) who keep private archives.

In addition, in recent years some new independent archives have been created, usually attached to research institutes focused on a particular problem, a group of people, or a place. The new Holocaust Museum in Washington, D.C., is one such example. In The Netherlands, a center was founded in 1945 for research and study of the Second World War; in its collection is the original Anne Frank diary. Germany has special archives for business affairs in Cologne and Dortmund, and the United States has, for example, a Ford archive in Detroit.

Until recently it was generally accepted that public archives should hold only public documents, that they should not, in fact, acquire the holdings of private families and private institutions, no matter how important historically. Now that has changed. Since 1959 the British Public Record Office has welcomed gifts of private papers, and a law of 1955 allowed the Royal Archive of Belgium to collect private papers of families, firms, and political figures. But these efforts are in many instances too late. As a result, the collections of many private individuals and institutions, if they have been preserved at all, are held in universities (Harvard University, for example, houses an archive concerning the industrial history of the United States), in private archives (the presidential archives in different locations of the United States), or in museums (Gladstone's papers are in the British Museum Library).

Sources of other kinds, most of them unwritten, are typically held in other depositories. Museums, for example, are the usual repositories for archaeological finds, artworks, and similar objects; libraries often house coin and medal collections; film and record libraries have been established for special collections (the Museum of Modern Art in New York, for example, collects dramatic films made since 1936; the Federal Archive in Coblenz, Germany, archives films made during Hitler's Third Reich).

Archives in Europe and North America today follow generally standard practices in organizing their holdings. For the historical archive, the most important principle of organization is place of origin, or provenance. No principle is more important because any isolated document, without such information, is practically worthless to the historian, just as a potsherd or a coin is of little historical value unless we can identify its provenance. We have to know where a document was found and where it was stored if we are to assess its import—its intellectual origins, its place and time of creation and use. Let us take a banal example: the address book belonging to James McCord, one of the men convicted of breaking into Democratic headquarters in the Watergate Building in 1972, with its reference to "Howard Hunt, White H(ouse)" would have had a different (and probably trivial) significance had it been found anywhere but in the rooms McCord and the other Republican burglars had hired in the complex. Having been found there, it played a decisive role in the history of this seminal case, since the address book suggested that the White House and even the president were involved in the affair.

The key notation for each piece of archival material is, thus, its provenance, and archives typically classify their holdings according to their (bureaucratic or physical) location at the time the archive was "living." This was not always the practice, however; in the early nineteenth century, archives usually classified their collections according to date order or by topic, thus without regard to their provenance. It is only since 1841 in France, and somewhat later elsewhere in the West, that new protocols prevailed under which collections were kept intact and, within each collection, the provenance was carefully noted.

The kinds of documents on which historians have traditionally relied are preeminently the creation of states and statelike institutions (the church, charitable and educational establishments, etc.) because by their very nature these bodies produce and must keep records of their existence and their operations. It is thus no wonder that the first archives of real significance in postclassical Western history come to us from the first great state-builders, for example from the twelfth-century pope Innocent III, or the French king Philip Augustus. So important were these archives to such princes that they carried them with them, housed in specially guarded trunks, as they voyaged throughout their realms. How fragile, how unsatisfactory, this system was becomes apparent when we consider that during the battle of Fréteval in 1194, the entire French national archive went up in smoke! It is even less surprising that the best collections of documents that come to us from this age treat fiscal and legal matters, for it was documents of this nature that evidenced (and assured) political authority.

Notarial documents (documents written and authenticated by specially trained and licensed professionals, rather like modern-day lawyers) created to secure property and legal rights constitute the bulk of the traditional private archival record. The documents have survived so well not just because they were important to the people involved, but because notaries were typically obligated to preserve them and to pass them on, at the end of their service, to their successors or to the state that licensed them. The office of notary was created in Roman times and was revived in thirteenth-century Italy, spreading into the rest of Europe during the fourteenth and fifteenth centuries.

Business enterprises and private institutions had equally good reasons to create and preserve documents of this kind, but because their institutional lives were typically shorter or more precarious than those of states themselves, few archives of this kind remain from the period before 1900. The survival of documents of other kinds—literary, artistic, personal—depends very much on the fortunes of the individuals involved and on historical chance.

Archives are also the creations of scholars and intellectuals who have organized to collect and preserve documents relating to the history of particular places, groups, or movements. Labor organizations have, for example, been particularly active in creating archives and making them available to scholars, as have certain religious and ethnic groups, such as the Mormons and American Jewish organizations. The process of archive creation is continuous, as history creates new sources and new needs for their preservation. For example, today the African National Congress is creating an official archive at both the University of Fort Hare in South Africa and the University of Connecticut in the United States. It will house documents that were for years hidden in three dozen countries during the party's underground struggle against apartheid in South Africa.

Although there are a dizzying and growing number of archives in the West, they have, in fact, preserved only a very small number of the documents and other materials actually produced in the past. One reason is simply that so few events were actually recorded. Events considered too banal, too obvious, were not recorded by contemporaries and were noted only in conversation. The same thing still occurs today, of course, especially as the telephone and Internet replace the letter as the primary means of private communication; even the fax is no improvement, for the quality of the print of most fax machines assures the ephemerality of the messages so transmitted.

Second, it often occurred that the official who produced or originally collected a given document did not think it worth saving. It is modern historians' great loss that, for example, medieval princes typically did not keep copies of the letters they sent to vassals calling them to serve or the invitations to councils delivered to the mighty of the realm. Even trained archivists have made choices we would surely lament; a social historian might, for example, have treasured the nineteenth-century sewer plan that an archivist discarded once the modern sewerage plant was built.

Third, archives are frequently destroyed in catastrophe, fire, and war. In World War I, the entire municipal archive of the important medieval city of Ypres was burned down; the library of Alexandria, one of the great intellectual centers of the ancient world, was lost as the city declined in the late antique period; the municipal archive of Naples was demolished in 1943.

Fourth, many institutions and individuals simply do not seek aggressively enough to preserve their records. Private firms are notorious in this regard. It takes, therefore, a rare combination of favorable circumstances for a premodern private archive to have survived for us: a bankruptcy that creates a court case and thus moves business papers from private hands into the public realm, as happened in 1368 in the case of the banker Willem Ruweel of Bruges; a private firm that is transformed into a foundation, as happened in the case of the Datini of Prato; the operations of a single enterprise that remain for many years in the same family; an individual family member who collects the papers of his relatives, with an eye to posterity.

Fifth, there are basic technical reasons why an archive does not last, namely the quality of the material on which the record is kept. The ink used today, which is based on aniline, becomes virtually unreadable after about thirty years—and the ink from a typical ballpoint pen becomes unreadable after a few hours in the sun! Today, the original documents produced in the Nuremberg trials of 1945 are almost undecipherable. The quality of the paper used has as great an effect on the durability of documents. Paper manufactured before about 1840, being made of textiles ("rag") and of glues derived from the bones of animals, was long-lasting.

Most of the paper made during the next century was not, for the pine resin used as glue destroys its cellulose fibers (the paper being a wood product). While deacidification processes have since been developed and are being gradually applied to the most precious surviving records, and while much of the paper produced since 1945 is not similarly vulnerable, a huge proportion of the documents stored in libraries and archives today is threatened with extinction simply because the paper is rotting. We might well ask ourselves just how durable are the photocopies of our present-day letters—often the only version that is saved—and the faxes on which we are so dependent. Wallpaintings in caves—some of them of inestimable historical and artistic value—become very vulnerable once they are discovered, for the light that enters the cave, once it is opened, allows the growth of organisms that consume the paintings.

Sixth, and somewhat paradoxically, archives can fail scholars because there is *too much* to collect, and archivists become overwhelmed by the task of deciding what to save, what to discard. Since World War II, this problem has become acute. The huge influx of material into small archives with overworked staffs has meant that files cannot be cataloged and prepared for use quickly enough and become, in effect, inaccessible. By the 1960s this situation throughout the West had reached the crisis proportions described by Alvin Toffler in his *Future Shock*: the point when information is accumulating at so dizzying a pace that we are at risk of losing our social memory. Solutions are being sought by technical means (compact disks, microfilm) and by editing processes (sampling, selective triage). Microfilms can serve as a durable substitute for paper that is vulnerable to the effects of humidity or light. Microfilm has another advantage as well, for it can store vast quantities of information in relatively little space; it has also been used to create a kind of shadow archive, a duplicate copy of documents which might be in danger of loss or destruction (as in war).

Another solution is to create storage centers for documents that have lost their official use but cannot yet be properly archived. Such Record Centers have existed since 1941 in England and the United States. In this system, a document produced by a government agency is sent to the Record Center once it has lost its direct, short-term official use. In this intermediate Record Center the documents retain the cataloging system used by the originating institution. They can easily be consulted both by the officials of the administration whence they came and by researchers. At this stage, the archivists of the Record Center work with specialists from the historical archive to select those documents for transfer to the historical archive and to decide on the final cataloging system. At the end of the process, which may require as much as thirty years to complete, the documents are transferred from the Record Center to the historical archive. In the meantime, however, they have been available to historians and other scholars.

But sources not only disappear; they also appear or come into existence. The boundaries of knowledge and expertise shift constantly, whether because new material is found or discovered, because material once closed to scrutiny becomes available (think of the archives in the former Soviet Union, many of which became available to Westerners only after 1989), or because the codes necessary to decipher a text are rediscovered. Michael Ventris's decoding of the Linear B alphabet in 1952 made, for example, Greek history before Homer newly comprehensible. Historians themselves sometimes create sources, when, for example, they conduct interviews with people who lived though the events being studied.

Many aspects about the past will, of course, never be known to us or to any historians because the questions we or our successors might ask are so different from those that might have occurred to the people we are studying. In the eleventh century, rulers did not take censuses because the size of the population they ruled was neither their concern nor a problem. And people were extraordinarily vague about such matters. In 1371, for example, the English Parliament declared a tax which was to be paid, they said, by the 45,000 parishes in England; in reality, there were at that time only 8,600 parishes in the whole realm!

Thus, to the extent we can produce estimates of population size for the premodern era in the West, we have to rely on sources produced for other purposes. Tax registers or other documents recording fiscal matters are the usual sources used for this purpose (but they can be very hard to mine for this information); parish records of births and deaths were not required in Christian Europe until the sixteenth century (the French were obliged, as of 1539, to keep such records; for the rest of the Catholic West, it took an ordinance from the Council of Trent, in 1563). Civil records of this kind were not kept until after the French Revolution.

Even when an archive exists, it is not always available to scholars. Private archives are technically closed and can be consulted only with the permission of the owner. Even public archives are often restricted. According to mutually agreed upon international conventions, access to documents less than thirty years old can be denied; in practice the limit is often closer to fifty or a hundred years. When private owners donate a collection to a public archive (such as a state archive), they typically require that access to those papers be closed for thirty to fifty years, usually because they do not want the embarrassment that could come with public use of their documents. The Vatican archive (Archivio Segreto Vaticano) was made partially available to the public only in 1881, and there are still parts of it that are closed. It was only in 1987 that the United Nations made the files of people involved in war crimes during World War II available to the public. Occasionally, exceptions are made, as in the Watergate crisis in 1973–74 when a portion of the infamous Nixon tapes was opened to the press and the courts (additional parts were released in later years).

Historians are not, however, limited to archives, museums, or libraries for primary written source material. With the advent of printing (ca. 1450), scholars began to publish sources so that they could be consulted by numerous individuals, in many places. This method of dissemination has obvious advantages, but its value depends entirely upon the quality of the editing process, and scholars have over the years developed strict protocols to guide editors and assure that the sources are reliably transmitted (see chapter 2 for further discussion of these processes).

The earliest published sources were, by and large, critical editions of important philosophical and religious texts (the New Testament, for example). A few were intended as supporting evidence for historical arguments, offered to satisfy skeptics; typically, these were excerpts from original texts or summaries of them. It was only in the seventeenth century that entire volumes devoted to editions of historical sources were published, and these were usually collaborative efforts. The Bollandists and the Maurists were the first to take on such projects. The Bollandists began in 1643 with their renowned *Acta sanctorum*, critical editions of saints' lives (hagiographies) from Christian Europe. The Maurists published the saints' lives of the Benedictine order. One of their number, Dom Jean Mabillon, published the first scholarly study of editing techniques (*De re diplomatica*, 1681), demanding close attention to matters of paleography (handwriting) and diplomatics (the structure of the document) and emphasizing as well the need to consult the originals as well as the edited version of a document. It is no surprise that the eighteenth century—the age of enlightenment—saw an outpouring of critical editions of secular texts. Thomas Rymer's edition of papers regarding England's relations with Europe (*Foedera*, 20 vols., 1704–1835) is a fine example of this age's work.

The nineteenth century is, however, the golden age of text editing and source publication, a flowering that had its roots in both romanticism and positivism. The romantic influence is evident in the fact that most editions were founded as national projects, efforts to record and celebrate the national history. The *Monumenta Germaniae Historica* was the creation of the Society for the Study of German History (Gesellschaft für ältere Deutsche Geschichtskunde), which was founded in 1819, during the euphoria that followed the end of French occupation; the volumes contain important (Latin) sources for German history. The *Recueil des Historiens de la France*, although first begun in 1738, was reedited and republished in 1899 as a celebration of the French state; like the *Monumenta*, the *Recueil* is a collection of Latin texts from the French past. Elsewhere, such publications had a somewhat less nationalist impulse, there more often being the products of learned societies such as England's Camden Society or its Selden Society.

Whatever their roots in romanticism's nationalistic impulses, all these editions are positivist in method in that they rigorously limit themselves to the "provable fact" and seek, in the famous words of Ranke, to tell the story "as it actually occurred" ("wie es eigentlich geweren [ist]"). They owe to positivism as well the high editorial standards employed, the incorporation of learning and technical skills borrowed from philology, classics, and Germanic studies.

Although these published collections have long served and will long continue to serve scholars, it is clear that we will never be able to edit and publish "all" the known historical sources, and in recent years scholars have begun to explore new ways of getting archival sources into the public domain. Microfilms have been made of serial data like fiscal accounts and census data; indexes of archival holdings have been printed and published. Texts have been reproduced electronically so that they can be searched and indexed by means of sophisticated software programs, a procedure which allows unparalleled scrutiny of a text's rhetorical and linguistic features and thus promises to open entirely new avenues of research and analysis.

\u2767

Technical Analysis of Sources

I n order for a source to be used as evidence in a historical argument, certain basic matters about its form and content must be settled.

First, it must be (or must be made) comprehensible at the most basic level of language, handwriting, and vocabulary. Is the language of the document archaic, its vocabulary highly technical, its handwriting or typeface unfamiliar? Obviously, these issues are more important for some documents than for others, and always more problematic when the source is very old or has originated in another culture, but they are never absent. A scholar using letters written in the early twentieth century must be as attentive to these matters as must any medievalist working with handwritten parchments.

Second, the source must be carefully located in place and time: when was it composed, where, in what country or city, in what social setting, by which individual? Are these apparent "facts" of composition correct?— that is, is the date indicated, let us say, in a letter written from the front by Dwight Eisenhower to his wife Mamie the date it was actually written? Is the place indicated within the source the actual place of composition? If the document does not itself provide such evidence—or if there is any reason to doubt the ostensible evidence—is there internal evidence that can be used to determine a probable date, or a time period within which the document was created? Can we tell from the content of the document itself or its relationship to other similar documents where it was composed?

Third, the source must be checked for authenticity. Is it what it purports to be, let us say an agreement for the transfer of land from a secular lord to the church or—to mention one of the famous cases of forgery from recent history—the personal diary of Adolf Hitler? Can we tell from the handwriting, the rhetoric, anachronisms of content, from the ink or the watermark or the quality of the parchment—or from the typeface or the electronic coding of the tape—that the document was not composed where it presents itself as having been composed? Is it, perhaps, a forgery from the period, a forgery from a later period, or simply a case of mislabeling by archivists?

A. Clio's Laboratory

Historians have at their disposal a wide variety of tools to help them identify and authenticate sources, to help them answer those vital first questions of when, where, and by whom? Obviously, most of these tools were developed by historians studying documents from former times or exotic places, for it is documents such as these that usually present the greatest problems of identification. But it is not just classicists and medievalists, scholars of Native American peoples or of nineteenth-century peasants in the Caucuses, who require such tools. Every historian, at one moment or another, must be a technician. In the sections below we have listed and described the essential tools available to historians as they confront sources. The bibliography attached to this book provides further guidance for scholars whose sources demand such technical analysis.

1. Paleography

Paleographers study handwriting. Humans use many different alphabets to write, as they use countless languages to speak. The alphabets change over time, as fashions, aesthetic taste, and the technology of writing develop in different ways. Alphabets are also determined by social and cultural context. In the late antique period, for example, Roman scribes simultaneously used two different calligraphic styles for texts carrying high literary, philosophical, or religious status. The first, *capitalis elegans*, was used for the famous non-Christian Latin authors such as Vergil, and the second, *uncial*, was employed for Christian texts like the Bible. The system was not formally prescribed, but was nevertheless in constant use, because it expressed cultural assumptions about the differences between these kinds of texts and their intended audiences. In both cases the individual letters were perfectly constructed and so perfectly legible, and each word was respected as a unit, because these texts were designed to reach many readers. In contrast, for daily business, the Roman bureaucracy used the Roman new cursive, a quickly penned, scarcely legible script in which graphical connections were made between letters in the interests of efficiency, and words were often disaggregated into pieces, without respect for their integrity. All this reduced the legibility of the text, but that was not the issue: the intended readers were all members of the same bureaucracy, all able to decipher the script.

Each century of Western history has produced a variety of scripts that differ according to the degree of cursitivity, the quality of the modulus (i.e., the ratio between the height and the breadth of a letter), the character of the ductus (i.e., the structure of a letter as determined by the number of the strokes, their direction, and their sequence), abbreviations, and ornamentation. At certain moments in time, a style will be very widely used (for example, the Carolingian minuscule in the ninth century); at others a style will be narrowly employed but exist in thousands of variations (for example, the gothic script of the twelfth to eighteenth centuries). In fact, any particular script is a mix made up of the dominant style of the age and the individual characteristics and stylistic tendencies of the particular writer. When the basic style is cursive (a style which, being penned so quickly, is easily varied), the personal idiosyncrasies of the writer pronounced, and the abbreviation system unusual, it takes a very skilled paleographer to decipher a given text.

Someone so skilled can, however, often use these stylistic and morphological variations in script to date an undated manuscript by comparing these features with dated texts from the same period. Of course, a date thus derived is always somewhat hypothetical, usually at best only within twenty to forty years of the actual date, since the trained scribes who penned most of the manuscripts that have come to us from premodern Western society used the same script throughout their professional lives. A skilled paleographer can also spot fakes, for such professionals can often identify peculiarities in a script that betray a date of composition different from the purported date. To be sure, the skilled falsifier can often ape the conventions of an age, and some falsifiers come, of course, from the period in which they are dating their fakes. But paleographers working in periods when most surviving documents were produced by teams of scribes can often tell not just when, but where, a document was written. They can thus identify fakes that claimed authorship by a certain ruler but were demonstrably not penned in the scriptorium used by that ruler.

Technology also comes to aid of the paleographer. Today we even have tools for making the ink visible on parchment and paper so old that its ink is too faded to read, even with the help of magnifying aids. The Wood Lamp, developed in 1914, uses ultraviolet rays to reveal the invisible ink. In 1979, J. F. Benton adapted the digital image processing technique developed by NASA in Pasadena, which permits decoding of texts that have deteriorated with age and dirt.

2. Diplomatics

Diplomatics, or the science of charters, is the study of the formal properties of such sources. Each section of such a document employs a style that varies depending upon the legal conventions and more general stylistic tastes of the age. During the Middle Ages, every chancery developed and preserved its own terminological conventions and formulas. In the secular chanceries (the legal and drafting offices of a political authority) of the twelfth century, for example, the formulas and stylistic conventions that had dominated in ecclesiastical chanceries typically fell into disuse as these secular chanceries developed their own conventions. Understandably, however, change came unevenly, erratically, and historians often find that certain conventions survived well beyond the institutions that gave them birth. The expression "servus servorum Dei," for example ("servant of the servants of God"), was constantly used in the opening section (the *intitulatio*) of papal documents until the twentieth century.

Scholars who work with such materials regularly become very familiar with these conventions and can use them, along with more external characteristics such as ink and handwriting, to help date undated documents (for an expert will recognize its affinities to those produced at the same time in that chancery). These techniques are an important part of the arsenal of historians who work with old documents. Throughout the Middle Ages, as we will discuss on more detail later in this section, especially in the period between 900 and 1300, documents were regularly forged or misidentified, sometimes leading to political reorderings and legal changes of immense significance.

3. Archaeology

During the Renaissance, intellectuals developed a keen interest in the artifacts left by the ancient world, but it was not until the eighteenth century that historians gave up their exclusive reliance on the written source. Their change of heart was brought about principally by a couple of spec-

tacular finds—Pompeii and Herculaneum, which were discovered, re-
spectively, in 1748 and 1738.[1] Both sites, which were destroyed by vol-
canic eruptions in 79 C.E., the first by a lava flood and the second by mud
that covered the site for centuries, are magnificently preserved. The sites
offer scholars unparalleled evidence about daily life in classical Rome. As
a result of these discoveries, Europeans of the eighteenth and nineteenth
centuries became increasingly interested in preserving old monuments,
often by removing them from their original sites, where they were
thought insecure, and placing them in museums. In 1816, for example,
Lord Elgin brought friezes from the Parthenon in Athens to the British
Museum in London, where they still reside (to the outrage of many
Greeks). Other scholars set out to discover ancient sites and even cities of
legend, sometimes with spectacular results. In 1871, Schliemann discovered one of the incarnations of the ancient city of Troy; in 1900, Sir
Arthur Evans uncovered Crete's civilization.

Archaeological evidence is, of course, most precious for lost civilizations, and is sometimes effectively the only way to know about their histories. Ancient Egypt, the Aztec civilization or the Mayan, the Cretan or Etr-
uscan—all these are known to us principally through the archaeological
record. This is true, in fact, for the bulk of human history; its first four million years left only material evidence of this kind, and it is only during the
last 5,000 years that humans created written sources.

Archaeology has little by little become a discipline of its own, related to
its sister disciplines of anthropology, history, and art history on the one
hand but also closely allied with the harder sciences such as geology,
chemistry, physics, and biology. Despite its emergence as a separate discipline, archaeology's importance in historical studies is in no way diminished. In fact, since the Second World War, archaeological studies have
become ever more crucial for historians of literate societies; medievalists,
for example, now regularly work closely with archaeologists in studying
twelfth-century agriculture; early modernists turn to archaeologists for
help in understanding the ruins of sixteenth-century military fortifications; historians of the colonial period in U.S. history depend on archaeologists for much of their knowledge about Jamestown.

What is sometimes called the "new archaeology" has further strength-
ened the relationship between archaeology and history. This approach to
archaeology shares much with contemporary developments in social and
cultural anthropology, archaeology's close cousin. Here the emphasis is

1. For this history, see P. Zanker, *Pompeii: Public and Private Life* (Cambridge, Mass., 1999).

more on the ways individuals experienced their culture and the way the objects or constructions found by archaeologists express those meanings. Hence, practitioners of this type of archaeology are considerably less positivist in methodology than those associated with traditional archaeology, in that they do not look just for systems or structures but for meanings and symbols as well.

In chapter 4 we will return to these larger methodological questions and the ways they have affected all social scientists' work. Here we want to pause, however momentarily, to consider the techniques employed by traditional archaeologists, for no matter how valid the criticisms of the epistemological assumptions made by traditional archaeologists, there is no doubt about the significance of the evidence they have unearthed.

Let us begin by looking at how sites are chosen and excavated. Many archaeological sites are discovered by chance, as roads and houses and subways are built, or as farmers work and rework land, thereby unearthing long-buried objects. A huge Gallo-Roman burial ground was discovered near Ghent, in Belgium, in 1968–69 during the construction of a new highway; a Native American burial ground was recently unearthed in New York City as a new subway line was being dug. Farmers in Brittany regularly turn up pieces of pottery and household implements used during Carolingian times; farmers in the American west frequently unearth the relics of Native American settlements.

Professional archaeologists have developed strict methods for excavating potential sites. They first mark off and enclose the area in some way, protecting it from contamination from the surrounding civilization to which it has suddenly been joined—and protecting it from looting. They label and register everything they find. They make detailed maps of the site and keep diaries recording every step in the process. Once a site has been studied as thoroughly as possible by means of noninvasive methods, scholars begin the laborious process of excavation itself. Usually, a site contains many different settlements, one on top of another, each having grown up on the ruins of the former. The modern archaeologist seeks to respect each of these layers and to manage the excavation so that one settlement is not polluted by objects and structures from another. By respecting the layers, archaeologists can date them, relative to one another, and can thus date the objects found in each.

In the course of the excavation, archaeologists apply various techniques to help identify the objects they find. Artifacts are categorized according to the materials which compose them, according to function, and then further according to peculiarities of form and style, all of which help in the laborious process of dating. Increasingly, archaeologists also make use of scientific tools such as special photographic techniques, chemical and physical analysis, and radiology. Skeletal remains are of even more interest, for the bones of humans and animals yield important data about body size and type, about the ways of life and death in a culture. Special techniques employed by paleopathologists reveal the diseases that left their traces on bones. From them scholars have learned, for example, that certain maladies common in our day were rare in the distant past—ancient peoples, for example, knew little syphilis, cancer, or tuberculosis of the spine. Tooth decay was almost unheard of until the Mesoliticum and did not become a significant problem until the Middle Ages, when Westerners began to eat a lot of sugar.

The problem of dating is, of course, the archaeologist's major concern. Absolute dating means that the object can be placed in a specific moment (a year) or century. Relative dating, in contrast, simply relates one object to another, classifying it as "before," "in the same period of," or "after." Sometimes archaeologists must be satisfied simply with a relative date, with being able to say, for example, that this settlement is older than that one. If they know the date of "that" one, they can thus give a terminus ante quem to the first. Better, of course, is a date based on evidence internal to the particular site, sometimes derived from comparison of artistic or industrial products with those from areas which can be dated but sometimes—in the best case—available from specific information found in the site itself. Most often, archaeologists use a combination of methods.

As in all their work, archaeologists seeking to date objects are very much helped by modern science. Archaeomagnetic analysis, for example, allows scholars to determine the date at which the clay or limestone used in an old pot was baked, for the baking set the iron filings in the material in a pattern that was determined by the electromagnetic force at that moment in time. The even more sophisticated techniques available today have improved this method, and are used for very small amounts of organic remains, allowing scholars to date, for example, the famous Shroud of Turin.[2]

Nature itself also yields clues that cannot be interpreted without the aid of modern science. One of the most widely used techniques for dating archaeological finds is dendrochronology, the study of tree rings. Each ring

2. On the application of scientific method to dating the shroud, see Harry E. Gove, *Relic, Icon, or Hoax? Carbon Dating the Shroud of Turin* (Bristol—Philadelphia, 1996), and Joe Nickell, *Inquest on the Shroud of Turin: Latest Scientific Findings* (Amherst, N.Y., 1998). Some commentators still insist on the shroud's authenticity: Ian Wilson, *The Book and the Shroud: New Evidence That the World's Most Sacred Relic Is Real* (New York, 1998).

in the trunk of a tree (visible when the trunk is cut horizontally) corresponds to a year of growth, and each ring has individual characteristics that reflect annual changes in growing conditions. Thus, when a tree that is, say, sixty years old is cut, scholars know something about the weather and other factors affecting the tree's health during each of those years. They can use these data to go back in time, by matching the earliest rings of that tree with the latest rings of a tree cut many years earlier, perhaps fifty years ago. And so on. Pollen analysis, another technique used to study past growing conditions, involves study of the yearly deposits of pollen grains, which are often well preserved in the layers of earth accumulated in nature preserves.

4. Statistics

Historians of the past few generations have increasingly turned to statistical methods, in the hope of providing more exact measures of events in the past, to make history more like a science, and to reduce the impressionistic quality of much of narrative history writing. Statistics can also help uncover hidden relationships among events, allow scholars to make historical connections, or reveal historical patterns that would otherwise not have been seen. Historians have, for example, used statistical methods to study sexual mores in the past, to go beyond the direct reports about sexual practices that appear in narrative sources such as letters and chronicles or the prescriptions contained in moralists' tracts. By analyzing the marriage and birth records of populations of the past, for example, historians have discovered that significant sectors of the European population began to use birth control methods systematically, apparently first in aristocratic circles and somewhat later among townspeople, in the seventeenth century. This is a full century before narrative sources give clear hints that such practices were usual, an indication perhaps of how much cultural expression can lag social practice. In fact, statistical analysis has shown, it was only the peasantry who by the eighteenth century did not employ some kind of birth control on a regular basis, and that group adopted such means in the course of the century.

Not all data lend themselves, however, to such statistical analysis. In order to take averages, measure trends, compare points in time, or calculate the incidence of correlation—the usual kinds of statistical analyses historians do—scholars must have homogeneous and continuous data. Like must be compared to like. If one wants to assess relative standards of living, the wages of unskilled workers in one time and place, for example, must be compared with the wages of similarly unskilled workers in a different (but comparable) time and place. If one wants to make a claim about English demographic exceptionalism, one must compare the birth rates in an English agricultural village with those in, say, a French agricultural village—not with birth rates among Florentine merchants!

Constructing a valid comparison is not always, however, simply a matter of comparing like with like in a mechanical way. Consider, for example, the problem of comparing living standards over long time periods. A simple—but not necessarily very good—method would be to compare average wages (or family income) in one period with those in another (in "real" wages, that is, in money prices adjusted for inflation, etc.). This method does not work, however, when the material importance and the relative price of a basic commodity changes dramatically from one period to the next, for instance, when a culture in which bread is the "staff of life" is being compared to one in which bread is a relatively minor part of subsistence and in which, consequently, the relative price of bread has fallen dramatically. To address this problem economists construct "baskets of goods" appropriate to the time and place—collections of essential materials of life, in proportions to reflect average expenditures; they then convert wages into these "baskets" and compare one worker's ability to buy her basket with another's ability to buy his. Thus, if scholars were comparing, say, living standards in fifteenth-century London with those in twentieth-century Chicago, they might measure a London family's living standard, to a large extent, in terms of how much bread the family could buy with, for example, a week's wage. In contrast, they might measure a Chicago family's principally in terms not just of food and rent but also of durable and consumer goods such as cars, washing machines, and movies. A comparison between the two periods thus becomes relational, allowing the scholar some insight into each family's socioeconomic status in the society.

Good statistical work also typically requires long runs of data; a few isolated birth rates or the occasional wage quotation will not suffice. These limitations make it very hard for historians working before the nineteenth century to do studies of this kind, for records of that era that can be mined for significant results are difficult to come by. This does not mean, however, that historians have been unable to undertake such studies; as the example mentioned above concerning birth control practices shows, historians of early modern Europe have had some great successes with these methods. It does mean, however, that they have had to be especially careful with their data and have had to search long and hard to find useful material.

It is also true, however, that extensive runs of data can be very difficult to manage, and historians are thus often obliged to take averages, usually of about five or ten years each. Sometimes they also sample their sources, choosing for close study a small number of cases among the hundreds or thousands contained in their source; they can legitimately do so when they are sure that the sample is in fact representative of the whole. The historian here is in the position of a pollster, who cannot pick just anyone to interrogate about political preferences; the persons chosen for a poll are carefully selected representatives of the various subgroups (age, gender, social status, etc.) within the entire voting population. It is often a difficult and time-consuming task to establish the necessary legitimacy of a sample. To do so, the historian must, as always, know his source: how were the cases that made up the entire record assembled? by whom? why?

This raises the issue of whether the historian is using a data set he or she has constructed or deploying data assembled in the past, by the society under study. In both cases, similar questions about the data and the statistical methods apply, but in the first instance the historian must take into account the fact that he or she is producing an interpretation about the past in the very act of assembling the data. For example, a historian might want to collect grain prices from markets all over Europe, during different years, decades, or centuries, and might want to run those data against information about weather patterns collected from chronicles. To do so usefully, however, the historian would have to find some way of taking into account the differences in the markets in which grain was traded, the accuracy of weather reports in chronicles, and a host of other "historical" factors that would profoundly affect comparability of the data. In contrast, the historian using birth records assembled in a single parish over two centuries would have many fewer such problems to worry about.

All historians, however, no matter whether they are constructing their own data sets or mining ones made by the people being studied, have to pay careful attention to the character of the sources from which the data come. An example from eighteenth-century Denmark can help make the point. Historians have long used a shipping register produced there to study the economy and politics of the period, but some have done so without sufficient understanding of the source. The register identifies the ship according to the nationality of its skipper, not that of the owner of the ship; it thus dramatically understates the importance of The Netherlands in this trade (for most of the ships in the register were, in fact, Dutch) and dramatically overstates the role of the countries that provided skippers. Only a historian who understood this peculiarity could have used the source to say anything useful about relative economic powers in the period. The historian's first job, then, is to do what historians must always do first: study how the source was constructed, by whom, where, and for what purpose. Only then can statistical methods, no matter how sophisticated, be fruitfully employed.

Statistical methods can, moreover, mislead. Thomas Malthus, for example, famously misjudged Europe's demographic future when he applied statistical reasoning in too simplistic a manner. Projecting from his understanding of the past relationship between the food supply and the population and his observation of the birth rate in colonial America, he reasoned that because the former progressed at an arithmetic rate and the latter at a geometric, demographic catastrophe in Europe was imminent. In fact, the relationship between the food supply and population growth is considerably more complex than his model allowed, and in the event a moderate increase in the food supply in the late eighteenth century (Malthus wrote in 1798) was associated with a flattening of the population curve. Nonetheless, Malthus's theories had an enormous influence on politicians and economists—including John Maynard Keynes.

Let us, however, end this section more positively. Although there are real dangers in using statistical methods, there is no doubt that they have made many new kinds of studies possible and opened the way for important methodological innovations in the profession.

As we have already indicated, statistical methods have proved particularly useful, indeed essential, in demographic history. Although historians of all periods and all cultures have benefited from these studies, their import has been particularly marked for students of the premodern and modern West. Let us return to Malthus to pursue this point, this time by pointing out a place in which he turned out to be right. He was one of the first to hazard that in eighteenth-century Europe late marriage was the major factor in limiting births; his guess has since been proved by several generations of demographic historians who have shown that by about 1500 (with wide geographical variation) in the West (up to 1750), the average marriage age for women had risen to at least 25–26. By marrying (and beginning sexual intercourse) some eight to nine years after menarche these women would have two to three fewer children than their counterparts in other times and places (such as colonial America, where women typically married earlier—and had more children). Thus, in this age, a low fertility rate was achieved, not by contraception, but by late marriage. What this example reveals is the usefulness of statistics not just to describe patterns of change accurately, but also to point to new questions. In this case, we have seen, the new questions concern social practice and cultural norms, areas of inquiry that require different kinds of analysis.

One of the most productive applications of statistical methods has been in the field of family reconstitution. In these projects, historians mine serial birth and marriage records, using the computer and statistical programs to construct family networks. With this information, scholars have been able to plot socioeconomic and political connections onto kinship ties, showing how in particular cultures these networks overlapped—or did not.

Statistical methods have been as widely and as profitably used to trace patterns of criminality, in different time periods and from region to region or state to state. It has been reported, for example, that in sixteenth-century England there were five to ten times the number of murders than in the twentieth century, and that the sixteenth-century figure was itself only half the thirteenth.[3] Fascinating as this statistic is, however, it has raised a host of questions which require historical work that is not statistical in nature—demonstrating again how statistical analyses of historical data both answer and raise research questions. For instance, some scholars have explained the apparent decline by arguing that in the movement from medieval to modern times, Europeans have better learned to control themselves, to adopt "civilized" behavior, to respond to injuries not with violence but with law. Others have proposed that the decline is simply an effect of the state—that murder rates have fallen to the extent state power has risen. Still others have thought that human behavior has changed less than the public institutions designed to control it; the high crime rates of the early modern period are, in this logic, simply the result of the emerging state's first efforts to police public space, a reaction to the sudden oppression. In this argument, it is also pointed out that as "crimes of blood" have declined, so have "crimes against property" risen. One interpretation of this shift is that the nature of the misdeed has changed, not the fact of crime itself; another is that one kind of crime is being more aggressively punished in one period and less so in another. In either case, the argument goes, the records do not tell historians anything about the actual incidence of crime. And—just to confuse the matter further—it has been also argued that all these statistics are suspect, for most crimes go unreported.

Cliometrics and the new economic history constitute a related subfield, a child of the 1960s when statistics and the computer were first enthusiastically taken up by historians. Methodologically, it is an application of economic theory to history; procedurally, it involves reducing historical events to quantifiable elements whose relationship to one another can be

3. T. Gurr, "Historical Trends in Violent Crime," *Crime and Justice: An Annual Review of Reference* 3 (1981): 295–353.

studied with sophisticated statistical methods, especially those measuring correlation. The object here is to remove the observer from the process—to expose significant relationships between historical phenomena by means of statistics, rather than by the usual means of argument or reasoning employed by historians. Studies by D. C. North (*The Economic Growth of the United States, 1790-1860,* 1961) showed, for example, that U.S. economic growth between 1790 and 1860 was closely correlated with growth in exports during the same period. North tested the strength of that correlation in ways that convinced him that the latter was a "cause" of the former. Less radically, historians have used these methods to "test" the association between, for example, social position or class and religious values, reducing both qualitative elements to numbers that can be statistically manipulated. Obviously, the value of such studies depends crucially on the degree to which something like "class," not to mention religious values, can be represented by a number, or even a series of numerical measures.

Statistics have also been used in fields where their applicability seems less expected. At the Max-Planck-Institut-für-Geschichte in Göttingen, for example, a group of historians has imaginatively applied statistical method to analysis of qualitative data of various sorts, including textual material. Scholars elsewhere have even tried to quantify religious sentiment, for example by counting the number of hosts used in medieval masses, by studying membership lists in Reformation churches, and by tracking the sale of Bibles in twentieth-century America. In some cases, their work has proved highly controversial: Jacques Toussaert, for one, has argued from evidence about the consumption of hosts that medieval people in Flanders attended mass less often than one would have expected in a fully Christianized society (*Le sentiment religieux en Flandre à la fin du Moyen-Age,* 1963). Needless to say, his critics have jumped first on the assumption that religious feeling can be deduced from participation in the mass—again a measure of how statistical studies produce new questions.

Scholars have also used statistics (and the computer) very profitably in purely textual studies, typically to trace the way certain words, phrases, spellings, rhetorical devices, and the like appear in a given text. Such information can provide telling evidence about authorship or provenance, and can also help scholars relate one text to another, showing the influence one had on the other or how both were influenced by other, related texts.

5. Additional Technical Tools

The historians' tool box has still more in it, instruments designed for very specific purposes. Here we provide a necessarily incomplete but suggestive list, along with brief definitions of terms. Researchers requiring these tools will find references to technical literature in the bibliography.

- *Sigillography* or the study of seals—the science and art of identifying and decoding the seals that were used until modern times to identify issuers and authors of documents. Today they are studied as much for their iconographic interest as for the information about authorship they provide.
- *Chronology*—the study of the different ways people have kept and marked time. The Hebrew calendar is, we all know, different from the Gregorian (which is based on Christian dating). In premodern Europe, the year began at different times; in some places, people reckoned from January 1, just as we do, but in other places the new year began with Easter, or on March 25, or on Christmas.
- *Codicology*—the study of handwritten books as archaeological objects, including the study of the materials (parchment, paper), of the bindings, of cataloging, and of preservation problems for manuscripts.
- *Papyrology*—the study of writing on papyrus.
- *Epigraphy*—the study of texts written on hard materials, such as stone and metal.
- *Heraldry*—the study of coats of arms.
- *Numismatics*—the study of coins.
- *Linguistics*—in the technical sense, the study of grammars, vocabularies, etc. Specific branches of this field include etymology, the study of the origins of words; toponomy, the study of place-names; anthroponomy, the study of personal names; semantics, the study of change in the significance of words; and semiology, the study of signs (to this important topic, we will later return).
- *Genealogy*—the study of family relationships, the basis of studies about social groups based on blood or marriage ties.
- *Prosopography*—the use of biographical material to construct group portraits; this kind of research is regularly done in social history to discover, for example, the professional or ethnic or residential characteristics that define a group.

Many of these technical tools are called into service when historians turn to the very first question facing them in source analysis: the "authenticity" of the document. Sources that come from the past, especially the distant past, are frequently "false" in some sense, although the degree of their falsity varies enormously. Historians need to distinguish between those sources that are false in the sense that they are not genuine and those that are false in the sense that they contain inaccurate information. In the first case, the question is whether documents do in fact originate as they claim (i.e., that were produced by the institution—the chancery, governmental agency, or firm, for example—or by the individual claiming authorship). If so, historians consider them authentic or genuine. In the second case, the question is whether the documents provide reliable information. Thus, an "authentic" document may contain "inaccurate" information, and an "inauthentic" document may contain utterly trustworthy data. The Middle Ages provides many examples of both types—in the first case, for instance, a chronicle that is authentic but attributes deeds to the king that were patently impossible; in the second, a reconstruction of a lost charter made by scribes who knew and closely followed the missing original. But such "falsifications" are not peculiar to the Middle Ages. Western governments today regularly issue reports containing inaccurate information (whether by design or error), thus creating what we have classified as "inaccurate" documents. And filmmakers regularly reconstruct events in films purporting to be "documentaries."

In analyzing sources for their accuracy or authenticity, historians commonly classify them according to the following schema:

- sources about which there is no uncertainty regarding form or content, i.e., that are both accurate and genuine.
- sources that are "false" in an intellectual sense, in that they were written to mislead contemporaries or to claim illegitimate rights or privileges (i.e., inaccurate). It should be noted, however, that what we might label "false" in this sense was often not so deemed by contemporaries. In the Middle Ages, for example, people took a document issued by the ruling authority to be "true," even if it claimed powers that had been illegitimately won (by usurpation of office or the like) or overruled rights that previous authorities had authenticated.
- sources that are "false" in that they are faked (i.e., inauthentic). The typical case is when someone makes a false original of a document, aping the form and language of similar legitimate docu-

ments issued in that period. They are sometimes called pseudo-originals. The Hitler diaries are a perfect example of the genre.

- sources that combine elements of the original with additions that are designed to mimic the original (pastiches). Sometimes such "falsifications" are deliberate, intended to trick, as when an author plagiarizes the words and thoughts of another. The most skillful of these falsifications combine elements from many different originals, mixing them creatively with their own material. Some use raw materials from the past—old wood, for example, to make a carving that mimics old art work. Others so faithfully reproduce the style of the age that they are very hard to distinguish from originals—a falsifier of documents may, for example, almost perfectly reproduce the handwriting conventions of the age.

Sometimes, however, such "pastiches" are more innocent, the products of an overzealous or overimaginative mind or hand. And sometimes they result from the art itself, as during the Renaissance when sculptors combined ancient forms with their own, to create pieces that passed as ancient. Similarly, during the nineteenth century neo-gothic architecture was made indistinguishable from, and was partly composed of, the original medieval. In these cases, it is very hard to distinguish the deliberately false from the creatively inspired. Today, restorers often inadvertently create such "falsifications," so expert are they at restoring old artworks to their original form.

- sources that are copies. Some such copies are, of course, "authentic" in that they were expressly made (and notarized or otherwise authenticated) at the time of issuance, usually to provide the issuer or recipient a record of an agreement. Sometimes too scholars make copies of documents for their own use. But sometimes the copy is made with an intent to deceive, as when an artist fakes a Rembrandt or when someone purports to be providing a "true" copy of an original that never existed (in this case historians speak of "pseudo-copies").

Thus, the "false" or inauthentic character of a source lies not so much in its material qualities as in the intention of its creator and the uses to which it is put. Any object is, in itself, authentic. A nineteenth-century copy of a fourteenth-century painting is "genuine" in some sense because it is a genuine artifact of the nineteenth century. And, whatever the degree of deceit involved in its composition, a falsification can have historical value, for it bears witness to the spirit of an age—its artistic interests, perhaps, but also its obsessions, its manipulations, its usurpations. The real falsification begins, then, not with composition but with intention and representation, even innocent misrepresentation as when, for example, a sixteenth-century original is misidentified by a scholar or archivist. In this case, the term "false" implies no calumny; it indicates only that the object was falsely labeled. A famous painting called *The Storm*, which is held by Vienna's Kunsthistorisches Museum, Gemäldegalerie, was long attributed to the sixteenth-century painter Bruegel; it was only in 1987, when it was discovered that the painting had been made on a panel of wood that postdated the painter's death (in 1569), that the misattribution was corrected.

It sometimes requires great skill to identify such falsifications. In general, historians look for anachronisms, whether of language, form, or content. The "Bruegel" painted on wood that did not exist during Bruegel's own life is one such anachronism. The art world is full of similar stories. There is, for example, a portrait of Willem van Heythuysen by Frans Hals, the dating of which experts have begun to doubt. There are two bases for suspicion. One is the wood on which the painting was made; scientific tests have shown that the wood was cut after the presumptive date of the painting. The other concerns the paint itself; traces of Prussian blue have been found on the canvas, a color that was not invented until 1703 and not generally available until about 1720.[4] Anachronisms of writing (or typeface) are also frequent. Sometimes, for example, it is possible to show that a particular "hand" did not exist when a document was purportedly written or that printers had not yet designed letters in the form used in a printed text.

The most interesting anachronisms are probably not, however, formal in this sense. They are mere slips, moments when the plagiarist or falsifier let his guard down and included a phrase, a reference, or, if a painter, perhaps a color that the avowed author or painter would not have used. A nineteenth-century Italian physician, Giovanni Morelli, made this argument explicitly, proposing that forgers of paintings tend to copy the most

4. The original study exposing the inaccurate dating was published by Seymour Slive (*Frans Hals* [London, 1989]). He explains there that the portrait in question (of Heythuysen, now in the Musée des Beaux-Arts in Brussels) could not have been painted in 1638, the original date of attribution, because dendrochronological tests showed that the tree from which the wood plank was cut had been felled about 1642. He also discusses the problem of the Prussian blue. Slive argued, however, that the painting was indeed by Hals, made sometime after 1649 (the earliest date at which one could have used a plank cut from a tree felled in 1642, seven years being the necessary curing time). A more recent study by Claus Grimm, however (*Frans Hals, the Complete Work* [New York, 1990], pp. 54–56) presents more recent dendrochronological evidence that dates the tree's felling to 1650–60. It also argues that the painting was not of Hals's quality and thus must have been a copy from the period, which was retouched in the eighteenth century (thus the Prussian blue paint).

striking elements of the original very well (Mona Lisa's smile, for example), but miss small details—the earlobe. Thus, he concluded, scholars should focus on the small, the apparently insignificant, in search of clues for falsifications, whether of handwriting, literary style, or painting, because a forger will rarely be able perfectly to ape every element of the original and is likely to miss on the smaller, less obvious points. In many ways, this method parallels those employed in the clinical practice of psychiatry associated with Sigmund Freud and in Conan Doyle's Sherlock Holmes stories.[5]

B. Source Criticism: The Great Tradition

Sources must be evaluated not only in terms of those external characteristics on which we have been focusing, the questions of where, when, and by whom a source was created and whether it is "genuine" or not. Traditionally, they have also been evaluated in terms of what historians have thought of as internal criteria. These include questions about the intended meaning of a source—was the author of the text in a position to know what he reported? did he intend an accurate report? are his interpretations "reliable"? These are the kinds of questions on which nineteenth-century historians concentrated, and these scholars developed very sophisticated tools for addressing them. All of them concentrated on the source itself—essentially on a written source, the text, and especially on those sources considered the queens of sources, charters or *Urkunden*.

But historians are not reporters or detectives. They are interpreters of the past, not its mediums. Hence, many historians today are ever more skeptical about the appropriateness of these questions, even about our ability to answer them adequately. The questions ignore important epistemological issues concerning the kind of knowledge any source can reveal, about our ability to have unmediated access to the past, about intentionality, outcome, and the relationship between the two. Seriously as we take these criticisms—a matter to which we will specifically return in the last two chapters of this book—we do not think that these older tools should be discarded. If used carefully, with full knowledge of their limitations, the tools can help us make good use of sources, make them produce meaning in responsible ways. Let us, then, turn, to the chief elements of source criticism as traditionally practiced.

5. We owe this example to Carlo Ginzburg's *Clues, Myths, and the Historical Method* (Baltimore, 1989), pp. 96–102.

1. The "Genealogy" of the Document

Once a document is determined to be genuine in the sense just described, the next obvious question is whether it is an original, a copy of an original, or a copy of a copy. Most copies announce themselves as such, but of course that is not always the case, and it is exactly those cases that can be the most treacherous, for a "copy" is not always a perfectly accurate rendition of the original. This is particularly true in the case of handwritten documents, but it is true even in our day, for the photocopies, faxes, magnetic tape, and digital processing used today to make copies are often imperfect because of unintentional technical failures or because of voluntary manipulations. There are even instances when more than one original exists, as for example in the case of international treaties or medieval business contracts, when an "original" is made for each side. While such duplicate originals can today easily be made identical, this was not always the case in manuscript cultures.

Copies contain all kinds of "faults," most of them unintentional. Manuscript (and even typed) copies regularly repeat words, for example; they reverse letters; if the copying was done in a scriptorium where copyists wrote down what was read to them, they can mistranscribe homonyms ("to" and "too"); they can drop syllables or words. Some mistakes were more easily made by copyists who were transcribing a text being read to them; others characteristically occurred when the copyist was working from a written model. Sometimes a copyist did not understand the meaning of what he was copying and thus mistranscribed the text. Occasionally, we find deliberate emendations to an original text, conscious efforts to change meaning or to insert new material.

It is for that reason that historians always prefer the original and sometimes go to great lengths to get it. But very often historians have to work with a copy, or even a copy of a copy, sometimes with several different copies. For historians working with older manuscripts, it is often not clear how the copy or copies relate to an original "archetype" which may be lost. Given the importance of such questions in certain kinds of historical inquiries, it is no wonder that historians have devoted so much energy to developing techniques that help them make such connections.

Unsurprisingly, it is medievalists who have developed especially sophisticated methods of this kind. Let us give just one simple example of a technique widely used to position copies in relationship to one another and to an "original." If two copies of a text contain common errors, they can be assumed to have been derived from the same "original" (or copy of a previous generation of texts). Using such methods, historians can often map complex family trees of texts, even identifying the characteristics of "lost" generations in the tree. Specialists have been working with these techniques for about a century, and in the process they have developed ever more sophisticated ways of relating texts by comparing such stylistic and paleographic variations. The details of any particular method can be quite complex and are, of course, useful (and worth the effort) only when one is working with manuscripts that are very difficult to place historically. For those scholars, however, the tools can be a godsend.

Once the "best" text has been located and its genealogy ascertained (to the extent possible), historians edit it, seeking to reproduce the text's meaning as clearly as possible. Here historians are very often tempted to improve the text, to correct it, to make it conform to the imagined original. But it is exactly here that they should be very cautious. While some corrections are obviously necessary—and the burden of all this tracing of copies was of course to decide which corrections should be made—it is always a great risk to intervene too energetically. And in any case, editors must base any proposed corrections to the basic text on another copy of the same text (what is then called an emendation) or on a good argument (called conjecture). Such care is necessary, not just to respect the original, but to preserve its "errors." These "errors"—misspellings, grammatical faults, transpositions, even apparent omissions—can be significant historical evidence, occasionally about the politics that informed the creation of the particular text and always about the literary technology of the age, about linguistic conventions, about the status of the written word itself in that culture.

It is crucially important that the historian doing such editing make every intervention evident to the reader, usually by means of footnotes and editorial prefaces. And, of course, she must introduce the text with all the information she has about the text's history—its location, its relationship to any known (or hypothesized) original, previous editions of the text, its place of composition, its date, and so on.

2. Genesis of a Document

Here we return to the question of where the source was produced, by whom, and when. But our interests now are slightly less technical; the questions are not so much literally about time and place and author as they are about the significance of this information. What kind of institution or individual produced a source, with what authority, under what circumstances? What surrounding events gave the date or the place special meaning?

Sometimes the source itself gives direct answers to these questions, at least in the literal sense. Juridical sources such as charters usually explicitly state the issuer and the date of issuance, unless they are delivering a message requiring immediate action (such as an invitation to a meeting or a call for military aid; in such cases the document typically mentions only the month and day, not the year). Literary sources very often fail to report such information.

The identifications provided by the source itself are, however, often misleading. We have discussed this issue before, in the introductory section of this chapter: sometimes authors are deliberately faking a source, sometimes they are disguising the real place and date of issuance. Our concern here is slightly different; here we want to investigate the notion of authorship itself. What does it mean to say that a certain person or institution "authored" a document? Is he the person who conceptualized the document, ordered its production—the person usually called the "intellectual author"? Is he the person who gave institutional and juridical impact to the document, by means of his authority or influence? Historians think of these authors as "juridical." Or is he the person who drafted it, crafted its language, rendered it in a form which made it legal—the person referred to as the "material author"? What is the relationship between the three?

For some kinds of documents, this is an easy question. A woman who pens a letter to her friend is the intellectual, the juridical, and the material author of the text in the sense defined here. A queen who orders a written copy of her commands is probably the intellectual and juridical author of the resulting document, while her chancellor is only her executor, the material author of the document. But in such situations this is not always the division of labor. Historians have long pondered the extent to which Lord Cecil was the intellectual author of certain texts supposedly authored by Elizabeth I of England. Who authored, and in what sense, Ronald Reagan's speeches? These examples should make it clear that any document, both those for which no "official" author is stated and those for which authorship is explicitly claimed, can have many authors. The alert historian can learn a lot about the significance of the document by discovering just who these authors were—the ruler or his ministers? his private advisers? his wife?

3. The "Originality" of the Document

Most of the documents that come from the past—whether a law code, a contract, a philosophical text, or a hagiography—are products of an intellectual tradition, and historians using an isolated text must know something about this tradition in order to read their text responsibly. They must know whether a section in a law code that reserved rule for males, for example, was the first instance of such a principle in the culture being studied, whether it was a convention copied from a neighboring political system, whether it was a revival of traditions that had lapsed. They must know, to offer one more example, whether the form of a particular contract—perhaps its requirement that the agreed property transfer be witnessed by family members—had previously appeared in other similar documents, whether the form was the imposition of a legal bureaucracy, whether it was an innovation that seems to have come from society itself.

In some cases, the historian can address these questions only by comparing the particular text with similar texts from the same period or from the past (if there is no independent record of the legal or institutional or intellectual history to which this text belongs). The further back in time the historian is working, the more difficult this process typically becomes, because the text with which she might be concerned may well be the only one of its kind from the period and the possible antecedents or parallels to the text are few and far between. In such cases, the historian must use sophisticated techniques of textual analysis to "place" a document.

More specifically, scholars are concerned with the way the author of one text takes over language from another, sometimes unconsciously, sometimes fully consciously, perhaps with the intent to represent the purloined text as original but more often in a deliberate effort to transmit the information from the former. Law codes typically fall into the latter category, literary texts into the first. Naturally, it is one of the historian's jobs to identify these borrowings, to label them as intentional or not, and to make sure his readers know which parts of the text he is himself using were derived from other, prior texts.

Text editors have developed standard conventions for conveying such information. Typically they print the borrowed language in small type, to distinguish it from the language new to the text being edited; when the earlier texts are themselves made up of borrowed texts, the editor usually uses footnotes to indicate these previous borrowings.

4. Interpretation of the Document

To the nineteenth-century historians who founded history writing as a scholarly discipline, the problem of "interpretation" of a document was one of deciphering its intended meaning. This was not considered a simple task; indeed it was technically demanding. Today, however, thanks largely to the effects interdisciplinarity has had on our profession, historians can no longer define the problem as narrowly, and they employ a wider range of tools to "interpret" a document. In fact, as we shall see in chapters 4 and 5, many historians today would argue that the intended meaning of a text is in some sense never recoverable and is, in many cases, not its historically most significant feature. Hence we will defer the entire topic of "interpretation" to those later chapters, noting here only that our predecessors marked the problem and made important strides in developing techniques for addressing certain of its aspects.

5. Authorial Authority

With what authority does the author of a source, perhaps a newspaper reporter or a compiler of facts about a nineteenth-century harvest, speak? Was he an eyewitness to the events he describes or did he participate in the design of the system for collecting the information? Was he even alive when the events he records are meant to have taken place? Is his information second, or third, or fourth hand? Is some of what the source relates a firsthand account, while other parts of the document are based on information that is taken from others? The latter occurs very frequently, and the "reliability" of the entire text, as measured by this standard, thus has a variable quality. The English monk known as the Venerable Bede, left, for example, the most valuable account historians have of conditions in the English church during the eighth century when he wrote; his report of the situation in Rome during the same epoch is, however, considerably less reliable and less acute because he obtained most of his information about those matters from others.

Understandably, authors are usually reluctant to acknowledge that they do not have such firsthand knowledge, for the revelation diminishes their authority. And rightly so, for the greater the number of intermediaries between the original telling of an event and the version that our source contains, the more chance there is of distortion. Historians thus make strenuous efforts to locate the truly firsthand reports of an event and to trace the relationship of other existing versions of the report to that original record.

Still, however important it is to know the source of our text's information about an event, scholars must not imagine that a firsthand report is "true" or that later interpreters might not have understood the event better than firsthand observers. This is a mistake often made by nineteenth-century historians, who tended to overvalue the "eyewitness" account and dismiss as historical evidence any text without that status. In fact, of course, any observation has a very indeterminate quality, differing according to the abilities, the interests, the purposes of the observer. For example, how "reliable" are the reports of such privileged eyewitnesses as the Israeli minister for foreign affairs Shimon Peres, the PLO leader Yasser Arafat, or the American

president Clinton during the secret negotiations between Israel and Pales-
tine in 1993? What can a western journalist in Tel Aviv, an Arab intellectual
from Jericho, or a Hassidic youth from Mea Sharim in Jerusalem tell us
about what is "really" going on in that land at any particular time? Each has
his or her own perspective—a limited, distorted, partial view of events.

It is the same for a historian studying an event as it is for the eyewitness
observers of it or participants in it. Historians have only partial views and
are situated, minimally, at one remove away. While it is essential to determine at what remove they are situated, it is no guarantee of "accuracy" or
"fullness" to obtain the firsthand account.

6. Competence of the Observer

Although no account, no source, is completely "reliable," the trustworthi-
ness of an account, at least as a report of events, may vary enormously, depending upon a great many factors. Many of them have already been discussed; here let us construct a rather more systematic list of the kinds of
factors historians consider in deciding how much credibility to give a
source—in deciding on its "competence." Historians have traditionally
considered this issue from two points of view.

The first concerns the factors particular to the individual observer.

- What was the psychological state of the author of the source? Was
  he satisfied with life or bitter about the way it had turned out? Was
  he a pessimist or an optimist?
- To what extent was the author's report selective? What particular
  kinds of things would have interested this author? What events or
  nuances would she have been likely to ignore?
- What prejudices would have informed the account? People unconsciously bring their assumptions about society to their reports of it,
  often unintentionally reporting events in ways that simply confirm
  their own expectations of human character: women who weep over
  dead bodies are "hysterical"; men who do so are "filled with rage."
- Under what outside influences was the source created, especially
  those of higher authorities? Eyewitnesses regularly shape their rec-
  ollections to accord with reports from more "authoritative"
  sources, not out of a conscious response to pressure (although that
  of course happens as well) but out of an unconscious need to conform to the dominant narrative. Many of the "eyewitnesses" to the
  assassination of John F. Kennedy, for example, changed their ac-

count about the number of shots they "heard" after the TV news reported other counts.

A slightly different set of questions about "competence" pertain to the climate of the times in which the observer lived.

- Was the moment at which he reported one in which people could have absorbed information critically? In times of emergency— for instance, during natural disasters or warfare—people lose all objectivity. Every rumor, every absurd story, is taken seriously. An eyewitness observer in these circumstances is, obviously, not "reliable" in the usual sense.
- Could the observer have understood what she saw? Here we have in mind the incapacity of people outside a culture to understand events within it. What, after all, do British observers in the United States make of baseball? What do Americans understand of cricket? What do Westerners think is going on in the public baths in Japan? What do Hindus from New Delhi who are visiting Texas report home about cattle yards?
- Was the observer technically or socially qualified to understand what he saw? Can the average American deliver a useful account of a Senate hearing on tax reform? Could the typical medieval merchant accurately describe the rituals of the joust? Could the medieval monk tell us much about married life among twelfth-century peasants—even if he had wanted to?
- Could the observer actually believe what she saw? Thomas Mann has reminded us that very often people simply cannot absorb the information before them, that they are paralyzed by what he called "Glaubensunwilligkeit"—an unwillingness to believe. Usually, this occurs when the events are too horrifying to contemplate. Consider, for example, the inability of many European Jews to accept that the German state was organizing their mass extermination. The Nazis had formally taken this decision on January 20, 1942, and the information was circulated by the Polish resistance in 1943-44 and even broadcast, with some delay, by the BBC. Nevertheless, almost no one in Europe believed that such a monstrous horror was possible, including the Jews themselves.
- Finally, historians must consider the difference between what an observer might consciously know and be able to report and the way this consciousness is affected by the culture he inhabits. The latter

question concerns the mentality of the age ("mentalité"), the way the physical, social, and cultural environment of a person determines what he "knows" and how he "knows." Understanding this aspect of "consciousness" is, of course, a central task of historians and one that requires study of many sources, over many years.

7. The Trustworthiness of the Observer

People—and thus sources—lie, of course, sometimes consciously but sometimes unconsciously. Here historians are interested not so much in the lie as in a more subtle form of falsehood, the suppression or shading of knowledge to conform to orthodox opinion. The personality of the observer is key here. Hence, the scholar must, to the extent possible, study the life of the individual; she must compare this observer with others treating the same or related events; she must be attentive to inconsistencies, lapses, suppressions in the story the document tells. A checklist of factors to consider would include the following:

- Political commentators, by their very nature, shade their reports, making them conform to the party line in one way or another. But even people without direct political connections to the events being reported have political views, and these will inevitably shape the way a person reports, and what is reported.
- Very often, politics are more evidently at play: an observer may not dare tell what he considers the truth. Sometimes, of course, the observer must fear for his life or the well-being of his family; more often, however, the pressure is more subtle—what is at stake is a job, influence, connections.
- The vanity of the observer will play a role as well, for every author puts herself center-stage, implicitly or explicitly. The historian's problem is to figure out just how center-stage this particular observer would have put herself.

❧

CHAPTER THREE

Historical Interpretation: The Traditional Basics

H aving assembled their sources and subjected them to the technical investigations described in the last chapter, historians face
the task of explaining them, of connecting them into a story
about the past. This process can be analyzed from several perspectives,
ranging from the fundamental question of how a historian might go about
reconciling the often conflicting information that is found in a group of
sources to the most sophisticated questions of what kinds of knowledge
about the past the historian is in a position to offer. In this chapter, we will
take up basic questions of how historians traditionally choose among facts,
how they decide what evidence to privilege, which to suppress, which to ignore. In the two succeeding chapters we will turn to larger issues of interpretation, concerning the kinds of questions historians ask and the ways
these questions determine their approach to evidence.

A. Comparison of Sources

Typically, historians do not rely on just one source to study an event or a
historical process, but on many, and they construct their own interpretations about the past by means of comparison among sources—by sifting
information contained in many sources, by listening to many voices.
Sometimes the information they have from various sources is contradictory, sometimes mutually confirming, but the historian's job in any case is
to decide which accounts he or she will use, and why. In the previous

chapter, we considered the various ways that historians evaluate sources individually. Here we want to look at some of the techniques they employ to choose among different texts or to rank them in order of usefulness.

The essential problem here is distinguishing among the useful, less useful, and useless source. Generally, historians consider sources to be useless (for reporting purposes) if they derive from other, usually older, sources. Although it is sometimes hard to decide if a source is in some way derived from another, once that assessment is made, eliminating the dependent source is usually easy. It is much harder, however, to rank sources that all seem to be "original" in that each provides an independent account of the particular events in question.

Nineteenth-century historians developed systematic rules for making such comparisons. Two of the best-known rule books of the age, that of E. Bernheim, published in 1889 (*Lehrbuch der historischen Methode und der Geschichtsphilosophie* [*Guidebook for Historical Method and the Philosophy of History*]), and Charles Langlois and Charles Seignobos, from 1898 (*Introduction aux études historiques* [*Introduction to the Study of History*]), provide a seven-step process, which we have summarized below. As we shall see, the procedure hardly guarantees the kind of scientific proof these scholars and their contemporaries imagined as the historians' goal (only numbers (2) and (6) seem uncontroversial), but it can, nevertheless, provide entry into the challenging world of source comparison.

1. If the sources all agree about an event, historians can consider the event proved.
2. However, majority does not rule; even if most sources relate events in one way, that version will not prevail unless it passes the tests of critical textual analysis (explained in chapter 2, section B).
3. The source whose account can be confirmed by reference to outside authorities in some of its parts can be trusted in its entirety if it is impossible similarly to confirm the entire text.
4. When two sources disagree on a particular point, the historian will prefer the source with the most "authority"—i.e., the source created by the expert or the eyewitness (again, see chapter 2, section B, for a discussion of this assessment).
5. Eyewitnesses are, in general, to be preferred, especially in circumstances where the ordinary observer could have accurately reported what transpired and, more specifically, when they deal with facts known by most contemporaries.
6. If two independently created sources agree on a matter, the reliability of each is measurably enhanced.

7. When two sources disagree (and there is no other means of evaluation), then historians take the source which seems to accord best with common sense.

To illustrate the application of these rules, let us take an example from recent history, the Watergate affair of 1972–74.[1] The story begins in June 1972, when five men were caught breaking into an apartment rented by the Democratic National Committee for its campaign headquarters. The headquarters were being used in preparation for the upcoming presidential election, in which President Richard M. Nixon (Republican) was the incumbent. The investigative journalism that followed, led by the *Washington Post* and ending in a formal Senate investigation and impeachment hearings, would lead to President Nixon's resignation in August 1974.

The course of this investigation can be divided into three periods: the first from June 17, 1972, until June 25 of the following year, during which Nixon denied any knowledge whatsoever of the break-in; the second, which began on June 25 with the confession by John Dean, one of Nixon's advisers, stating that the president was implicated in the cover-up; and the third, between July 13, 1973, and August 1974, when Nixon gradually confessed to his involvement, until the climax of his resignation.

During the first phase of this drama, all witnesses reported the president's version of events—all, that is, were inclined to accept the lie. This might have been because all the sources were derived from the same source, Nixon, and were, as we now know, also lying. It might also have been the case, however, that the agreement reflected a situation like that described in (6) above—that all agreed because all had independent confirmation of the same (true) fact. At that stage in the drama, there was no way of knowing.

By phase two of the history, we are in another situation. Then, with Dean's testimony, we are faced with contradictory sources—Dean's account, and the account of other top advisers to the president such as John Mitchell and John Ehrlichman, who disagree. Neither is, on the face of it, more "reliable" than the other in the sense intended by rule (4) above (they were all equally competent), and Dean's account has not yet passed the critical tests of rule (2).

In phase three, however, the situation changes. Another of Nixon's advisers, Alexander Butterfield, let slip in the Senate hearing that Nixon

---

1. On the Nixon tapes, see S. Kutler, *The Wars of Watergate* (New York, 1990) and *Abuse of Power* (New York, 1997). The tapes can be consulted on-line at www.hpol.org and in print (a slightly different version from the Web-based text): William Doyle, *Inside the Oval Office: The White House Tapes from FDR to Clinton* (New York, 1999).

had kept tapes of private conversations held in the oval office. At first, Nixon refused to release these tapes, and it was only after enormous legal and political pressure was applied that he consented. The tapes provided the necessary hard evidence. At this moment, Dean's testimony (A) was vindicated by independent witness (B)—the tapes—in the sense implied by rule (6) above. Never, however, would rule (7) have helped Dean's case, for there was no way for outside observers to determine the "common sense" of either position. The "proof" came only with the corroborating evidence.

Another more recent political scandal provides an even more spectacular example of how a single piece of outside evidence can resolve a stalemate between competing sources. On February 7, 1983, an Israeli special commission (called the Kahane Commission after its chair, a prestigious member of the Israeli High Court), which had been formed to uncover Israel's role, if any, in the massacre in the Palestinian camps of Sabra and Shatilla in Beirut that had taken place on September 16-18, 1982, issued its findings. Until then, the press reports had all been in conflict on the question, and no one appeared to have definitive information. For his part, Prime Minister Menachem Begin had on September 18, when the massacre first became public, firmly denied any official involvement. The commission, however, was able to supply a critical piece of evidence: the report of a cabinet meeting on the 16th in which, it was revealed, the Israeli cabinet had discussed the planned attack and decided to let it occur, by authorizing the anti-Palestinian Phalangists in Lebanon to enter the camps and by providing them Israeli military support.[2]

What, however, when there is no "smoking gun," no external piece of information that renders one account "correct" and another "incorrect"? Are historians then compelled to throw up their hands? Not always. Let us look at several different situations that typically face the historian who has assembled a group of sources bearing on a particular problem.

What is often called a "stalemate" occurs when the sources (or particular witnesses) flatly contradict one another and when the historian has no obvious independent way to verify either version. Sometimes these stalemates can be resolved, at least with some degree of plausibility, by reference to the larger context in which the sources were created. Let us consider, by way of illustration, a case from recent political history. On July

2. For the official report, see Abba Eban, *The Beirut Massacre: The Complete Kahan Commission Report* (Princeton, 1983). For commentary, see Claremont Research (ed.), *The Beirut Massacre Press Profile*, 2nd ed. (New York, 1984); Claud Morris, *Eyewitness Lebanon* (London—New York, 1983); and Walter Prevenier, in J. Art and L. François (eds.), *Docendo discimus: Liber amicorum Romain van Eenoo* (Ghent, 1999), pp. 445–62.

25, 1990, the American ambassador in Baghdad, April Glaspie, was invited to a private meeting with Saddam Hussein, the Iraqi president. Neither took notes. One week later, on August 2, the Iraqis invaded Kuwait, and the Americans organized the Gulf War, which led to an Iraqi retreat.

Glaspie and Hussein gave different reports of their meeting. In a press conference held just after the invasion, Hussein insisted that Glaspie had told him that "Washington, wanting friendship and not confrontation with Iraq, had no opinion about the border conflict between Iraq and Kuwait." Glaspie's version comes to us from much later, from a Senate hearing held in March 1991 to determine whether the war could have been avoided by diplomatic means. She claimed that Hussein's version of their conversation omitted a key sentence: "The United States insists that you resolve your conflict with Kuwait peaceably." Both witnesses had, of course, good reasons to insist on their version of events, and both continued to do so.[3]

Is there a way for the historian to resolve this conundrum? It probably can never be known just what was actually said. It is hard to imagine, however, that a skilled diplomat such as Glaspie, who was familiar with the culture of the Middle East, would have said anything other than something like what she reported, and it is even probable that Hussein either listened selectively or that he simply did not take the U.S. warning seriously. Is this then a case of "Glaubensunwilligkeit"? Could Glaspie simply not believe that Hussein would ignore her threat? Was this a failure of diplomacy, a collision of two political logics, or was it a case when diplomacy had no chance because both the political leaders—or at least one of them—wanted the war or thought it was necessary for his domestic position? The latter explanation acquires plausibility when we consider that the efforts of competent diplomats such as Yevgeny Primakov, James Baker Jr., and Tarik Aziz in January and February 1991 were equally unsuccessful in averting the conflict. The two presidents, it seems, had reasons of their own for wanting the war. Invoking rule (7), we can see that the stalemate between Glaspie and Hussein, in itself irreconcilable, becomes comprehensible when we consider it in light of the diplomatic failures that followed.[4]

3. Hussein's version was printed in unabridged form in the *New York Times*, September 23, 1990. Glaspie's version is available in *Publications of the Center for Security Policy* 91 (page 22 of the March 20, 1991, testimony and page 63 covering July 14, 1991). For additional views, see R. Clark, *The Fire This Time: U.S. War Crimes in the Gulf* (New York, 1992) and E. Sciolino, *Outlaw State: Saddam Hussein's Quest for Power and the Gulf Crisis* (New York, 1991).

4. A more recent and equally well known stalemate occurred in the Senate hearings surrounding Clarence Thomas's Supreme Court confirmation. For an analysis of that event, see Sandra L. Ragan (ed.), *The Lynching of Language: Gender, Politics, and Power in the Hill-Thomas Hearings* (Urbana, Ill., 1996).

Historians often face, however, another kind of problem, a problem created not because the sources disagree but because some of the sources report a piece of information and some do not. In such cases, historians can often surmise that the silences are deliberate, and further research can explain just why the authors of those sources would have suppressed that information. The silence speaks, in fact, of the motivations of those who chose to be silent on that particular issue.

Once again, the case of Israeli's role in the 1982 attack on the refugee camps in Beirut provides an example. On September 17, 1982, Yitzak Shamir, then Israel's minister for foreign affairs, was interviewed by Belgian TV. In the interview he talked about the general situation in Lebanon, making no reference at all, however, to the slaughter that was then taking place (it had begun on the 16th), although he surely knew its details (the attack was still unknown to the world). The Kahane investigation shows, indeed, that he, as the second most important member of the Israeli government, had attended the crucial cabinet meeting that had made the decision. Thus, in this case, his silence was ominous, almost certain proof that he was covering up.

Of course, an argument from silence can serve as presumptive evidence of the "silenced" event only if, as in this case, the person suppressing the information was in a position to have the information, and was purporting to give a full account of the story from which he omitted the crucial information, and if there were no compelling reasons why he should have omitted the information (other than the wish to conceal). Hence, it is usually a considerably greater leap to conclude that "silence" means "concealment" than it was in the case of Shamir's selective omissions during his interview. In most cases, historians have to guess a bit more. They must presume that a suspected fact was an integral part of the story being reported and so central a part of such a story that the reporter would automatically have included it. That he did not becomes, then, presumptive proof that he was deliberately suppressing this piece of information.

Another difficulty with an "argument from silence" is that historians cannot assume—as nineteenth-century scholars such as Seignobos would have assumed—that an observer of a particular "fact" would have automatically recorded the fact. Authors regularly observe all kinds of events, but they deliberately record only those which seem important to them. For example, historians ought not conclude —as some have—that because the erotic plays a small role in some traditional African literatures, the erotic itself is unimportant in those cultures. In addition, it is clear, silences can be inadvertently created when texts are partly obliterated, lost, or changed in unexpected ways. And, conversely, it is naive to assume that everything that a text reports was actually observed—much less that it occurred!

Thus, the discovery and interpretation of "silences" is both a fine art and a science. In the so-called third phase of the Watergate scandal, for example, the editors of the famous tapes, editors who were aides to the president, pretended that in 1,075 places on the tapes they could not decipher Nixon's voice—while there were in total only 595 such places, involving 11 different speakers (other than Nixon), on the rest of the tapes. This disproportion was explained when the tapes were finally in the hands of the Senate committee. The Senate's technical experts then were able to determine that the tapes had been selectively edited by the "president's men" who, no doubt at Nixon's request, had manipulated the texts by erasing the compromising sentences.

Although historians must often reason from silences, they more commonly reason from positive evidence, and in their accounts they employ a number of logical processes. Very often historians reason by interpolation or by analogy, as though inserting missing pieces in a puzzle whose overall pattern they can discern by comparison with other, analogous situations. Historians have, for example, learned a great deal about the 1991 putsch in Moscow by comparing that uprising with the failed revolt against Boris Yeltsin in 1993. In the first, Vladimir Kryuchkov of the KGB attempted to take control from Mikhail Gorbachev, a move that gave Yeltsin his opening and led to Gorbachev's downfall. In the second, Yeltsin was himself under seige but in the end prevailed.[5]

Comparison of this kind can be a useful technique, but it is also a treacherous one. Comparisons are never perfect. Historical actors are creative; they learn from former events. At first glance, the putsch of 1991 and the subsequent uprising seem quite similar events. But looking more closely we realize that superficial similarities conceal fundamental differences. In 1991, Yeltsin had managed the putsch by mobilizing thousands of Muscovites before the Russian parliament building. Just over two years later, on Sunday, October 3, 1993, Yeltsin himself was facing exactly the same kind of crowd, this time mobilized against him. Reasoning by anal-

5. For background to these events, see the following: U. Gosset and V. Fédorovski, *Histoire secrète d'un coup d'état: Moscou 19 août 1991* (Paris, 1991); V. Frangulov, a.o., *The Coup: Underground Moscow Newspapers from Monday, August 19 to Wednesday, August 21, 1991* (Minneapolis, 1991); S. White, a. o., *The Soviet Transition: From Gorbachev to Yeltsin* (London—Portland, Ore., 1993); S. Hersh, "The Wild East?" in *The Atlantic Monthly* (June 1994), 61–86; M. Gorbachev, *The August Coup: The Truth and the Lessons* (New York, 1991); P. Goble, a.o., "The Situation in Russia," *Briefing of the Commission on Security and Cooperation in Europe* (Washington, D.C., October 1993).

ogy, the historians might expect 1993 to have ended as 1991 had, with the overthrow of the sitting government. It did not happen that way, however, for Yeltsin survived the challenge. Nor did Yeltsin behave as we would have expected if we relied on his behavior in 1991 to predict his actions in 1993. On the first occasion, he was in charge of the media and the crowd. On the second, at least on that Sunday, he was "running around like a chicken with his head cut off," in the words of the Russian journalist Sergiy Parkhomenko, in a CNN broadcast of October 3, 1993. It was not until that night that Yeltsin took control, effectively ending the revolt.

Reasoning by analogy, although useful and often necessary is thus often inadequate. Hence, historians employ other kinds of logical processes as well, often turning to what is labeled "the scientific method." In these instances, historians construct testable hypotheses and marshal evidence to test them, following the principles of the physical sciences. Claude Bernard, a nineteenth-century positivist scientist, was one of the first, in 1865, to lay out these steps systematically: (1) observation, (2) hypothesis, (3) fit between the hypothesis and the given facts, (4) verification of the hypothesis with new facts. For historians who would follow this method, "observation" consists of critical analysis of the sources using the methods we have considered in chapter 2. The "hypothesis" is an effort at explanation—an attempt to make causal connections between the observed "facts." The process is dialectic, so that the resultant hypothesis is then tested by new facts, revised if necessary, and retested. And so on.

To illustrate this method, let us return to the Moscow coup of 1991, the KGB-led coup against Gorbachev. Even a child, let alone an experienced journalist, could see that the leaders of the failed coup handled the Soviet TV very badly, that they should have blocked CNN, that they should not have allowed Yeltsin to speak to President George Bush on the telephone. From these facts (Bernard's first step) it is easy to form a hypothesis (Bernard's second step): the coup failed because the organizers did not handle the press skillfully, because Yeltsin did, and because the Russian public never once believed that the leaders of the coup were serious. Analyzing the fit between the given facts and the hypothesis (Bernard's third step), we see that the Russian public had good reasons for their "Glaubensunwilligkeit." They lay, we can surmise, in the six years of glasnost that had preceded the attempted coup; it was simply impossible to set the clock back. We can verify this hypothesis (Bernard's fourth step) with other evidence, such as the analogous political processes leading to the collapse of communism throughout the East Bloc in 1989.

The uprising of 1993 provides another illustration. Yeltsin's silence the entire day of Sunday, October 3, prompted a great many hypotheses: some supposed he was paralyzed, others that he was drunk; his aides reported that he consulted feverishly, but rationally, for hours with his military, which did not want to move against his opponents. There is good evidence for the last hypothesis, for the next day, Monday, the old Yeltsin was back. He ordered the tanks to fire on the parliament building; he wounded or killed many victims as well; and he had his opponents arrested. Evidence available since then has confirmed this hypothesis, for a government report secretly obtained by journalists revealed that on Monday morning at 5 A.M. Yeltsin had made a deal with the army leaders that finally set him free to act. Months later, in December 1993, it became clear what price Yeltsin had had to pay for the support: a guarantee of privileges and increased budget allocations for the military, which since the Afghanistan debacle had suffered budget cuts and loss of prestige.

Although it is a simple process to think up hypotheses, it is no simple task to formulate hypotheses that actually link the observed pieces of evidence—that can explain the facts available, not those that the scholar might wish to have. Often, it takes many tries before the scholar can formulate a hypothesis that really works—one that satisfactorily accounts for the known evidence. There is no formula for success in this difficult venture.

The entire process of scientific discovery is, in fact, considerably less "scientific" than scholars sometimes imagine. This does not mean that scientific progress occurs randomly, by accident, by some alchemy we cannot comprehend. It means that scientists belong to, and are dependent upon, a community of scholars that is itself politically and culturally constituted. A recent example illustrates the point. Janssen Pharmaceuticals (a Belgian company, now a division of Johnson and Johnson) had by 1966 developed a drug (Levamisole) that happened to be very successful in treating animal parasites. Years later, in 1977, a French researcher at the University of Tours noticed, by chance, a chemical similarity between Levamisole and a product that he was testing for its usefulness against cancer in humans. This led Janssen's scientists to suspect that Levamisole could work on human cancers, and they began tests on human subjects. In both 1981 and 1991, they published their results (very positive) in scholarly journals. The interesting element in this story for historians is not, however, the wonders of the drug, but the process by which the drug's usefulness in treating human cancers was established. The original tests for the drug's effects on cancer were done in the 1980s, both in the United States (the Mayo Clinic) and at the University of Antwerp, and in both sites the results were encouraging. The U.S. Food and Drug Administration refused, however, to allow the clinical trials on humans required for licensing. In 1989, the issue came to a head during a meeting of the Division of Cancer Treatment (of the NIH) and the FDA, with the FDA arguing that the indications of possible effectiveness in humans were not strong enough to warrant the risks of clinical trials. The story of the debate was reported in the journal *Cancer Letter* and picked up by the *Washington Post*, which invoked the Freedom of Information Act to get access to the notes from the meeting. That publicity, along with pressure from AIDS activists, who were simultaneously lobbying for a loosening of restrictions on human trials for drugs of possible use in fighting AIDS, forced the FDA to back down and revise its policy on human trials. Thus it was that Levamisole's benefits for cancer patients were established and the drug licensed—an enlightening story of the politics of science.[6]

The difficulties of applying the so-called scientific method to historical research means that historians must often satisfy themselves with rules of logic that appear less watertight, making statements that seem probable, not "proved" in any "scientific" sense. This is particularly true when the historian is trying to decide between two equally compelling explanations. Let us say, for example, that a historian is studying a cluster of events around 1900 and concludes that two possible arguments seem equally good. To avoid the stalemate, the scholar may turn to similar clusters of events that happened, perhaps, in 1800, 1700, or 1600. In effect, this is a kind of reasoning by analogy, for the argument is that a situation in one time or place is enough like a better understood situation in another time or place so that the first situation can be explained in terms that have been accepted for the second. This is, needless to say, a very risky process, and gains credibility only to the extent that the historian can make a persuasive case about the similarity between the two situations.

Let us give an example, using Geoffrey Blainey's *The Causes of War* (3rd ed., 1988), a history of relations between Russia and Turkey. These two countries, Blainey pointed out, had fought ten wars in the two hundred years between 1678 and 1878, none of them with a decisive conclusion. They fought so regularly, Blainey argued, because they both miscalculated their respective military potential, and were thus always willing to reopen the conflict. Reasoning by analogy, we would argue that wars be-

6. Early reports of the drug's effectiveness are found in W. K. Amery and D. A. Gough, "Levamisole and Immunotherapy: Some Theoretic and Practical Considerations and Their Relevance to Human Disease," *Oncology* 38 (1981): 168–81. Also see Rebecca S. Mutch and Paul R. Hutson, "Levamisole in the Adjuvant Treatment of Colon Cancer," *Clinical Pharmacy* 10 (February 1991). The story of how the drug became available for human use is reported in Ezra M. Greenspan and Rodrigo Erlich, "Levamisole and the New Era of Chemoimmunotherapy," *Cancer Investigation* 9, 1 (1991): 111–24.

tween the two would continue, and that they would continue for the same reasons. What Blainey pointed out, however, was that when Russia decisively beat Turkey in 1878, matters changed. Then the power differential became evident and, as a consequence, the situation stabilized because Turkey was no longer willing to risk open conflict with Russia. Since then, just as Blainey predicted, the two have fought only as part of more general conflicts, as in World War I. Analogy, thus, works only so long as the fundamental circumstances producing the similarities remain unchanged.

All the techniques we have discussed are, it should be clear, flawed. Each, no matter how "scientific" in form, requires historians to make assumptions, to fill in blanks, to make intuitive guesses, to reason from the specific to the general. This is, in the crudest sense, the essence of historical interpretation, and such interpretation is just that—interpretation. This does not mean, however, that historians do not hold each other accountable for the way they reason. No historian's work will survive if it is based on sloppy reasoning in the judgment of colleagues in the profession. Among the many fallacies of reasoning that are guaranteed not to pass this test of plausibility are the following: reasoning from the isolated case to a general rule (all Irishmen have red hair); confusing correlation with cause (taxes were cut and the GNP rose; hence the tax cut caused the economy to grow); the use of two unconnected and unproved facts to prove a third (the Star Wars defense system planned by the United States in the 1980s would have made the country impregnable to missile attack, and the huge investments the Soviets made in their military caused the nation's economic collapse; hence, Star Wars brought about the end of the Soviet empire); and the adduction of evidence that has no established relevance to the case (X is not a good parent; hence, he will not make a good president).

B. Establishing Evidentiary Satisfaction

At what point do historians (and their professional critics) think they have enough evidence to support their arguments? Given that no interpretation is ever fully secure, when is it "secure enough"? While perfect certainty is never achievable, there are gradations of plausibility—some kinds of evidence are better than others, some kinds of interpretations are easier to support. In the first two chapters of this book, we considered the credibility of individual sources: whether, for example, the source was intentionally or unintentionally created; whether it presents data of a social bookkeeping kind that have a certain reliability because they report patterns of social action; whether the source speaks from a personal voice, as does a diary; whether it purports to relay a political judgment; whether the source relates what people were supposed to have done (i.e., a normative law) or what they did (i.e., police records). Here we want to consider the issue of evidence more generally, isolating those factors that seem to most historians crucial in judging the quality of evidence. While we can offer beginning historians no formulas for deciding "how much" evidence is enough, we hope to provide some useful aids for making that decision.

To a large extent, the amount or quality of evidence required depends on the kind of event being studied. Nineteenth-century positivist historians thought that the problem of "true" or "false" in historical interpretation was a matter of deciding whether something actually happened ("true") or not ("false"). For Ranke, true facts would have included easily establishable events such as the birth and death of Chancellor Otto von Bismarck. But there are, it hardly need be said, few events of interest to historians that can pass this Rankean test, not even the simplest "fact" of "what happened." Let us take, for example, a question that seems quite straightforward: what did Boris Yeltsin do on the morning of Monday, August 19, 1991, in order to telephone the White House in Washington from his home outside Moscow? Still harder to establish with certainty are the "facts" surrounding the KGB's decision not to prevent his calling. Even statistical "facts" are seldom as uncontroversial as the numbers imply. Exactly how many people died in the Nazi concentration camps, and how many among them were Jews? No numerical answer given to a question like this, no matter how plausible, can ever be absolutely proved. Even if historians were to gather all the archival material in the world about this matter, they would still not be able to answer that question with full certainty, for the records are simply not good enough for that level of precision, and those that once existed often do not still survive.

"Facts" that imply knowledge of an actor's intention are considerably harder to verify and will never pass the positivist test of "true" or "false." Why did Gorbachev, in 1991, continue to believe that the Communist Party would survive, even after the putsch and the dramatic confrontation with Yeltsin in the parliament? While we can be sure that he had certain objectives in mind, and a logic that could explain his actions, we can also be sure that what he would later claim to be his motives do not constitute the whole story. Our certainty about the patterns, the causes, and the effects of general processes will be even less secure. What forces were unleashed by the 1991 putsch in Moscow? The principal problem with a question like this is that the "forces" are many—social, political, economic, and ideological—and each observer will give different weight to each, will assess each differently. Finally, there are certain events of the past that can never even be subjected to this test of true/false. An essay by Jean-Paul Sartre, a novel by Ernest Hemingway, a poem by Maya Angelou, these are all "true" in the sense that they exist and that they exist as the "truth" of their text.

Historians also apply a kind of quantitative measure in assessing evidence, in general following the principle that the more evidence, the better. But historians never have just what they want or need. At one extreme is the historian limited to one source. Einhard's *Life of Charlemagne* is, for example, the only source scholars have about the private life of Europe's first emperor. Like many of the political biographies written today, this one is more hagiography than critical biography, and in the best of worlds historians might well refuse to use it as evidence about Charlemagne's life and his character. But historians, although conscious that they are prisoners of the unique source and bear all the risks that this involves, use it because it is all they have. At the other extreme are historians studying the recent past. They have a great many sources, and in many ways their problems are thus fewer. But even here there is no certainty. The historian studying the American war in Vietnam has plenty of "evidence," but there are still a great many issues that remain murky, even at the level of simple event.

Oddly, moreover, it is often the case that some of the sources treating the matters historians of the contemporary period are studying have not yet become available and that there is still the chance of getting new, absolutely crucial evidence. For example, the historian who is now, in 2001, studying the peace accord negotiated in 1993 among Israel, the PLO, and the Arab world might rightly suspect that useful information about this event, such as deals made between Shimon Peres and Mahmoud Abbas, still lies secret and might someday be released. Today, however, this information is still too delicate, too raw, for public opinion and cannot be permitted to surface.

In contrast, the classical historian's problem is typically scarcity of sources, not abundance. The paradox here is that because the scarcity is irremediable, this historian has to spend little time searching for or worrying about undiscovered documents. Of course, this does not mean that ancient historians or any other historians of the distant past can imagine that all they need to know on a subject is collected in archives and neatly labeled, passively awaiting their arrival and their questions. Like all historians, these scholars must decide what kinds of sources could provide relevant information and must seek it out, often moving from archive to archive, from dossier to dossier. The crucial difference between them and someone working on the recent past is, then, not so much that they have few sources and the modern historian has many; it is simply that they are much less likely to come upon previously unknown sources.

Even when all the sources available agree, even when there are a lot of sources concerning an event, even then historians cannot be sure about the facts because it is often the case that the sources available represent the opinions, or the versions of the events, of the winning party in a contest or the dominant powers in a system. From the early to the high Middle Ages (roughly from the sixth century through the twelfth), for example, almost all the sources that survive were produced by ecclesiastical institutions—monasteries, the papacy, bishops, and their officials. None of these sources had very much good to say about merchants; none of them knew much about the ordinary life of secular people or thought to say much about it. Hence, what they reveal about any of these matters has to be taken with handfuls of salt. And it is possible, as some historians have recently argued, that the profession's reliance on these sources for views of this half-millennium has radically distorted understanding of religious life in this period, luring historians into imagining that Europe was uniformly Christian and that people lived according to well-understood Christian precepts.[7] Similarly, what historians know about workers' movements before the nineteenth century in European history comes to them almost entirely from records produced by their repressors or opponents. Conservative newspapers of the day unanimously portrayed the early leaders of socialist movements in Europe as dangerous and subversive; police files repeated the story. The socialists' own voices are extremely difficult to find; scholars have only a few personal letters and diaries, a few reports of proto-socialist movements. The situation regarding the German peasants' revolt of 1525 is similar, for it too is described largely in the words of its enemies.

Another factor to consider is the historian's personal distance from the events, for that very much determines the way he or she uses the evidence and thus its "sufficiency." In general, we would expect that the closer a historian is to events, the better he or she can judge the available evidence; thus, he or she will require less evidence than would someone

7. For a recent study arguing that the Middle Ages was in many respects more pagan than Christian, see Ludo Milis, *Heidense middeleeuwen* (Brussels, 1991; *The Pagan Middle Ages* [Rochester, N.Y., 1998]).

studying a more distant period. Some commentators have even argued that *only* participants in an event can reliably tell its history. Elie Aron Cohen, a Dutch physician who was himself in the Nazi concentration camp in Auschwitz, published a study in 1979, *De negentien treinen van Sobibor* (*The Nineteen Trains of Sobibor*), which investigated the events at Sobibor, one of the most notorious camps, where certain Jews assisted in the exterminations in exchange for their own lives. For Cohen, these were inexplicable events, comprehensible only to those who had experienced them. He concluded, "someone who had not experienced [such an] event, cannot write about it," thus constructing an impenetrable barrier between those who survived the camps and those who did not. In recent years some scholars have similarly argued that only women can write women's history or that only African Americans can teach African American history.

This barrier is too high. While it is certainly true that participants in an event, immediate observers of it, and scholars who share the social identity of the group being studied have a particular—and uniquely valuable—perspective, their knowledge and understanding of it are hardly perfect. The historian who is distant from the history he or she is relating is sometimes in a better position to comprehend certain aspects of that history, even to have better evidence about the events. Such scholars have another advantage as well in that they know the aftermath, and that knowledge helps them identify the significant features of the event. Sometimes information that contemporaries could not have known will become available to later generations—secret files will be opened, stories once too shameful or too dangerous to relate will become tellable, facts that no one at the time saw as relevant will be revealed as significant. In 1971, for example, the *New York Times* published the famous "Pentagon Papers" leaked by Daniel Ellsberg, which, among other things, showed that the decision to bomb North Vietnam had been made long before the Gulf of Tonkin attack. None of this was known in 1964, and the historian writing between 1964 and 1971 would have told a very different story about the war than would someone studying this event thereafter. Other barriers hinder historians who are personally involved in the history they are writing. They are less able to distance themselves from the politics of the events they study, more likely to inject their own views or wishes into the story they are relating. For such historians, it is often too easy to interpret the past in terms of the shared ideology rather than in terms of the ideas and circumstances that shaped the ideology of that past. Sometimes, indeed, the historian who is not in sympathy with her subject is in a posi-

tion to provide a more nuanced analysis, for, being conscious of her preferences, she will be especially careful to present her subject's views.

C. The "Facts" That Matter

As we shall discuss further in the following two chapters, the status of any
"fact" available to the historian is always insecure. Nevertheless, however
self-conscious they are about the limits of their knowledge, about its par-
ticularity (to this issue we will also return), historians must construct their
interpretations about the past out of information that they deem to be of
factlike status—information that is available to them for the purposes of
their inquiry.

No historian, however, not even those uninterested in questioning the
epistemological status of their "facts," treats every fact equally. Even when
a piece of evidence available—the dates of a battle, a tax roll, a political
memoir, a love letter—has passed the necessary tests of authenticity and
reliability, that "fact" does not necessarily play a significant role in the historian's interpretation. Only certain "facts" acquire that status.

Often, historians will privilege evidence that seems to point to a recur-
ring picture, to add to a story that seems familiar or repetitive. Always,
however, this is a risky choice. In some sense, all events are unique, and
every fact about an event is unique. There can never be another Hitler in
Germany as there was in 1933. Nor will the same event, replayed in different contexts, produce the same result. The events of 1989 in Europe,
when the countries that had been ruled under the same monolithic Soviet
system for more than forty years broke free of that system, all had the
same starting point: Gorbachev's glasnost and perestroika, begun in 1985.
Yet the aftermath of communism's collapse was experienced very differently in each of these countries; it had different results in Russia, Poland,
and Hungary, and different still in East Germany and Czechoslovakia.

This is not to say, however, that there are not patterns in history, similarities of circumstance that allow the historian fruitfully to compare one
place and time with another, to look for patterns of recurrence and thus
patterns of causality. Only when one considers how similar people behave
in similar situations can one begin to make generalizations about the relationships between events that we call cause and effect. Only then does
history become more than the banal repetition of events. The historian,
for example, who does not place the Luddite revolts of the early nineteenth century in a longer history of social protest against unrestrained
economic growth can understand very little about how it was that people

like these workers could have been moved to collective violence. The same historian, observing the warnings of the Club of Rome and the actions of the ecological movements after the Second World War, might well keep in mind the history of the Luddites two hundred years ago. If he does, he is able to make better sense of the Three Mile Island disaster of 1979 and the catastrophe in Chernobyl of 1986. Thus, it is patterns of recurrence that typically interest historians, the ways that events seem to repeat themselves, the ways that generalizations become possible. The "facts" in such patterns thus acquire special importance.

Historians are, of course, interested only in the "facts" that pertain to the events they consider important, or interesting. While such selectivity is an essential part of the historian's job, it is not simply the analytical process that leads historians to treat some information as "data" and to ignore other sorts. It is also a reflection of the judgments historians implicitly make about what kind of events actually matter.

Nineteenth-century historians typically took account only of political events at the level of the state (or statelike institutions) because history, in their view, happened at this level. The coronation of Charlemagne, the battle of Waterloo or of Gettysburg, the signing of the Declaration of Independence—these were the events worthy of historical study. After 1900, historians became interested in the history of industrialism and capitalism because of the spectacular economic performance these processes unleashed in the nineteenth and twentieth centuries, and suddenly information about technology, money supplies, world trade, and labor practices seemed vital. After World War II, with the emergence of the European welfare state, historians mined the archives for facts about social life—the family, health, poverty. More recently, the history of what the French call mentalités (attitudes, patterns of thought, culture in its most general sense) has become a central concern of the profession, and historians read newspapers, letters, diaries as they never did before; they study paintings and films and photographs in new ways; they analyze parades, folk songs, and rock concerts with the care their predecessors gave to parliamentary debates and peace treaties.

Each kind of history thus not only privileges certain events, certain kinds of information; each tends to ignore other events and to suppress other data. For the nineteenth-century historian, the birth rates of seventeenth-century peasants were of no interest—and whatever information about these patterns might have appeared in their sources was not given the status of "fact." For the historian of the family today, in contrast, the sixteenth century is studied for its parish registers, not for the story of the

Armada. A cultural historian working today on the 1880s is likely to find the Jack the Ripper story a more important event than Disraeli's death. Just as historians ignore the information that they do not qualify as "fact," they ignore any historians who are out of sync with the times. It was in 1939 that Norbert Elias published his wonderful *The Civilizing Process*, a study of manners and the rules of social conduct among the European ·aristocracy and bourgeoisie; it was not until the 1980s, when his topic became *au courant*, however, that the work became required reading in graduate schools throughout the West (1979–82; orig., *Über den Prozess der Zivilisation*, 2 vols., 1939). In contrast, Ranke's *History of the Popes*, once considered the epitome of scientific historiography, is now hardly read, except for its historiographical or encyclopedic interest.

To a certain extent, to be sure, historical questions are determined by the sources available to study them. Historians do not have many studies of bathing habits in the fifteenth century in part because there are few sources that can tell us much about these apparently simple matters of daily life in that age. In contrast, scholars have lots of information from this period about philosophical and theological disputes, about church administration, and about politics around the courts of Europe's monarchs. But, as historians of the last twenty or thirty years have demonstrated, one can learn much of interest about the fifteenth century by studying its bathing habits, and they have also managed to find out a surprising amount about these habits. All that was required was to treat this past "as a foreign country," and to observe it with the eyes of a wondering child.[8] Once the topic became of interest, the sources that could reveal something about it became visible.

So what historians do is, in some sense, treat the ordinary as extraordinary. They must do so because ordinary facts, called "quotidienneté" by the French, do not normally catch the eye. Even repeated atrocities are invisible to contemporaries, principally because these people become immune to them. To Adolf Eichmann, after all, the deportation of Jews was a banality. The history of women's history provides a perfect example of how a shift in interest can lead to the discovery of sources, or of new ways of reading sources, and thus to the production of "facts" that were once invisible. A mere thirty years ago, historians simply did not write the history of women. Any graduate student, whether in Europe or the United States, who proposed such a dissertation topic, was dismissed with assurances that "the sources did not exist for such a study" (or, occasionally, she [or he] was told that whatever could be done on this topic "had al-

8. On the past as a "foreign country," see David Lowenthal, *The Past Is a Foreign Country* (New York, 1986) and Leslie P. Hartley, *The Go-Between* (London, 1953).

ready been done," presumably by the few turn-of-century scholars who, under the influence of that epoch's women's moment, had thoroughly mined the archives). The shelves of every university (and secondary school) library in the West today are eloquent witness to how wrong that assessment was.

Historians make still another distinction among facts that matter, or between "facts"—reliable information—and "nonfacts"—unverifiable information: they have also traditionally distinguished between "facts" and "opinions" about facts, by which they have typically meant individual judgments about these facts. Nineteenth-century positivist historians were especially concerned to distinguish the two and even eliminated from their purview anything that smacked of an "opinion" because such opinions were in their view not verifiable. Thus, in its extreme form, this kind of history writing limited itself to records of what people did, not what they thought about what they did or even what they said they did. The terms of a peace treaty, the amount of taxes collected, the outcome of a battle—these were potentially verifiable pieces of information, potentially "facts." A letter damning the peace terms, a newspaper editorial lamenting the tax increase, the burial records of the men lost in battle—these were also potentially "facts" but they were of considerably less interest unless it could be shown that they produced other "hard facts"—a new peace treaty, a change in the tax laws, a decline in the marriage rate. They were not considered possible indicators of nationalist sentiment, social consciousness, or attitudes toward death simply because these matters could not be sufficiently well known to rise to the level of "fact."

Those days are long past. Even the most methodologically conservative historian of today happily takes such material as evidence, recognizes it as possibly valuable information about the very opinions, dreams, hopes, and attitudes that his predecessors thought not knowable. There are many important moments in this history of history writing, and in the next chapter we will discuss some of its key episodes in greater detail. Let us end here by commenting that the "fact" as the object of historian's study has, in the process, been diminished almost to the point of disappearing, at least as our predecessors generally understood it. What is left? To that question we will return.

CHAPTER FOUR

❦

New Interpretive Approaches

H istorical interpretation is not simply about assembling and ordering facts. It is as much art as science, as much intuition as technique, always some of each. It is not, however, always a mixture in the same proportions. At different moments in its long history, professional history writing in the West has taken various approaches, and at each of these moments it has thus tended to treat sources in particular ways, at one time selecting certain kinds of sources, at another a different kind—at one time searching for information about coronations and wars, at another attempting a statistical analysis of inflation and deflation; at one time dissecting sources as though they could provide unmediated access to truth, at another reading the same sources with the skepticism of a poststructuralist critic.

It was during the second half of the nineteenth century, when Western history writing was first professionalized and moved to the academy, that many of the techniques of source criticism were first developed. As we have described, history was imagined as a pure science during this epoch, the science of source criticism. Using these techniques, historians such as Leopold von Ranke hoped to create objective renderings of the past, narratives constructed of unadorned "facts" which had passed the severe tests to which their trained eye subjected them. Ranke's effort to tell the tale "as it actually happened" was labeled "historicist," a rendering of the past strictly on its own terms, without grand theory about social systems, causality, or purpose; in this version of historiography, the narrative itself was the explanation.

Since Ranke's day, historiography has gone through many changes.

Historians no longer study the same subjects, in the same way; nor do they imagine they have obtained the same kind of understanding of the past that Ranke and his contemporaries thought possible. Among the many reasons for these changes, the many influences that have helped transform historiography so radically, sociopolitical factors loom very large, and we shall discuss them in a bit more detail at the end of this book. As important as social and political developments were in changing historiography's course, however, even more central were intellectual currents that fundamentally altered the way historians think about, read, and interpret sources. Here we want to discuss some of the principal motivations for these intellectual changes and the directions they have taken.

A. Interdisciplinarity

Most of these influences have come from historians' encounters with other disciplines. One source was the social sciences, preeminently sociology but also economics, political science, and psychology. More recently, there has been an equally productive exchange with anthropology. The second principal source of methodological innovation was the humanities, especially linguistics, philosophy, and literary criticism. Whether these encounters were with literary scholars or sociologists, economists or philosophers, all have affected what historians study, and it is largely thanks to these influences that they have today a much broader range of inquiry than they once had. The most important effect of these encounters has been, however, not on what is studied, but on how historians study it—in short, on what they think they can know and how they think they can know it.

1. The Social Sciences

Historians' engagement with the social sciences goes back at least to the early days of social science itself, back to Marx, Weber, and Durkheim whose works constitute, still today, the bedrock of sociology. Their social theories have given history new ways of thinking about how human beings organize themselves into groups, whether by family, community, class, caste, or political party. They have helped historians think about how these groups change and how membership in them gives meaning to human life.

Although the influence of Karl Marx (1818–83) on history writing itself would be more direct in the second half of the twentieth century than it was in the late nineteenth, his theories about the relationship between economic structure, social change, and the political order gave birth to entire schools of sociology. In turn, this sociology provided historians with powerful conceptual tools for analyzing the relationship of the economy to human experience at the most complex level. According to Marx, the aspects of our lives that make us human—that distinguish us from other mammals and give us our history—are constituted by our material existence, which he defined as the ways we transform the natural world to secure our physical and social existence, and our consciousness of this capacity. In his interpretation, these relationships necessarily change over time, as human beings organize themselves in ever more complex and hierarchical ways, and they change in predictable directions. The nineteenth century in which Marx wrote was, he argued, both the end of one epoch, in which a capital-owning class (the bourgeoisie) controlled the production process, and the incubator of a new, in which there would be no separation of capital and labor (communism).

Although Marx's theories had a huge impact on all the social sciences (and somewhat later on the humanities as well) few historians of the late nineteenth and early twentieth century were in full agreement with Marx because his theories about historical change seemed to deny human agency, to remove individuals—the very focus of traditional historical scholarship—from history. In addition, Marx's own politics and the critique of capitalism on which his historical and political theories were based alienated many scholars, whose own views about capitalism, its benefits, and its likely future were very different. Nevertheless, no historian after Marx escaped his influence. Even those among his successors such as Henri Pirenne and Karl Bücher, who made quite different arguments about the history of market economies and capitalism, were in conversation with Marx. Since the Second World War, Marx's influence has been even more visible. Marxian methodology, rather than his theories of history, has, for example, provoked fascinating work by Jan Romein concerning the way people in all societies regard such issues as labor, authority, time, and nature, and by Karl Wittfogel on the link between despotism and irrigation systems. Marxian theories of class and social change have informed some of the most important debates in social history of this century, including interpretations as far apart as E. P. Thompson's already mentioned 1963 *Making of the English Working Class*, Eugene Genovese's *Roll Jordan Roll: The World Slaves Made* (1971), Mary Ryan's *Cradle of the Middle Class: The Family in Oneida County, New York, 1790–1865* (1981), and Albert Soboul's *Les sans-culottes parisiens en l'an II* (1958; *The Sans-*

Culottes: The Popular Movement and Revolutionary Government, 1793–1794, 1972).

Max Weber (1864–1920) followed Marx in time, publishing his most important works around the turn of the century, but his effect on historical scholarship was felt almost immediately. His basic methodology, to abstract "ideal types" from close observation of empirical data, transformed the way that many historians conceptualized their research projects on society, economy, political order, and even culture itself. Analytical frameworks borrowed from Weber, especially from his great *Economy and Society* (orig., *Wirtschaft und Gesellschaft,* 1922; Eng. of Ger. 4th ed., 1968), allowed historians to make generalizations about societies of the past; to see social systems as integrated wholes, inseparable from economic, political, and ideological structures; and to make comparisons among societies, both across time and across space. Weber also wrote historical accounts, most famously *The Protestant Ethic and the Spirit of Capitalism,* (1930; orig., *Die Protestantische Ethik und der Geist des Kapitalismus,* 1904–5), which argued that capitalism was the product, in part, of a particular "Calvinist" psychology that valued savings, hard work, and individual accomplishment over display, leisure, and birth. While Weber's argument on this particular issue has been much criticized, it has proved one of the most important historical studies of the twentieth century, not just for the way it combined a structural analysis with a cultural, but for its challenge to the more determinist marxist accounts of the evolution of capitalism. Marx had argued, in *Capital (Das Kapital,* 1867) and elsewhere, that the blind passion of capitalists, born of their need to survive against ruthless competition, would drive them ever forward in search of profits. This process, he claimed, could be slowed but not halted, diverted but not aborted. The inevitable result would be collapse and revolution. Weber, in contrast, left this abstract world of possibility and focused on the social, political, and even cultural institutions in which capitalism was embedded.

The list of scholars and of books that bear the direct imprint of Weber's *Protestant Ethic* is very long. Richard H. Tawney, for example, reworked Weber's argument in *Religion and the Rise of Capitalism* (1926); Henri Hauser built upon it in *A propos des idées économiques de Calvin* (1926; Concerning Calvin's economics). In *The Theory of Social Change* (1964), Everett E. Hagen argued that religion was not the dominant mover in capitalism, putting his emphasis instead on the psychological need for achievement that minorities feel (in the case he studied, Jews in western Europe). David McClelland (*The Achieving Society,* 1964) and Anthony C. Hepburn (*Minorities in History,* 1978) developed this idea, claiming that it is the marginal condition itself, rather than ideological or psychological factors, which produces great achievement. The list could go on; the point here is simply to underline how productive Weber's argument has been.

Emile Durkheim's (1858–1917) importance for historians rests on his theories about collective consciousness, about how entire societies imagine and experience the world. This consciousness, Durkheim argued, is brought by institutions and their workings, and is materially represented in symbols that are themselves located in cultural systems. The main thrust of his work was a resistance to reductionism, that is, a refusal of the then dominant idea in much sociology that culture was a reflection or a product of socioeconomic structure. Durkheim insisted, instead, that social phenomena are "social facts," and these he thought were the subject matter of sociology. Social facts are those ways of acting, thinking, and feeling which exist outside the consciousness of the individual and which have enormous coercive power. When, for example, a woman performs her duties as mother, wife, worker, religious observer, or citizen, she will usually adhere to norms of behavior that seem to her entirely natural, given, and thus inalterable. But these norms are neither self-imposed nor natural—they are learned via membership in the society that defines the roles. Social facts are thus determinant of individual experience, they are external to any particular individual, and they perdure over time. In later work, Durkheim went on to argue that social facts and the moral rules they instantiate become effective in individual lives to the extent they are internalized in the consciousness of individuals, while also continuing to exist independently of them. In this sense society is both something beyond us and something in ourselves. Much of Durkheim's work focused on how these rules develop and gain power, and it was those questions that led to his well-known studies of religion, ritual, and work.

The influence of the social sciences on history writing is not, however, limited to the impact of great theorists such as Marx, Weber, and Durkheim. An equally important effect was methodological.

One debt is obvious: historians owe their discovery of statistics and quantitative methods to the social sciences. It was from colleagues in sociology and economics, above all, that historians acquired skills to render evidence in forms that made it susceptible to quantitative analysis. From them historians learned how to take samples, how to measure correlation, how to think more rigorously about the relationship between correlation and causality. It is also from them that historians first acquired the software needed to manipulate massive amounts of data and from them, by and large, that they learned how to use it.

Economists and other quantitative social scientists, for example, have taught historians to measure—to quantify—what they once only described. In doing so, historians have not only acquired much needed precision; they have discovered trends and patterns that were hitherto invisible, not just to the people who lived through these events, but to their historians as well. For example, scholars studying economic cycles have produced several models describing (and to some extent explaining) patterns of change that have proved quite useful to historians seeking to understand economic history. In 1939, to mention one of the best-known studies, Joseph Schumpeter identified three kinds of business cycles: short cycles, which last about three years; intermediate cycles, of ten years' duration; and long-term cycles, which last about fifty to sixty years (*Business Cycles: A Theoretical, Historical, and Statistical Analysis of the Capitalist Process*). These last cycles, specifically defined by Nikolai Kondratieff and hence usually called Kondratieff cycles, begin with a period of upswing, which implies rising production and prices, and end with a downturn, accompanied by declining production and falling prices.[1] Many different explanations have been offered for these cycles. Some economists have argued that monetary policy plays a key role; others credit overinvestment or underconsumption. Historians have added political and social factors, such as war or demographic developments.

Other debts are perhaps less easily recognized but just as important. For example, scholars such as Robert Berkhofer have developed an analysis that focuses on what people in the past *did* rather than on what they thought or felt.[2] The argument here is that the historian cannot re-create the mental world of the past except by means of studying what these people did, since historians bring too much of themselves into interpretations of what another age thought or felt. Thus, scholars must firmly distinguish the historical actor from the observer (i.e., the historian). They must also distinguish the motive from the act, deducing the motive from the visible actions. Finally, Berkhofer insists that acts must be placed in time and culture; in that way historians can divine something of the historical personage's relationship to his or her own age. For example, the historian studying the evolution of ideas about religious tolerance in early modern Europe would begin by studying the general climate of opinion in that age. Then, he would observe the way a particular person who lived in that period behaved with respect to people of different beliefs. Having considered these action in the context of the period, the historian can then, and only then, judge that person "tolerant" or "intolerant."

1. For a recent edition of his work, see Natalia Makasheva, *The Works of Nikolai D. Kondratiev* (London, 1998).
2. Robert F. Berkhofer, *A Behavioral Approach to Historical Analysis* (New York, 1969).

Social science methodology of this kind rendered a great many historians fully "positivist" in that they, like the sociologists or political scientists
on whom they modeled themselves, sought to transform their craft into
something like a laboratory science. In this vision of history writing (discussed in chapter 3 as well), the historian is like the chemist or physicist in
that she is imagined to discover general rules governing the behavior of
"data" by means of close observation of those data. While the physicist, for
example, studies the behavior of electrons in order to posit general laws
about the structure of the atom, the historian studies voting patterns in
nineteenth-century America to discover general laws about development
of popular democracies. In their strictest form, neither the techniques of
positivist history nor its assumptions about the kind of knowledge available to the historian are creditable today. Still, the influence of positivism
on history writing has been deep and lasting. Historians may no longer
imagine that evidence can be rendered "data" or that their inquiries will
produce (or test) general laws regarding human behavior, but they still
employ many of the methods of research and of analysis borrowed from
this model of scholarship, and many historians still long for the level of
certainty promised by the positivist social sciences.

Historians also evidence their enduring debts to the social sciences
when they borrow the typologies developed in those fields. The charis-
matic theocracy, such as that of the precolonial Incas or the Iran of
Khomeini; the city state such as that of classical Greece or late medieval
Italy; the bourgeois democracy of nineteenth-century Europe; the post-
capitalist democracy of late twentieth-century America; the welfare state
of western Europe; the totalitarian bureaucracy of the former Soviet
Union—all these are concepts borrowed from other social sciences. In
some historians' hands, such typologies have become the stuff of theory.
Roland Mousnier, for example, has used a three-part system (*Les hiérar-
chies sociales de 1450 à nos jours*, 1969; *Social Hierarchies, 1450 to the Present*,
1973) for analyzing the way that any particular society organizes social hierarchy: by castes (as in traditional India), by social rank (as in early modern Russia), or by class (as in seventeenth-century Holland). According to
Mousnier, castes are based on levels of religious purity, rank or honor is
linked to social function, and class is tied to wealth. With the aid of this ty-
pology, he has explained the collapse of ancien régime France as the shift
from a society of orders (social rank) to one of class.

Historians borrow almost as freely from other branches of the social sciences as well. Sigmund Freud, Carl Jung, Erik Erikson, and countless
other theorists of the human psyche have given historians powerful tools
for thinking about the way that an individual—or an age—understands

and approaches the world. Scholars today have studies of feelings in history—anger, distrust, compassion, and love—that no nineteenth-century positivist could have imagined. Historians now seek to discover the anxieties of an age, its dreams and hopes and desires, and they use the tools of psychology to help them do so, sometimes reading the letters and memoirs that have come to them from ages past as though they were psychiatrists and the past their patients.

The enduring connections between the social sciences and history have contributed to what many scholars today would characterize as a blurring of boundaries among the disciplines, a gradual conflation of interests and of methodologies, at least among some branches of historical studies and some branches of the social sciences. Social historians have, naturally, long been deeply invested in the methods and theories of sociology, to the point that some historians have seemed almost retrospective sociologists. Political historians have long been in deep conversation with political scientists; economic historians use formulas developed by contemporary economists to chart and explain economic change in the past.

But historians are not social scientists *manqués*, and not all of historians' encounters with the social sciences have been successful. We have already mentioned the positivist inclinations of much traditional social science— the notion that "facts" are unmediated truth and that historians are like scientists, discoverers of general laws of human behavior. Leaving aside for the moment the problematic question about the status of a "fact," let us remember that in some sense there are no general laws of human behavior except trivial ones (that, for example, we all are born and we all die) and that the historian is the caretaker of the memory of how different, how unique each moment in the past was. While historians must work with generalizations ("the bourgeoisie," "feudalism," "Christianity," "capitalism") and while they must work toward generalizations that provide explanations (the emergence of bourgeois democracies, the collapse of feudalism, the implosion of Latin Christianity at the end of the Middle Ages, the globalization of capital)—and while their owe their facility with such generalizations, sometimes even the generalizations themselves, to colleagues in other social sciences—such generalizations sometimes disguise more than they reveal. What, after all, does it mean to talk about the "rise of the middle class," the "crisis of liberalism," or the "patriarchal system of male dominance"? When historians use those terms, they must make sure they know what they mean by them—*precisely* what they mean, for it is the historians' principal job to provide that kind of textured account of the past and the people who made it. Although historians may want to talk about feudalism and may want to use its "collapse" as an explanation for some other event (perhaps the rise of the territorial sovereign and the national monarchy), they must always be clear about just what was "feudal" about the society whose "collapse" they are invoking and what elements constituted its "collapse."

The risks of blindly adopting social science methodology might be best considered under three categories. First is the danger of anachronism. It is entirely appropriate to use terms to describe a group or a process in the past that the people of that period did not use, so long as the historian is clear—and makes it clear to readers—that the term and the concept are his. For example, historians have coined the term "patriciate" to describe urban elites of medieval cities (borrowing it from the Romans); they do so, however, in full consciousness that the term is their own, that it describes a social group for which medieval people did not have so specific a label. It is also perfectly correct to use questions from the present to interrogate the past, but scholars should not expect people of the past to have experienced or understood the world as they do. Thus, historians might rightly inquire about GNP/capita or land/labor ratios in ancient Rome, borrowing these categories from present-day economics. They would be at serious risk of anachronism, however, if they expected to find that first-century Romans conceptualized their world in these terms, let alone employed this terminology. Similarly, they would be wrong to imagine that these same Romans imagined, or experienced, childhood as they do. Thus, while historians might want to use Freudian concepts to think about individuation and socialization in ancient Rome, they would err if they assumed these people had the same oedipal experience that Viennese bourgeois may have had in the early twentieth century, or that Western children have today. Freud's theories, if they work at all, work only for the culture in which the psyche he studied was created.

A second risk is an overdose of conceptualizing, to the point that the empirical detail is suppressed. Marc Bloch once warned his fellow historians: "les méchants faits détruisent les belles théories" ("nasty facts destroy lovely theories").

The third risk involves the naïveté of too much model building on too narrow a database or of gross generalization. Alan Macfarlane's theory about the etiology of witchcraft persecutions in early modern England, which argued that the persecuted came from the poor working people and the persecutors from their rich employers, turns out, Robert Muchembled has shown, to have little relevance to France and Flanders.[3]

---

3. Alan Macfarlane, *Witchcraft in Tudor and Stuart England* (New York, 1970); Robert Muchembled, *Le roi et la sorcière: L'Europe des bûchers, XVe-XVIIIe siècle* (Paris, 1993).

There both victims and accusers came from the same class. Models, historians must remember, are just abstractions from selected data and are seldom directly transferable to another historical situation. Human life is too complex.

This is, of course, the contribution that history makes to the social sciences, and it is important to keep in mind that social scientists are probably as indebted to historians as the reverse. Because historians today approach the past as the past, as a time and place that were different, that changed, they can illuminate the ways in which the human experience cannot be reduced to "rules" and "systems." Thus, to the extent that social scientists have made use of historians' skills and learning, their own work—whether on state formation, voting behavior, poverty, or investment patterns—has become richer, more nuanced, more useful. We can see the potential uses of history, for example, when we consider how differently theorists of international law and scholars specializing in conflict resolution regard the notion of violence. For the former, "violence" (i.e., war) is inevitable in societies, while the force or threat of force deployed by states and statelike institutions is effectively ignored. Theorists of conflict resolution, in contrast, do not see violence (i.e., war) as inevitable but recognize institutional force as being on a continuum with more covert forms of violence.[4] They also insist that people do not "naturally" resort to violence to settle disputes. Both groups would have benefited by closer study of the historical record, for the past can teach much about the history of violence and its (variable) role in creating and sustaining a society. Similarly, during the Vietnam War, American military strategists might well have designed better simulation studies had they taken the more complex view of warfare that historical study provides. As it was, the Pentagon designed elaborate models simulating the outcome of the military campaign, which took into account troop size and preparedness, military contingencies, and the like, but failed to understand the culture of war in Vietnamese society and its particular history. The simulation models thus failed to simulate the reality that lay before the American soldiers and their generals.

Although history's first and perhaps deepest connections with the social sciences is by way of sociology, political science, and economics, historians of more recent generations owe their most direct debts to anthropology. The two disciplines were not always, however, as close. Anthropology was

4. See, for example, Frank Marsh and Janet Katz, *Biology, Crime, and Ethics: A Study of Biological Explanation for Criminal Behavior* (Cincinnati, 1985); David F. Farnington, *Psychological Explanation of Crime* (Aldershot, U.K.—Hanover, N.H., 1994); and Peter B. Answorth, *Psychology of Crime: Myth and Reality* (New York, 2000).

born, after all, as the study of non-Western societies which were seen both as fundamentally different from Western society and as repositories of information about human social organization so fundamental, so basic, that it was almost timeless. In that incarnation, anthropology seemed quite different from history, for it dealt largely with preliterate societies and was in search of what was enduring about human society, not what changed.

The form of social and cultural anthropology dominant today has a much closer relationship to history. First, the tools anthropologists have developed for studying nonliterate societies—studies of ritual and performance above all—have proved to be extremely useful in historical research. Historians of premodern Europe, understandably, were the first to see the potential of this work, but it is not they alone who have borrowed heavily from anthropological theory and method. Second, anthropology's focus has shifted from the study of what were imagined as the "primitive" forms of human society to examination of how any sociocultural system creates and reproduces itself, thus in many ways intersecting much more directly with the interests of historians.

Both these shifts are part of a more general transformation in the field, a transformation that is, in paradoxical ways, the product of a profound crisis in the discipline that has both political and intellectual roots. The political crisis is associated with anthropology's birth as a discipline in which the West studied the non-West and, in particular, the developed world studied the undeveloped. The politics of that stance have been subjected to severe critical scrutiny in the last few decades, with the result that Western anthropologists now also examine their own cultures in much the same way they once studied others. Anthropologists have also become much more self-conscious about the position they occupy when they observe other cultures. Much recent critical work in anthropology has focused on these latter issues, calling into question the most basic methodologies of fieldwork—the very questions anthropologists pose, the sources of the information they gather in interviewing "informants" or otherwise interrogating other cultures, the presumptions they make in deciding what is to be studied.

During the same period, anthropology has undergone a series of invigorating debates about the relationship between social structure and cultural meanings, between practice or experience (what anthropologists regularly refer to as "on-the-ground" experience) and ideology, between cultural *systems* and an individual's position in a particular culture, between high and low or "popular" culture. These debates, and the productive work to which they have given birth, have had an important impact on historical studies (to which we will return later in this chapter). The great French scholar Claude Lévi-Strauss played a key role in these developments, but he was not alone: more recently, Clifford Geertz, Pierre Bourdieu (actually, a sociologist by training), and Victor Turner have had been at least as influential. We will turn to some of those influences in the pages below.

This new self-consciousness about method is just one of the strands of a larger epistemological crisis in anthropology, one that has also affected all the other social sciences, none more so than history. It has its roots, however, in linguistic, philosophical, and literary studies and is today generally (and loosely) referred to as poststructuralism. Let us now turn, too briefly, to that history.

2. The Humanities

Historians' reliance upon written sources has long made them natural partners of scholars who study language and texts. And they have generally shared with the traditional literary critics among them the assumption that language was decipherable—that words referred to real things and that the scholar's task was to discover the "codes" of a particular text or a system of language. We will momentarily turn to the ways that structuralist and poststructuralist theories of language and texts have undermined these assumptions, but first let us review some of the theories or strategies involved in this more traditional way of addressing the problem of how to read texts.

Generally, historians have followed those literary scholars who emphasized that the meaning of a word or a symbol in a text, a painting, a film—in any cultural production—is dependent on context. To establish the meaning of a word, a phrase, or an entire text, scholars have typically begun with the words or the phrases themselves. What, for example, did Shakespeare mean by the phrase "a rose by any other name would smell as sweet"? To answer this question, scholars would ask what the words could have meant when Shakespeare used them, how Shakespeare might have used them elsewhere, what particular meaning they acquired in the poetic line and in the text itself. They focused both on how contemporaries in Shakespeare's culture could have interpreted the phrase and how he could have intended them to interpret it. Understandably, historians have traditionally been especially attentive to context as "time and place," that is, to the ways that the conventions of a particular time and place determine the meaning of language. They have borrowed heavily from a rich array of methods and strategies developed in the humanities to help them explore these issues.

Historians turned first, as early as the seventeenth century, to the critical method of Jean Mabillon, and as early as the nineteenth century to the philological method of Karl Lachmann.[5] They also employed the work of the scholars studying the history of languages, the meaning of words in historical usage, and the formal properties of literary and nonliterary genres, in the hope of understanding the original and conventional meanings of the words. In particular, historians have relied upon students of what is usually called historical semantics, the history of words in use. For example, the French word "grève" referred, in the late Middle Ages, to the actual place where workers could be hired, a sort of hiring hall for casual help. It was not until the nineteenth century that the word acquired its present meaning of "strike," an evolution undoubtedly linked to the fact that "strikes" started in "grèves." Any scholar reading municipal ordinances from the 1300s must, obviously, be aware of this history and read the word with the eyes of a person from that century. But, as literary scholars can also teach historians, it is essential to be cautious with such techniques. An author from the 1300s might himself have anachronistically copied language or word usage from older texts, perhaps from classical texts that had little relationship to—and little meaning in—his contemporary world.

Historians can also learn a lot about a particular text by paying close attention to just the way an author employs a word whose historical significance they have learned to recognize. Jean-Pierre Faye has shown, for example, in his *Langages totalitaires* (1972; Totalitarian languages), that the term "totalitarian" was used in a very positive sense in Italian fascist circles from about 1925, when it had not yet acquired pejorative connotations in the rest of Europe. Scholars have also learned to be attentive to the appearance of new words, to regard them as indications of new ideas, new practices, new ideologies. Bernard Quemada has, for instance, shown that the word "erotic" was first used only in 1788; although this obviously does not mean that there was nothing like the erotic before that date, the appearance of the word does signal a new category of thought, and perhaps of experience. The French word "gauchisme" (being of the "left") likewise has a short history; first used in 1842, it has retained much of its orig-

5. For the latter, see Sebastiano Timpanaro, *Le genesi del metodo del Lachmann* (Padua, 1985), and Harald Weigel, *Nur was du nie gesehn wird ewig dauern: Carl Lachmann und die Entstehung der wissenschaftlichen Edition* (Freiburg, 1989).

inal meaning, but it is no accident that the French language had no such word prior to that date. Other words have longer histories, but their meanings have changed radically. The word "knight" meant one thing in 1300, another in 1800. A word can shift its reference: today the word "bright" is used with colors; in earlier days it was more commonly used to refer to sounds.

It is not just historians who have drawn upon such work on language. Sociologists specializing in communications theory have recently also attacked the problem of context, seeking methods for systematically analyzing the way words are used in particular texts. One of the best known is Bernard Berelson's *Content Analysis* (1952; new ed., 1971). Although based on a quantitative analysis, this method involves much more than counting the number of times words, tropes, phrases, grammatical constructions, or the like appear. It also looks outside the text, in order to analyze the ideology in which the text is embedded. More recently, this method has been expanded to include analysis not just of the message, but of reactions to the message. For instance, scholars have analyzed the public's reaction to the famous debates between Nixon and Kennedy in the United States presidential election of 1960. Those who saw the debates on TV tended to think Kennedy had performed better; those who heard the radio broadcast gave the prize to Nixon. The difference, scholars have argued, is that the reaction to the TV performance was determined not just by the arguments but by the facial expressions, body language, and the like.

The problem of "context" is not, however, limited to the problem of understanding the meaning the words could have had in the text when it was created. In addition, scholars must be attentive to the way phrases, sentences, entire passages acquire meaning in relation to other phrases, sentences, and passages. They must also listen for silences in a text, be ready to recognize shifts in voice and mood. Such meanings are discernible only when the reader can immerse herself in the thought-world of the text, when its logic and ideology are familiar. To read a text, scholars must thus be armed with many skills, many techniques. They must be able to interpret the symbols of the culture in which a particular text is located: its slang and idiom, its jargon, its forbidden words, its formal language, what counts as humor, what works as irony.

Linguists have done extremely useful work on these problems. Noam Chomsky has, for example (*Aspects of the Theory of Syntax*, 1965), developed a model for analyzing a speaker's (or writer's) utterances that distinguishes the speaker's competence in the language (passive knowledge of it) from his performance of it (ability to deploy the language). Because different individuals achieve different levels of competence and different performative abilities, no two utterances are given or received exactly the same way. Paul Grice, building on Chomsky's work, has developed tools for analyzing the way that in conversation people deploy a language system's rules to create new meanings. In Grice's analysis, a dialogue between a young man and a young woman might involve the following exchange: he suggests, "Let's go to the movies"; she responds, "I have exams to study for." Implicit in her response is a refusal, but it is up to us to supply an explanation for her refusal. Most of us would fill in the blank with "I would like to go, but . . . ," thus operating exactly as we do when we watch a conventional western movie, knowing that when the bad guy is about to shoot the good guy, the sheriff will intervene (or that somehow things will come out right). We know the conventions; we can apply the rules to what is unsaid or not yet done.[6]

Philological and philosophical studies have also helped fuel what is generally known as the hermeneutical approach to interpreting the past. First and most famously developed by Wilhelm Dilthey (1833–1911) and Wilhelm Windelband (1848–1915), this was a reading strategy that emphasized the scholar's empathy with a text, an understanding of the meanings constructed by the text's language. Although dependent upon a high degree of philological erudition—study of language and words and of the historical circumstances of the text's creation—this approach is also philosophical in that it presumes that the reader of the text can re-create the thought-world of that text and its culture, can intuit what the author intended, what the text meant to the age in which it was created. The historical understanding thus achieved is a kind of re-creation, a re-capturing of the past. Typically, it does not presume that the historian is in search of grand theory or even of causal explanations, only of understanding. Underlying this approach is, however, a bold theory about knowledge, about the knowability of the past and the historian's access to the past. Some of the twentieth century's greatest historians have worked in this way; Johan Huizinga's *Waning of the Middle Ages* is, in many ways, a hermeneutical study of late medieval Burgundian culture.

More recently, this tradition of hermeneutical study has been revised by Hans Georg Gadamer (*Wahrheit und Methode*, 1960), who argues that historians' chronological distance from the texts they study renders their

---

6. This argument appears in Paul Grice, "Logic and Conversation," in P. Cole and J. L. Morgan (eds.), *Syntax and Semantics*, vol. 3, *Speech Acts* (New York, 1975), pp. 41–58. Grice is famous for a line, "Say no more than you are in a position to say," that is often quoted by historians.

readings fundamentally different from any a contemporary of the text would have given. Historians are simultaneously able to understand what a contemporary witness would not have understood *and* bound to read the text through the culture they themselves inhabit. Arthur Danto has also contributed to this discussion with an analysis of how historical explanation works. The historian's task is to report events, as they happened, in the order of their occurrence, thus producing a narrative. If the narrative is satisfactory, it explains the movement from the beginning to the end of a known trajectory, or provides a "satisfying" account of the process.[7]

Although such techniques of text analysis have had a long and profound influence on the way historians approach sources, the linguistic, philosophical, and cultural theories that go, very loosely, under the names of structuralism and poststructuralism have had the most dramatic impact on the discipline in the past half century. The story is probably best begun with the great Swiss linguistic scholar Ferdinand de Saussure (1857–1913). His lectures published in 1916 as *Cours de linguistique général* (*Course in General Linguistics*, 1967), along with the work of the American Charles Sanders Peirce (1839–1914), revolutionized the science of language, almost single-handedly making the study of signs the center of linguistic analysis. Radically undermining the commonsense idea (one, we have seen, which long underlay literary studies) that words bear necessary relationships to things, Saussure argued that language is simply a mental system with no necessary relationship to the "world" of "reality," an arbitrary system of signs whose meaning is created through their relationship to one another, and to one another alone. The relationships that constitute meaning are, Saussure showed, binary in structure—black is not white, male is not female, in is not out, and so on. The sign itself is composed of the signifier—that which does the pointing—and the signified—that to which the reference is made; the noun "flag," for example is a sign made up of the arbitrary arrangement of letters f-l-a-g (the signifier), which refers to a banner decorated in a way that links it to a particular object, event, or group (the signified). Following Saussure, semiotics developed as the science of "decoding" these signs, understanding how they were constructed, how they changed, what mental gymnastics we go through to create the meanings embodied in signs. In addition to these techniques, semiotics gave Western scholars new ways to think about the relationship between what we know and what "is," between the "truths" we create through language (whether "flag" or "god") and those which might exist outside language. And, to the utter outrage of many ob-

7. See Arthur C. Danto, *Analytical Philosophy of History* (Cambridge, U.K., 1965).

servers, the conclusion was that there is no necessary relationship. And that we can never know what that relationship might or might not be, for all we can know is that which we "know" through language.

It is very hard to overstate the importance of this work on all areas of the humanities and, increasingly, the social sciences. Entire schools of art, film, and literary theory dominant in the West today depend upon semiotic theory, and even those which are more "historical" in that they seek to "decode" the symbols of a text, a painting, or a film by relating them to the "real world" employ the tools of semiotic analysis. Erwin Panofsky was one of the first to adapt the principles of semiotics to the decoding of iconography. His method, laid out in his *Studies in Iconology* (1939), involved three steps: recognition of real persons and events; identification of the represented individuals; and search for the intrinsic meaning and message. Nelson Goodman was among those offering a semiology of paintings, photographs, and films (*Languages of Art*, 1985), in his case focusing on the relationship between the icon and the reality it represented. He argued that Vermeer's scenes of street life in seventeenth-century Holland referred more directly to other works of Vermeer than to streets he was supposedly representing. In contrast, the famous portrait of Erasmus by Holbein contained a double truth: in one sense, it was a representation of Erasmus (or at least resembled other contemporary portraits of Erasmus), but it was also a commentary on Holbein's other portraits, for it also resembled many of Holbein's portraits of other people who looked nothing at all like Erasmus.

Iconographic studies remain central to the historian's craft, for many of the sources that historians use are visual. Medievalists, for instance, must be familiar with the symbols used to indicate personality or identity in medieval art. A dog at the foot of a person in a portrait is, for example, often an index of fidelity; a peach represents the erotic, for it evokes the female buttock. Important as these "readings" are, they are often difficult to do well. Paintings are frequently anachronistic, for example, often dressing characters of one age in the costumes of another (fifteenth-century paintings of ninth-century events, e.g., typically had the figures costumed in fifteenth-century garb). Frequently, too, the artworks are more complicated than they appear, containing irony, understatement, inside jokes that are difficult to interpret. One must be trained to look for and to recognize clues, what Carlo Ginzburg has called "spie," meaning innocent details that tell a noninnocent story. For instance, a seventeenth-century painting by Gerard Ter Borch long thought to be a sentimental domestic scene has now been recognized as something considerably more complex, for the female character holds a coin in her hand, the sign of prostitution.

Decoding films is still another matter, for a film works neither as written text nor as static painting or piece of sculpture. This point was made quite effectively by Peter Wollen in his *Signs and Meanings in Cinema* (1969). He distinguishes icons, indexes, and symbols as they function in film, arguing that an icon is a sign referring to well-known objects, that an index represents by association (a thermometer indicates heat, a symptom represents illness), and that a symbol functions by convention. Whether one retains Wollen's system or not, it is clear that "reading" a film requires special knowledge of its conventions and grammars. The director's and producer's roles are key, for they not only control the scene, but govern the way the scenes appear on film, during the process of cutting, splicing, and rearranging that goes into constructing a film. French structuralist film critics have been particularly attentive to these textual qualities of films, while the Anglo-American tradition of film criticism has tended to be more contextual, more interested in sociocultural significance than in form. Most historians have, understandably, tended to pursue the latter line of inquiry, emphasizing the way films bespeak cultural norms, influence public opinion, or simply record (or distort) current events.

Saussure's work focused on language and language systems, however, not on cultural products or a person's experience of them. His insistence that language was an arbitrary, self-contained, and self-referential system meant that language (as a system of codes) existed prior to experience, that it structured experience. Thus, Saussure's linguistics constitutes a radically *structuralist* system. In a general sense, the term "structuralism" refers to an entire mode of social and cultural analysis, which argues that "systems" precede and structure experience. In the language of its critics, structuralism presupposes metatheory—a theory to which all history, all culture, all language is bound and which it in some sense enacts. In other words, structuralism implies that there is a logic or order that exists, in some sense, prior to the event or the text under scrutiny; such events or texts are thus mere "epiphenomena." Saussurian linguistics is not, however, the only structuralist system, and certainly not the only one of importance to historians. Lévi-Straussian anthropology and marxian sociology are, for the same reasons, considered structuralist.

With Jacques Derrida (and post-Freudian psychoanalytic theory) linguistic structuralism entered the poststructuralist age. In his most important work, *Of Grammatology* (1976; orig., *De la grammatologie*, 1967), Derrida deconstructed the sign, showing that the relationship between the signifier and the signified was not just arbitrary but also unstable, sliding. As a result, meaning was never fixed, never certain, in some sense never fully possible. Deconstructionist textual interpretation, which follows from this critique of language, thus involves a close reading of texts, showing how the texts refer to others, uncovering what is left out or suppressed in the text, and revealing the illogic of what is presented as logical.

Derrida's claim is, however, not so much a methodological one as an epistemological one, a claim that radically undermines the dominant traditions of Western philosophy. Hence, his theory, and the method of deconstruction with which he is associated, have had an equally important—and equally unsettling—effect on all the humanities and, increasingly, on the social sciences, for in the hands of literary theorists and cultural critics the Derridian approach has been generalized to a mode of cultural theory. Poststructuralism, in this general definition, would thus deconstruct all systems of thought and representation, showing that they have no ontological existence, no prior position in time or logic, no history that is inseparable from the history of the event or the text. Poststructuralism is, thus, not so much a theory as an approach, a way of thinking about culture. Scholars and critics working in this way tend to eschew all "totalizing" theory (i.e., concepts that put all phenomena under one explanatory concept, such as "god" or the "social relations of production"), all essentialism (the idea that there is a knowable reality beyond language, ideology, or history), and all foundations (the notion that signifying systems are stable and direct representations of "facts"). They refuse the idea that "individuals" are separate from one another or their history, that there is anything stable or fundamental about the "person" so dear to Enlightenment thought; for that, they are considered antihumanists (although that does not mean antihumane).

Poststructuralism has transformed literary criticism in the West in the last thirty years. Today, no major literature department in the United States or the United Kingdom is without its "deconstructionists," and even those scholars who maintain some distance from the full implications of Derridian theory show its influence. In the hands of such scholars, the object of study is less the aesthetics of a poem or a novel or a play than its construction, the way meaning is created by the juxtaposition of binaries—good and bad (people, art, acts), high and low (objects, culture, purpose), clean and dirty (things, people, acts), male and female (people, values, things), and so on. And the way meaning escapes those binaries. Poststructuralist cultural studies have gone even further, making all the world a text, examining and subverting the hierarchies that structure the world, and bringing into scholarly focus topics, texts, and cultural products that were once ignored. Many cultural theorists of this "school" have directly influenced the social sciences, perhaps none more so than

Edward Said. His *Orientalism* (1978) deconstructed the cultural system through which the West had traditionally studied the (near) East, and has deeply influenced entire subdisciplines—branches of anthropology, history, sociology, and political science among them—that were undergoing their own self-criticism from a poststructuralist perspective just as Said's book was published.

It is not hard to comprehend why poststructuralist theory has elicited angry, bitter, outraged criticism, nowhere more so than in the field of literary studies where both its impact and its threat are greatest. Not only does this approach eschew aesthetic analysis; it also calls into question the very idea of beauty or art, treating both as "effects" created by the text that are dependent on the reader's interpolation in the system of meaning the text replicates, not on any external standards of skill, craft, or aesthetic perfection. It also denies, explicitly in some cases, any "truth" other than that created by the text (and the discourse in which it is embedded), thus opening the way for moral indeterminacy that frightens those literary scholars who would treat literary works as ethical achievements.

It is not literary criticism alone, however, that has been transformed by (and threatened by) poststructuralist approaches. Every kind of cultural study—even some, such as physics or biology, that have aggressively defined themselves as beyond culture—bears its traces: anthropology, as we have already mentioned; sociology, thus giving birth to a burgeoning subfield of cultural sociology; art history; religion. And history. Each of these fields has, however, felt the impact of poststructuralism somewhat differently, for in each the particular promise and the problems of poststructuralism are different.

In history, the work of the French critic and philosopher Michel Foucault (1926–84) has had the greatest influence. Although he repeatedly refused the label "structuralist" or "poststructuralist," his studies of Western "discourses" place him at the dead center of what we now call poststructuralist cultural theory. In a series of important studies of Western sexuality, criminality, bureaucratic institutions of the state, and of language and thought themselves, Foucault explored both the nature of "discourse" itself and the peculiarities of modern Western discourses. In his terms, the production of discourse, the way we know our world, is structured. It is governed by rules of exclusion, by internal systems of control and delineation, by conditions under which the discourse can be deployed, and by philosophical ideas that disguise these processes (ideas of the "individual," of "origins," of "truth"). Following Foucault, historians now regularly use the term "discourse" to mean more than speech or language; they mean systems of speech, thought, and action that constitute knowledge—that make knowledge. According to this kind of theory, no "facts" exist independently of the thought-world that makes a given fact knowable. "Homosexuality" did not exist, for example, as a category of human experience until the West had developed a certain understanding of (a discourse of) human sexuality, one that linked sexual acts to desire and desire, in turn, to identity itself. Similarly, "depression" as a psychological state was a creation of psychoanalytic theory and "genius" a product of an age that romanticized the individual.

Foucault is not the only theorist to examine the relationship between speech and knowledge in this way. Pierre Bourdieu, a French sociologist profoundly influenced by poststructuralism, has devoted his career to exposing the way people live and experience—and thus help create—a symbolic discourse that constitutes their reality. In one of his studies examining the sentencing documents of early modern French courts, for example, he argued that these documents are not merely the results of an inquiry on crime or of studies of past actions; they are statements which simultaneously create the power that condemns the crime and simultaneously create the crime. In Bourdieu's words, "le discours juridique est une parole créatrice, qui fait exister ce qu'elle énonce" ("the juridical discourse brings to life that which it pronounces").[8]

Surely we hardly need note that poststructuralist assumptions are anathema to many historians, for to many they seem to belie the very object of historical research—to uncover the meaning that a text had in the time and place it was written, to the people who wrote and read it. If deconstruction implies that "any" reading is possible, as some have thought, then the historian's project seems in vain. Most historians can go no further than Umberto Eco did in his 1990 *Limits of Interpretation*. There he argued that, while we can never isolate a definitive truth of any text, we can discern its relative location in the consensus reached by the largest body of competent readers. By competent readers he meant specialists, people who had mastered the languages of that age, understood its linguistic and cultural codes, and could relate the texts to the institutions that had produced them.

It is also true, as countless historians have pointed out, that Foucault and his colleagues have in some sense told historians nothing new. It is, after all, the very project of many cultural and intellectual historians to reveal how each age, each social group, has its own "ideology," its own

8. P. Bourdieu, *Ce que parler veut dire: L'économie des échanges linguistiques* (Paris, 1982), p. 21.

"mentalité," its own capacity for imagining reality. In the section below we will explore some of the most important of the "schools" of history writing that have taken up such questions. And scholars before Foucault provided many of the insights he would later elaborate; we have only to reread the works of Johan Huizinga or Norbert Elias to concede this point. Nevertheless, it is undeniable that Foucault has had an impact far greater than his predecessors; and that impact must be attributed, in part, to the fact that he offered a theoretical and methodological apparatus which historians had previously not had. To that impact, we will also return in the section below.

B. The Politics of History Writing

The heady mix of social science method and theory, of cultural theory, and of the sociopolitical changes that have defined the second half of the twentieth century in the West has produced kinds of history writing very different from that associated with Ranke and his colleagues. New "schools" of history writing, defined by both methodology and subject matter, have sprung up, and in the wake of their encounters with older traditions of history writing and with one another, have in turn produced other new schools.

Although, as we shall see, each of these approaches to historical inquiry differs from others, they all share a self-consciousness about the assumptions that propel their inquiry which was absent in older traditions of history writing. For the positivists and historicists who once dominated professional history writing in the West, the goal was a kind of neutrality before the "facts," the production of a historical account which simply related "as it actually occurred." Historians would now generally agree that such objectivity is impossible, and it is ironic that today Ranke's critics can easily show that he and his school did not even approximate the objectivity they sought. In fact, many critics have called Rankean objectivity a "pseudo-objectivity." Appearing only to recount the events concerning the powerful men on whom their narratives almost inevitably focused, they in fact implicitly endorsed even the most outrageous of their characters' actions—murder, pillage, deception. Ranke himself also regularly betrayed his own biases in his prose, displaying his anticlericalism with every paragraph he wrote about the history of Christianity; the French journal *Revue historique* shamelessly defended the French national state in the name of some "objective" rendering of its history.

1. The *Annales*

One of the earliest and most influential breaks with traditional historiography took place in the first half of the twentieth century, in France, in what has come to be called the *Annales* school (after the journal *Annales: Economies, sociétés et civilisations*, founded in 1929; originally called *Annales d'histoire économique et sociale*). Its two leaders, Marc Bloch and Lucien Febvre, mounted scathing critiques of traditional history writing (great men, great ideas, great deeds), of methodology (obsessive concentration on source analysis and "truth"), of theory (or the avowed absence thereof). Lucien Febvre gave birth to what would later be called the "history of mentalités" with his *Le problème de l'incroyance* (1942; *The Problem of Unbelief in the Sixteenth Century, the Religion of Rabelais*, 1982) an effort to re-create the mental world of the sixteenth century and to demonstrate that in that period there was no such concept as atheism. Marc Bloch launched his salvo with a structural analysis of feudalism called *La société féodale*, in 1939–40 (*Feudal Society*, 1961), a book that treated feudalism as a system of social relations and culture, not a set of laws about political obligations.

After World War II, practitioners of the so-called second phase of the *Annales* took up quantitative methods with a vengeance, producing extensive and meticulous studies of prices and wages, the economy, and demography, all in an effort to capture the historical experiences of ordinary people, to reveal the historical significance of everyday life, and to expose the material conditions that structured the mentalité or thought-world of the age. Fernand Braudel's great *La Méditerranée et le monde méditerranéen* of 1949 (*The Mediterranean and the Mediterranean World in the Age of Philip II*, 1972), which begins with a systematic (if wonderfully poetic) analysis of the material conditions of life in sixteenth-century Europe, is exemplary. It argued that because all historical experience was constituted at this first level, which in time took place during the "longue durée" ("long term"), historical interpretation had to begin at this level.

More recently, in what is often called the *Annales* school's third phase, the quantitative and statistical methods so typical of the second phase were subordinated to a new kind of social history, generally referred to in the English-speaking West as the "new social history." Here quantitative methods were combined with a focus on basic social units and categories (the family, marriage, the child, old age, death, the poor, the outcast, the woman) and, again, on mentalité. Obviously, sociological theory, particularly Durkheim's notion of collective consciousness (and his functionalism), was essential to this historiography, but theory and method borrowed from anthropology played as great a role. From the latter discipline, historians borrowed structuralist theories about the way human social identities were constituted, about the ways human beings organized the world mentally, about the ways roles and functions were assigned in human society. Ideas about space and time, about male and female, about life and death, for example, were examined as elements of this structure, and they were shown to be both fundaments of the sociocultural system being examined and products of the material and mental landscape.

A fine example of how historians used this kind of theory and methodology is Emmanuel Le Roy Ladurie's *Montaillou* of 1975, a study of a southern French village in the early fourteenth century. It was based on Inquisition records created during an investigation of ninety-four people accused of the Cathar heresy (documents that had for centuries been discreetly secreted in the Vatican archives, where the inquisitor Jacques Fournier, then bishop of Pamiers and later pope, had deposited them). Using this text, Le Roy Ladurie was able to reveal basic attributes of human experience in this culture—the passions and attitudes about everyday matters as well as about God and nature; the systems of social control, the ways social bonds were created, and the tensions inherent in these relations; the relations between men and women; the range of sexual practices, and the taboos and freedoms attending such practices. Le Roy Ladurie did not, of course, find these structures, these ideas, these modes of behavior presented as such in his Inquisition records. Rather, he had to read these documents ethnographically, looking for patterns of behavior, of language, of ways of telling a story. He had to place these texts against a larger model of preindustrial European agricultural societies that previous historians had constructed using material such as quantitative data on, for example, prices and wages, death rates, and marriage patterns or, perhaps, court records treating land transfers and disputes, inheritance and succession matters, or settlements of personal injury suits. He thus had to uncover the structures that lay hidden, to make visible what was visible neither to the inhabitants of Montaillou nor to historians who had come before him. Georges Duby's studies of marriage (*Le chevalier, la femme et le prêtre. Le mariage dans la France médiévale*, 1981; *The Knight, the Lady, and the Priest: The Making of Modern Marriage in Medieval France*, 1983), Philippe Ariès's investigations of childhood (*L'enfant et la vie familiale sous l'Ancien Régime*, 1960; *Centuries of Childhood*, 1962); and Michel Vovelle's explorations of death and the cult of the deceased (*Mourir autrefois. Attitudes collectives devant la mort*, 1974 [Death in another time: collective attitudes toward death]; *La mort et l'Occident*, 1983 [Death in the west]; *Idéologies et Mentalités*, 1982; *Ideologies and Mentalities*, 1990) mark key moments in the development of this historiography as well.

The methods, interests, and theories associated with the *Annales* school have had an enormous effect, not just in France but throughout the West, first in Britain, the United States, and Italy, thereafter in Belgium, Holland, Germany, Spain, and elsewhere. From anthropology has come, for example, the concept of popular culture, as distinct from the learned culture that had traditionally been the concern of historians. Peter Burke in England and Robert Muchembled in France argued that in early modern Europe the two existed side by side from about 1400 to about 1550, but in tension, and that slowly, over approximately the two hundred subsequent years, popular culture as a coherent category was suppressed.[9] The art forms, music, entertainment, and literatures of the learned would thereafter stand as the only real "culture" of Europe. Carlo Ginzburg's study of witchcraft persecutions in early modern Europe, *Ecstasies: Deciphering the Witches' Sabbath* (1990; orig., *Storia notturna: una decifrazione del sabba*, 1989), adopted this model as well, arguing that these persecutions were a result of a clash between learned ideas of witchcraft (demonology) and popular ideas of witchcraft (magic). Studies of popular culture did not, however, always concentrate on its struggles against a hegemonic elite culture. What is perhaps Ginzburg's most famous book, *The Cheese and the Worms: The Cosmos of a Sixteenth-Century Miller* (1982; orig., *Formaggio e i vermi*, 1976) was, in fact, a study of how the popular and the elite intersected, how ordinary people accessed, made sense of, and inevitably transformed elements of learned culture and Christian doctrine. In short, so influential has been method and theory from anthropology that many historians—Ginzburg in Italy, Natalie Zemon Davis in the United States, and Le Roy Ladurie in France among them—are often thought of as historical anthropologists.

2. The "New Left" and New Histories

In the English-speaking West, the impact of the *Annales* school intersected with independent developments. Most important of these was the so-called new left, a largely unorganized group of historians who, after World War II, adopted and revised marxist theory to found new kinds of progressive history. Like the *Annalistes*, these historians were interested in

9. Robert Muchembled, *Culture populaire et culture des élites dans la France moderne (XVe–XVIIIe siècles)* (Paris, 1978; *Popular and Elite Culture in France, 1400–1750* [Baton Rouge, La., 1985]); Peter Burke, *Popular Culture in Early Modern Europe* (New York–London, 1979).

the history of ordinary people and like them adopted many of the techniques of the social sciences to ask questions, pose theories, and conduct research. They sought, however, a considerably more politically engaged history—one self-consciously directed not just at recovering the history of those whom traditional history writing had ignored (the poor, the working class, women, homosexuals, minorities, the sick) but at demonstrating that their roles in historical change had been profound and uncovering the historical circumstances in which they had been able to take control of their lives. The leading journal in England associated with this body of historiography was *Past and Present,* but the historiographical concerns of the new left were not represented by a single journal, either in Britain or the United States (nor was all the social history associated with *Past and Present* so far "left").

Anglo-American new social history had many offshoots, many homes. Some scholars produced massive, quantitative studies of demography (Robert Schofield and Edward A. Wrigley's demographic reconstitution studies are exemplary: *The Population History of England,* 1981); some debated marxist historical theory (i.e., the famous Brenner debate concerning the collapse of medieval feudal society and the rise of modern capitalist society, conducted in the pages of *Past and Present* in the 1970s and republished as a separate volume in 1985[10]); some combined marxian socioeconomic theory with Braudelian method to posit "world-systems theory" which analyzed European economic imperialism (Immanuel Wallerstein's *The Modern World System,* 1974).

These countries and this "school" also gave birth to women's history, African American history, and ethnic history, now among the most important and fastest growing branches of American historiography. Women's history has obvious connections to the new social history, for it was the studies of birth and marriage, of families and domestic spaces, of children and old age, of poverty and illness, that first made it possible for that generation to see that women had a place in history, that women qua women made historical experience and historical change possible. Thanks to the work of many of these social historians, women entered the history books.

But women's history was also the child of a political movement, and many of the scholars who wrote women's history were feminists. As feminists, they were not content simply to uncover the roles of women in the past. In their view, the object of women's history was to reveal the ways that gender hierarchy was constructed in the past (as part of an effort to dis-

10. T. H. Aston and C. H. E. Philpin (eds.), *The Brenner Debate: Agrarian Class Structure and Economic Development in Pre-Industrial Europe* (Cambridge, U.K., 1985).

mantle such hierarchy in the present) and to explore the ways women had escaped the traditional roles to which a male-dominated system assigned them. Soon after these beginnings, women's history, especially in Britain and the United States, turned to questions of gender itself: How, such scholars asked, do "women" get assigned their feminine roles? What is the relationship between biological femininity and the feminine psyche or personality and feminine roles? What is relationship between sex, sexual desire, sexual practice, and gender position? And, finally, if women qua women have a history, do not men qua men?; that is, is not it as necessary to study the history of manhood as a cultural construct as it is to study the history of womanhood? It is no wonder that women's history or what is today more often called gender history became aggressively interdisciplinary, for it was only with the help of sociologists and anthropologists, cultural theorists and psychoanalysts that such questions could be addressed. As we shall momentarily see, it is also no surprise that women's historians were among the first to explore the possibilities of cultural history.

Lesbian and gay history emerged during the same period and in some respects had a similar historiographical history. At its beginning, such history writing was concentrated on documenting the lesbian and gay experience itself. More recently, scholars have turned to new questions about the history (and by implication, the nature) of sexuality itself, calling into question received notions about sexual identity and sexual categories. The effect on other subdisciplines of history, indeed on the discipline as a whole, have been profound.

African American history was, like women's history, born of a political movement and in some ways these two bodies of historiography have had close connections. But there were tensions as well, for the experience of women—especially the middle-class white women who dominated women's history in its early days (and still dominate today)—was "like" the experience of African Americans in the United States only in limited and sometimes superficial ways. Nevertheless, women's studies programs and black studies programs grew up on American campuses at nearly the same historical moments in the 1970s and 1980s, and women's historians and black historians have frequently worked together in establishing legitimacy for their fields.

Ethnic history, including Native American history, is a somewhat newer arrival, at least as a distinct subfield of historical study, but it shares with African American history the commitment to study the ways that ethnic groups have been created and marginalized, and how they have won civil, economic, and social rights in the past. Although originating in the United States, where the ethnic experience is so visible a part of the nation's history, ethnic studies have developed in Europe as well, particularly in the last twenty years as many of the European nations have seen their populations transformed by immigration.

3. The New Cultural History

If the term "the new social history" can be used to categorize all these branches of twentieth-century history writing, the term "the new cultural history" can be employed to describe its child. And child it is, for it was only after the new social history had so successfully unseated older traditions of history writing which had privileged "great" men, "great" ideas, and "great" events that historians could safely return to questions about ideas, meanings, language, and culture. But it is also a rebellious child, for the new cultural history is in many respects a reaction to the limitations of social history. For all its innovations and openness to new questions and new ways of working, social history method assumed some of the very historical categories some historians wanted to examine and denied historians access to the way people understood their world—and appreciation of why they behaved as they did. In short, the new cultural history was born in frustration with the assumption of social historians that "structure" was fundamental. To a large extent, this was a product of social history's focus on infrastructure—on material structure, on the economy, on social or political systems. While such studies did not eliminate the individual—some of the best social histories, such as Laurel Thatcher Ulrich's *Goodwives: Image and Reality in the Lives of Women in New England, 1650–1750* (1982), told the stories of individual lives—they did tend to see individuals as products of the systems to which they belonged. For a great many historians, even those who had no desire to write histories celebrating the individual, this was a problem.

So, social historians early began to modify social history method. Carlo Ginzburg, almost single-handedly, created what would be called "microhistory," a way of studying isolated events, individuals, or actions that derives from methods fashioned by the *Annales* school. In many ways, his studies (*The Cheese and the Worms*, already mentioned, is the most famous) resembled conventional biography, breaking from the methodological traditions of social history (while retaining its interest in social structure and social networks) and borrowing from anthropology the ethnographic method which emphasized close observation of small details, careful listening to every voice, every nuance of phrase—what the anthropologist Clifford Geertz called "thick description." By this Geertz meant that the actions of people in the past cannot be explained, as most social historians and *Annalistes* tended to do, by reference to "structures" or concepts these people would never have conceived, but must be viewed in terms of categories that were their own. Thereby, anthropologists and their fellow travelers from history sought to expose not just the social structure in which historical actors lived, but also the mental and social world they inhabited, seen from their point of view—the rational and irrational, the subjective and objective strategies by which they apprehended and manipulated family, community, political parties, and networks of clients. Ginzburg's methods have been widely adopted; Natalie Davis's well-known *The Return of Martin Guerre* (1983), for example, works in much the same way.

From anthropology comes as well the new emphasize on ritual, including ritualized behaviors such as ceremonies but also the ordinary rituals of everyday life—encounters on the street, behavior at table, bedroom etiquette. Norbert Elias's *History of Manners* (vol. 1 of *The Civilizing Process*) was one of the earliest histories in this tradition (he was, however, a sociologist!), but recent years have seen an explosion of such studies. The work of Edward Muir in the United States (for example, *Civic Ritual in Renaissance Venice*, 1981) and Virgilio Titone in Italy (*La società italiana sotto gli spagnoli*, 1978 [Italian society under the Spanish]) are exemplary.

Thus, in the last twenty or thirty years, we have seen what Lawrence Stone, one of the best known of the social historians associated with *Past and Present*, called a "revival of the narrative," a renewal of interest in cultural practices, in the way that people create meaning, understand and interpret the world, and with it a renewal of storytelling as the way to reveal and apprehend those meanings. A seminal moment in the turn to cultural history (at least in the Anglo-American world of scholarship) came with Edward P. Thompson's already mentioned *The Making of the English Working Class*, a study of the development of class politics in England in the eighteenth and nineteenth century. While never abandoning the marxist perspective from which he began, Thompson radically shifted the emphasis from structure to culture, arguing that the English working class emerged in a history made by workingmen themselves (Thompson was pretty much blind to women's place in this history), which they fashioned in a rather bricolage-like way, out of common experiences and their interpretations of those experiences. Class was not a "condition" "produced" by their place in the "system of production," as traditional marxist historiography had it. In such older studies, workers were too often prisoners of economic systems, unable to escape the social position to which their work condemned them. For Thompson, in contrast, class was a cultural product, made by men out the materials of their lives, and workers were thus capable of taking control of their history. Thompson's book not only facilitated the turn to narrative and fueled interest in cultural history; it helped create what is now generally called "cultural marxism," in which culture is seen not as reflection or even as a "semi-autonomous" system but as an agent in historical development.

Women's historians were among the first to take up these modifications to social history and to lead the search for ways to write cultural history. They did so because the social history paradigm in which many women's historians initially worked tended to see gender—and thus women—as subordinate to or outside of the system being studied: women "functioned" to enable capitalism; women played "roles" which produced and reflected their subordination; women "resisted" their oppression. There were no tools for asking what made "women" women, no tools for examining women as anything but elements in a social system determined elsewhere, by men. The questions on which women's historians increasingly wanted to focus would thus, it soon became apparent, require other methods of analysis, methods that allowed direct scrutiny of how gender is created, experienced, and changed.

These, then, were some of the key moments within the discipline itself that led the way to the "new cultural history," an invigorating mixture of older traditions of intellectual history ("history of ideas") with work on culture as understood anthropologically and socially. The methods of cultural history as it is now practiced owe a great deal to historians' encounters with cultural theorists in other branches of the humanities and social sciences, especially with literary critics, cultural anthropologists, and cultural sociologists. From them, historians have learned new strategies of reading documents, learned to be more attentive to (and more cautious of) language, learned to interrogate their own position as assemblers of "facts," interpreters of "evidence," formulators of "explanations." What is even more important here is that historians have learned to take culture more seriously, not just the culture or cultural products of the elite—that historians have always done—but culture as the system of meaning through which people experience the world. And they have acquired new skills for grasping those meanings.

Not all cultural historians work in the same way, of course, and all retain strong ties to older traditions of research and analysis. Some scholars have taken up poststructuralist theories, especially those of Foucault, but have deployed them in archival and institutional studies of the most traditional kind. Judith Walkowitz's study of Victorian London, *City of Dreadful Delight* (1992), Thomas Laqueur's exploration of the evolution of modern ideas about sex and gender, *Making Sex* (1990), and Isabel Hull's study of early modern Germany, *Sexuality, State, and Civil Society in Germany* (1996), are fine examples of the genre. Other cultural historians work quite differently. Caroline Bynum's *Holy Feast and Holy Fast* (1987) bears the marks of the social and women's historians who came before her and shows the strong influence of cultural anthropologists, but her method of reading religious texts owes perhaps most to hermeneutical traditions.

\(*

CHAPTER FIVE

The Nature of Historical Knowledge

H
istory as academic historians write it today would be almost un-
recognizable to scholars working even fifty years ago, let alone in
a past that is a century, two centuries—or twenty centuries—old.
In the previous chapter we sketched the ways historical methodology has
been transformed in the last century, and throughout the book we have
emphasized how frequently and how radically the craft and many of its
purposes have shifted course. At the close of this book, we will return to
the significance of the twentieth century's upheavals in the profession
and their implications for the next generation of scholars.

Here we want, however, to make a different, almost a contradictory
point. We want to emphasize the continuities that mark the profession—
continuities of purpose or intent and continuities of practice. While we
certainly do not wish to imply that history writing has been or should have
been always the same at some "real" level, we do want to consider the
kinds of questions that have driven and still continue to drive history writing in the West. We also wish to expose the kinds of assumptions historians make, usually implicitly, in pursuing those questions. Our discussion
focuses on two principal issues: change and continuity, on the one hand,
and causality, on the other.

A. Change and Continuity

No matter how much they may differ in the kinds of events they study, the
precise kinds of questions they pose, the research methods they employ,

or the reading strategies they use, all historians are in one way or another involved in studying change over time. Not all explicitly focus on change, to be sure; indeed, some of the best-known historical studies treat a moment in time—the ethos of an age, the patterns of social intercourse in a particular place and time, or the workings of a parliamentary system during a decade. Even such studies, nonetheless, assume change by exposing the distinctiveness of the practices being described and the ways they came into being. Typically, however, historians are more visibly concerned with change over time. Sometimes they provide full accounts of the theories with which they are working; more often they bury these assumptions in their narratives, seemingly unconscious that they are, in fact, proceeding with theory.

Most historians in the West have worked, explicitly or implicitly, with theories of change that are linear in form. In this approach, historical change is imagined to progress toward a predetermined end. In this sense, such theories are teleological. The most easily recognized version of such history is the Christian eschatological model; Augustine's already mentioned *City of God* is frequently invoked as the example. Recounting the struggle between the heavenly realm and the earthly, the book describes a preordained, already revealed struggle played out in the contest between the church and the secular world. In this telling, history is a manifestation of God's plan, a purposeful journey. This vision of history informed Christian thought for centuries—visible not just in Augustine, but in many other great Christian thinkers such as Sextus Julius Africanus, Eusebius of Caesarea, Isidore of Seville, and Bede.

Christian eschatology is not, however, the only kind of teleological historiography typical of the West. The marxist theory of history is, in its strict form, teleological as well, for it conceives of history as an inevitable progression toward communism. In this vision, human history is divided into distinct periods, defined by the "social organization of production." In the first, the ancient, there was no such thing as private property. In the second, private property emerged, but labor was not yet separated from capital (the means of production, such as land, animals, and tools); surplus was extracted from the producers (peasants) by force (or by the threat of force) under the feudal system characteristic of this stage. The third was capitalism, in which one class (the bourgeoisie) owned all capital and another class (the proletariat) labored for wages. The fourth, and final, was communism, in which private property was to be destroyed and, with it, classes and exploitation; capital and labor would thereby be reunited.

Teleological assumptions are very hard to avoid when one is thinking about time. Even the most neutral-seeming periodizations often embed a kind of linear thinking. The periodization that historians typically use to divide Western history—ancient, medieval, and modern—was, for example, devised during the Italian Renaissance and was intended to signal the dawn of a new age, one that would break free from the barbarity of the "middle" period and recapture the splendors of Greece and Rome. Implicitly, it imagined history as progressive, as moving toward a better future, even as it treated the distant past as the inspiration for that future. Often too, when historians set up contrasts between social or political systems, between societies or periods, they implicitly create a kind of linearity, a sense that one of the paired elements is more primitive than the other. The traditional division between preindustrial and industrial, or premodern and modern, for example, seems to grant a kind of superiority to the latter term. Emile Durkheim's contrast between caste and class societies, in fact, is tied to this premodern/modern dichotomy, for Durkheim credited the latter with dynamism and damned the former as "static." Fernand Braudel similarly set up an opposition between societies that were more or less urbanized and named the former "modern," the latter "premodern"; for him, the dividing line between the two was reached when at least 40 percent of the population in a given area was urbanized. The teleological bias of such reasoning is more evident still in modernization theory. In this model, a certain set of social and cultural characteristics—inevitably those that distinguish the modern West—are taken as definitive markers of modernity, and the rest of the world is evaluated in terms of its similarity to or distance from those characteristics.

Typically, linear theories of history presuppose a better future, a time when human misery is reduced, when political order is perfectly achieved, or when the human spirit is fulfilled. Most reflect the preoccupations of the age in which they were conceived. The notion, shared by the great eighteenth-century thinkers such as Condorcet, Kant, Voltaire, and Lessing, that mankind was progressively moving toward greater and greater enlightenment was as characteristic of their age as Augustine's Christian eschatology was of his. Hegel's idea that mankind was achieving maturity via the liberal national state, the realm of the ethical, was equally typical of the nineteenth century. In Hegel's view, mankind had experienced its moral childhood in antiquity (China and Egypt), its youth in Greece, its adolescence in Rome, and was coming of age in nineteenth-century Germany. The nineteenth century also gave us positivism, which, in the hands of thinkers such as Auguste Comte, looked forward to the day when science would transform the human condition. Modernization theory, the early and mid-twentieth century's typical form of linear social theory, reflects the optimism of that age.

By the time the Second World War had ended, the Eurocentrism that had defined Western culture since the Renaissance was fatally threatened by decolonization, the Cold War, doubts about economic miracles, hesitations about the effects of economic growth on the environment, and disappointment with modern science. Only in the United States, where prosperity had been promptly restored after the war, where no battles had been fought on native soil, and where science still seemed a blessing, was it possible to sustain optimism, at least for a few decades more.

The nationalist histories that characterized so much of nineteenth-century and early twentieth-century Western historiography were in many ways equally teleological. They were founded, however, on assumptions about the stability of culture that seem to deny history, for they all presumed that there was something eternal about the "national" character of a people. In a limited sense, that is true, for when a population shares the same language, traditions, social forms, and cultural practices, when all the people live under the same laws and are governed by stable political institutions, a unified culture—by definition—does develop. This is a teleological process, and, in the nationalist histories that celebrated it, the happy outcome of a long history of cultural and political development, with a unified nation-state as the goal. To borrow—and render benign—a phrase from Hitler's politics, what occurs in these processes is a kind of "Gleichschaltung" ("political coordination" or, more generally, homogenization), the kind of thing we have in mind when we casually speak of "those Italians," as though all Italians were alike. Today, of course, as individual western cultures are disrupted by the constant flow of people, information, and goods that characterizes global capitalism, those national differences—those distinctive national cultures—are being eroded. All of us are, to some extent, part of an unstable McDonald's culture.

Other theories of change, although also linear in form, seem less politically charged. Carl Ritter, for example, argued (in *Allgemeine Vergleichende Geographie,* 1817–18) that human societies go through progressive stages of ecological/economic organization. Early peoples settled in river valleys, as did the Egyptians and Babylonians. Later cultures took root on inland seas, as did the Greeks and Romans. West Europeans inhabited the oceans. Emil Spiess argued in 1939 (*Welt und Heimat im lauf der Zeiten geschildert* [World and homeland over the ages]) that human cultures have progressed from a preliterate stage (prior to 3500 B.C.E.) to a literate, and that the literate represents a higher stage of culture because it allows collective memory—a history.

The obvious alternative to a linear theory of history is a cyclical one, that is, one which imagines history to unroll in patterns that repeat themselves. In some sense, then, such theories deny time, or treat time as only a marker of place in a cycle that is in itself unchanging, repeating, rather than as an index of true change. Many such theories are pessimistic (just as linear theories tend to be optimistic), implying that no improvement, no progress, no real betterment is possible; such theories, understandably, are often formulated during periods of crisis, when society seems most threatened, the future most bleak. One of the earliest in Western culture was developed by Polybius in the second century B.C.E. He argued that all societies emerged, grew, and aged rather as people did, first growing to strength, accomplishment, and power, then slowly but steadily declining until they were replaced by another, more vigorous civilization. Some 1500 years later the great Islamic scholar Ibn Khaldun (1332–1406) argued that such patterns were determined not only by political organization, as Polybius had claimed, but also by climate, ecology, and geography and by religious or moral purpose. The twentieth-century German commentator Oswald Spengler returned to such themes in his *Untergang des Abendlandes* of 1918 (*The Decline of the West*, 1927) It is surely no coincidence that Spengler published the book in 1918, amid the catastrophic effects of the war. In it, he claimed that his beloved Germany was entering its old age, a period of decay and death rather like that suffered by human beings at the end of life—and rather like that earlier suffered by the Egyptians and Aztecs.

Perhaps the best-known today of such theories is Arnold Toynbee's, offered in his multivolume *Study of History*, which appeared between 1933 and 1961. Like many other authors of cyclical theories of history, Toynbee wrote his during a period of pessimism, when England (his native land) was losing its empire. Like others, he argued that England's experience would parallel those of great empires which had come before, going through four stages. In the first, the emergence, a primitive community faces challenges to which it must respond; if it does so successfully, it may reach the second stage, the stage of civilization. In this phase, the challenges are not so much material—they are not about mere survival or physical well-being—but spiritual, intellectual, and moral. In the third, the breakdown, the civilization loses its creative energy. In the fourth, the disintegration, it falls apart. Toynbee found that of the thirty cultures he studied, twenty-one reached the second stage or beyond; of them seven achieved full maturity and still existed when he wrote. Some civilizations, he also noted, managed to change enough in the fourth stage to avoid death; they remade themselves in some fundamental way so that continued survival was possible. Toynbee's model differed from Spengler's (and improved upon it) principally in that he did not imagine that these stages were inevitable, that they were governed by some external law analogous to that which governed the human life cycle. For Toynbee, Western civilization could survive so long as it retained its core set of beliefs and practices—in the case of England, he thought, these were Christian.

Although Toynbee's model has been roundly criticized, he earned the respect of his colleagues in the profession for his erudition and the attempt he made to take account of the actual historical record as he knew it. His approach has been echoed by important scholars such as Karl Rainard Popper and Pitirim A. Sorokin (not all scholars pursuing arguments like these, it should be noted, have displayed comparable scholarly skills). Edward Gibbon's much earlier and widely admired *History of the Decline and Fall of the Roman Empire* (1776–88) is also a kind of cyclical history, and in fact had a direct influence on Toynbee. Not a theoretical work, it is a study of high erudition that meticulously chronicled the collapse of the empire, the Roman state, and its confrontation with the culture emerging from the confluence of Christianity and "barbarian" cultures to the north.

Not all cyclical theories are pessimistic, however. Vico, for example, thought that human history could be understood as a series of cycles, but he thought each characterized by a different set of beliefs—the first, he labeled the age of the gods, the second the age of the heroes, and the third the age of man. Others emphasize the role of nonhuman factors in determining the cycle. An organization called the Foundation for the Study of Cycles has, for example, been exploring the relationship between astrological changes and changes here on earth. Alexandre Dauvillier discovered in 1960 that, from 1750 on, sunspots intensify in eleven-year patterns and that these patterns are replicated in the growth of trees as measured by tree rings (see chapter 2's discussion of dendrochronology). Some years earlier, in 1955, Derek Justin Schove had remarked that these cycles of sunspots are correlated with years of revolution, and suggested that the two events were causally linked. This research is, however, in very early stages, and it is far too soon to deduce cause from correlation.

Methodologically more promising is the use of climatology in historical research. Emmanuel Le Roy Ladurie in France is, for example, one of the leaders of research attempting to link climatic cycles to human history—a logical approach when one is studying preindustrial Europe, which was fundamentally an agrarian economy. He has used harvest dates of grapes in wine-growing regions as an index of weather conditions. Cold summers are presumably associated with a poor grain harvest and a rise in grain prices. In an ingenious twist on the usual logic, Le Roy Ladurie has proposed that if scholars do not have precise information about grain harvests they can use data about grape harvest to infer that information. Although this work has attracted a lot of well-deserved interest, it has rightly been criticized by agricultural historians such as Bernard Slicher van Bath, who has argued that weather conditions were not the same throughout Europe and that grain prices were equally affected by imports, demand, and other economic factors not related to the supply of grain grown in the region of consumption.

Historians are thus very far from having the kind of studies needed to establish clear connections between climate and larger historical change in preindustrial Europe. In particular, they still do not have the evidence necessary for decisively linking, as some scholars have sought to do, the shift in the European economy from south to north that occurred between 1000 and 1600 with climatic improvements. Nor can they be sure that the "little ice age" of the period between 1590 and 1850, when the glaciers slid south, can be linked with the crisis of the seventeenth century, another hypothesis favored by some. It is, however, certain that such factors played a role in the past, and not just over the long term. Two or three bad harvests in the short term were catastrophic for the European Middle Ages, for even this short cycle would produce famine and economic disruptions.

However attracted they have usually been to theories about change, historians have also been concerned about the structures and practices that seem immobile. Indeed, although history is about change, there are of course many things about humanity which do not change or which change so slowly that they fall out of the historian's view. But it is dangerous to assume, as people sometimes do in casual conversation, that "people are always the same." This is true only at the most trivial level: "humans are social beings"; "humans have to eat to survive"; "humans reproduce bisexually." Few statements of that kind will withstand historians' scrutiny. Let us recall that it is only during the past fifty years that we have come to appreciate how much the European family has changed in the last thousand years, how different the modern sense of privacy is from that of our medieval ancestors, how new the idea of "race" is as a biocultural category, how natural and thus permanent inherited social position seemed to sixteenth-century Europeans, how fair European-Americans living in the nineteenth century considered their occupation of Indian lands in the west.

Yet while no historian would deny the possibility of change in human society and in human beings themselves, historians today do regularly speak about what the French call "histoire immobile" (history that does not change). By this they do not mean unchanging in the sense that anthropologists once thought of the basics of human culture, elements so fundamental that they were common to all human beings or certainly to all members of a given culture, even over time. Instead, historians using the term "histoire immobile" mean that some changes occur so slowly that they are invisible within the lifetime of the individuals who experience them; they become visible only in retrospect. Such "immobilities" are of special interest to scholars such as social historians concerned with the basic structures of everyday life (the mode of production, the domestic unit, the community, etc.) and cultural historians studying the thought-world of the past.

One example of such "histoire immobile" is the medieval idea that society was divided into three "orders," which were defined by social function: fighters (the nobility), prayers (the clergy), and workers (the peasantry). By the time this notion had entered the European cultural imagination, the system itself no longer existed (Europe's nobility were no longer the sole warriors; merchants and artisans worked and fought alongside others; peasants had in some areas become market farmers, and everywhere the agricultural labor force included wage workers). Nevertheless, Europeans continued to imagine their social system in these terms—thus preserving in the collective mentalité a system that "on the ground" no longer existed. It is clear that this conceptual framework survived long beyond its capacity to describe social reality because it served to legitimize the privileges of the nobility and clergy. In this sense, cultural history was "immobile."

Le Roy Ladurie has also described the demographic system of Europe between 1300 and 1720 as an example of histoire immobile, for in this period the population stayed remarkably steady over the long term. To be sure, the long-run stability was achieved through dramatic short-run fluctuations: radically high natality balanced by equally high mortality. But grosso modo, the population was "immobile." Typically, such immobility is best observed when a break occurs, when some sudden upheaval disrupts the system of equilibrium. It is only when this happens that historians tend to recognize the character of the period that has just ended. The sexual revolution of the late 1960s in North America and Europe, for example, revealed the long histoire immobile of sexual norms that had dominated Western culture for more than a century.

The concept of immobility has also been usefully employed in studying the impact of cultures upon one another. Nathan Wachtel, for example, in *La vision des vaincus. Les indiens du Pérou devant la conquête espagnole, 1530–1571* of 1971 (*The Vision of the Vanquished*, 1977), investigated the reaction of the Incas to their Spanish conquerors. He acknowledged that Inca culture was profoundly altered by the conquest and that the

Incas adopted many of the practices of their conquerors, but he also showed that this was not a one-way process. In many ways the Incas' acculturation was superficial, and in a veiled way they retained many of their precolonial beliefs, practices, and institutions. In fact, the Incas privately mocked the Spanish, as they only pretended to have adapted to Spanish ways. There was, thus, a basic immobility in their history, a place of no change, of stasis, a place that both the Spanish and the Incas claimed.

Finally, the concept of immobility helps historians recognize those moments when cultures or parts of cultures are reactionary, when they resist innovation. The French refused margarine when it was developed by the French army in the nineteenth century; Europeans thought tomatoes poisonous and would not eat them when they were first brought from the New World; Europeans took years before they began to accept the ballpoint pen, an invention of the American army.

It is nonetheless not the immobility of culture but its mobility that motivates most historians' questions. Seldom, however, do they explicitly ground their studies of change in theory or seek to articulate one. Ironically, in this respect they share something with the historicist tradition associated with Ranke, for in that tradition every event, every historical moment is individual, unique; any explanation of change that the historian can offer must emerge from the data themselves, and no particular pattern of change is exemplary of a larger "model." While today's historians typically look for patterns and seek to make generalizations about the processes of change they observe—we will turn to some of these ideas in the section below—they share with this older tradition of historicism a distrust of grand theory, for in all such theories, they suspect, lurks a teleology. If the horrors of the twentieth century have taught anything, such scholars often remind themselves, it is that the world is not necessarily getting better, that science is not the new savior, that humanity is not progressing toward greater enlightenment. Many historians would further argue, on epistemological grounds, that they simply do not have access to knowledge of that kind, that any such "theory" is a mental construct, an imposition of meaning rather than a discovery of it.

B. Causality

Change, all historians would acknowledge, does occur, however slowly or quickly, however visibly or imperceptibly, however purposefully or purposelessly it might do so. And all change occurs, historians ineluctably assume, for some reason, even if that reason may not turn out to be rational. Whether they acknowledge it or not, historians thus presume cause when they write history, for to produce a chronology of any kind is in some way to locate causality in chronology. That is, historians select information and order it chronologically precisely to demonstrate (or hoping to do so) the causal relationships between the events described, to expose the weight of experience as generations succeed one another. Sometimes the sources that historians consult will purport to provide such explanations; a chronicle or newspaper report, for example, may give the reasons for the war in the same passage that it tells of the fighting. Of course, such explanations are not to be accepted without investigation, but they often provide historians starting points in their own search for causes. More often, however, historians must themselves propose the explanation.

Necessarily, then, historians confront the problem of cause as they consider change. As a practical matter, few historians ponder the philosophical implications of this issue—whether cause is ever knowable, whether what they call "cause" is simply their conclusion about the meaning of a correlation between events (Y follows X, therefore it is imagined that X causes Y). But even if historians do not push their inquiry that far—and few do—they must think seriously about what they mean by cause and how to assess it.

In such thinking, historians rely upon causal theories. Too often, however, they do so sloppily. In the typical history textbook, for example, we find lists of "immediate, medium-term, and long-term causes" of this or that event (World War I is a favorite) as though those definitions were clear. In fact, they are not, and professional historians must think about cause in a somewhat more sophisticated way. For example, an event X might be labeled a "cause" if the course of history would have been fundamentally different had that event not occurred. Such a "cause" is the student demonstration in Prague on November 17, 1989, which led to the Velvet Revolution; had it not occurred, the fall of the communist regime in Czechoslovakia would have happened differently (perhaps not at all?). Complex events have, however, complex antecedents, and historians must take account of that complexity in order to offer causal explanations of that event. This is no easy task, and it requires some careful thinking about just what is meant by "cause," even at a commonsense level.

Sometimes the word "cause" is used to refer to motive, as when historians talk about "hunger" as "cause" for popular unrest. The trouble with this use of the notion is that one and the same motive may have a range of outcomes. Hunger does not necessarily produce popular unrest; in fact, it usually does not. More frequently, probably, it leads to theft; in other cases, it encourages a shift in agricultural practices or forces emigration.

Another problem with the notion of "cause" in the sense of motivating event is that most events, historians know, are the product of actions by many people, each of whom may have very different intentions. An event, let us say Hitler's coming to power, was the outcome of a series of actions by groups of people who were, for various reasons, dissatisfied with the Weimar regime. These workers, middle-class people, retired soldiers, monarchists, captains of industry, right-wing activists—to name just the major groups involved—certainly did not share the same goals when they collaborated to put Hitler in power. The coup in Moscow on August 19, 1991, its collapse, the replacement of Gorbachev by Yeltsin—these events were the product of an complex of interrelated actions by men of the old bureaucracy, by reformers, by radicals linked to western organizations, by nationalists, by human rights activists; for all of them the planned agreement of August 20 to establish a less centralized government was the red flag. Their motives for the roles they played in the events were highly varied—and their degree of satisfaction with the outcome as diverse.

Obviously, then, in order to talk about cause, historians must have a more precise concept of what they mean. One way historians have approached this question is to consider whether there is an actor in the story who had the authority and power to directly affect the events being studied. When, for example, President Bush ordered the troops into the Gulf during Operation Desert Storm, historians can with some justification name him a causal agent in the war. Of course, it may well be that he could not have acted without the consent of others and that he would not have acted without their advice, but it is still possible to attribute "cause" to him in some limited sense. But that sense is, truly, fairly limited, and certainly "George Bush" is not an adequate explanation for that war.

Cause might also be thought about as the sum of all the factors that contributed to the outcome; the problem here, however, is to rank these factors, to decide which were most important, which less so. In situations like these, historians often employ structural arguments, reasoning, for example, that the class position of, let us say, workers who staged an uprising endowed them with certain aspirations, needs, abilities, and resources that set the terms within which they operated. These factors are then treated as primary, with the particular events surrounding the event (perhaps a pay cut, food shortages, workers' strikes in nearby places, a particularly oppressive boss) treated as secondary.

Some scholars have offered more rigorous strategies. Leo Apostel has argued, for example, that it is useless to think about cause in terms of antecedent, motive, means, conditions, influence, explanation, and the like, because the content of these terms differs according to the specific historical situation. Instead, he proposes to extract from a series of case studies the criteria by which historians can link events in the following kind of statement: in a historical situation of a certain type (a major event like the collapse of the Soviet Union in 1991), there is a causal relationship between events F_1 and F_2 if conditions X and Y (or X, Y, and Z or X, Y. . . n) prevail. Since in historical studies it is not possible to proceed as one does in a chemistry laboratory, by way of experiments, or as one does in philosophy, by way of deduction, it is necessary that historians proceed inductively. In other words, historians must formulate provisional causal statements in the form outlined above on the basis of many observations of concrete situations. In order to determine if event F_1 is a "cause" of F_2, it is necessary to study many situations like that under question and determine in how many individual cases with analogous political or social contexts event F_1 was indeed followed by event F_2, and in how many that did not occur. Using this logical process, Apostel argued that a political shift in a given country might be explained if certain essential prerequisites existed, specifically certain kinds of internal disintegration and the presence of organized political opposition. These conditions can then be elevated to the level of "causes."

Let us look, as an example of how Apostel's method might be applied, at the case of the Moscow coup in August 1991. In that case there were two power shifts: one structural, the shift from the old Soviet state, the Communist Party, and the old army to the post-communist Russia (and other new states), and the other the shift of personal power from Gorbachev to Yeltsin. The first confrontation was the initial purpose of the coup, the second the unexpected consequence. The causes of the structural change, the collapse of the old system, are clear (if complex). The historian can easily identify the "conditions" that worked in analogous historical situations. Apostel's first condition, that there be internal disintegration, is obviously met: the old party structure, although still in command, was nevertheless decaying and not ready for the change of mentality associated with glasnost; the entrenched authorities (the Soviet state and its government apparatus) were under pressure because of the failures of the economy and of perestroika. The second condition, that there be a center of oppositional power, is equally evident: power centers with popular support had grown up outside the government, especially around Yeltsin himself and the opposition mayors in Moscow and (what was then) Leningrad; other opponents were led by ethnic groups and antifederalist activists in the non-Russian states; the trust the army had traditionally enjoyed was undermined by the disasters in Afghanistan. It is no problem for historians to find comparable situations—similar coincidences of events, conditions, and outcomes—at other historical moments; in doing so, they can reason, with Apostel, that certain events, aligned with certain conditions, are "causes" of certain outcomes.

As Apostel's strategy seems to require, most historians attribute cause to factors that emerge within the society, country, or group being studied. But as Robert A. Nisbet pointed out in *The Social Bond* (1970), a political crisis cannot be entirely explained by internal political factors or by domestic social tensions. He argues, instead, that governments lose control over their population because of a combination of internal and external factors. In assessing the Moscow coup of 1991, for example, historians must consider that the old regime's failure was owed to both. The economic problems, especially in agriculture, and the restlessness of nationalist movements that were then taking shape put unbearable stresses on the political order. But historians must also look outside the Soviet Union as well: the frustrating war in Afghanistan, the disarmament negotiations with the West, and the collapse of the Soviet empire in eastern Europe, which occurred in 1989–90.

While Nisbet's general proposition seems entirely well taken, his related claim that most events cannot be anticipated, but occur suddenly and sporadically, with uneven effects, seems less generally applicable. In many cases, it should be recognized, such events could be anticipated. There were, as we have often mentioned, many warning signs in the Soviet Union before the August coup. On May 1, 1990, Gorbachev had been subjected to hisses and catcalls when he appeared in public in Red Square; on December 20 of that year his minister of foreign affairs, Eduard Shevardnadze, warned that "a dictatorship is approaching" and resigned. One could go even deeper, arguing that the putsch and its collapse were the inevitable results of glasnost and perestroika, which dated back to 1985.

1. Causal Factors

Given the complexity of most historical change, few historians have argued that there is a single lens through which the past can be interpreted; nevertheless, historians have over the years identified several fundamental processes or ideologies that they have at one time or another taken as principal agents in determining change. Below we list and briefly discuss several that are commonly invoked, cautioning that none in itself—no matter its particular relevance to one age or another—is sufficient and that none is operative in every circumstance.

a. Religious Ideology, Clericalism, and Anticlericalism

Some historians writing in the classical period and all during much of the Middle Ages assumed that human affairs were under the direct control of a deity who intervened actively in making history. For Augustine, and for many Christian thinkers after him, life on earth was a struggle between the heavenly and earthly realm. In the name of this faith many wars were fought and conquests won, including the centuries-long campaign of the Crusades. Such beliefs did not expire with the Middle Ages, however. Both Saddam Hussein and George Bush appealed to God (the same God) in the Gulf War of 1990–91, and Bush turned to his minister for spiritual support during the war; Hitler's army bore the slogan "God (be) with us." Many of the West's most devastating wars were fought over claims to control religious faith, most memorably those of the sixteenth and early seventeenth centuries.

Clericalism and anticlericalism have also been thought to set history in motion. Here the approach is somewhat different, for the claim is not that a divinity determines human history, but that religious interests here on earth are the motor for change. Scholars pursuing this line of inquiry often start with the French Revolution, for its attack upon—and eventual defeat of—the institutionalized church was the essential prerequisite of its success and the subsequent establishment of the liberal state. Thereafter, the church in such states was subordinated to the secular power, although even in these countries the church often retained control of education and social services, even in the face of strong opposition from secular groups. For instance, in France and Belgium after 1900—even after World War II—politics largely turned on questions of the church's role in education and on the more general issue of whether one professed Christianity or not. Today the fights are different, and the lines of division are largely between more fundamentalist or more liberal interpretations of the faith. It is not, however, within Christianity alone that these struggles take place; the same struggles divide Islamic peoples throughout the world.

b. Social and Economic Factors

Karl Marx's theory of causality, with the historiography it has spawned, is probably the most influential single body of work concerning socioeconomic factors and historical change. As we have previously discussed, Marx focused on tensions within the social system itself, regarding them as the essence of historical change. For Marx himself, of course, the central event was class war, which broke out when the system of exploitation (which constituted the class system) could no longer be sustained. During the early modern period, for example, feudalism collapsed because the nobility lost power to a rising bourgeoisie, as the aristocracy's traditional sources of income declined, their expenses rose, and the peasantry on whom they depended fought back. Capitalism will, in turn, collapse when the bourgeoisie can no longer extract enough surplus from the labor of the proletariat to sustain economic growth.

It is not only marxists, however, who have focused on tensions internal to the social system. In a rewrite of marxian theory that preserved Marx's emphasis on the socioeonomic structure, Ralf Dahrendorf (a liberal in his own views) argued in 1961 that the conflict of interest between the classes has a psychological as well as an economic character (*Gesellschaft und Freiheit* [Society and freedom]; see his *Modern Social Conflict*, 1988). In the early stages of the process, this tension is latent, but as soon as both parties are conscious of their respective positions, the tension becomes manifest. At that point, the ruling group seeks to preserve the status quo, the subordinated group seeks to change it. Charles Merriam (*Political Power*, 1934) added politics to the marxian mix, arguing that political revolution occurs only if the social tensions require political action, if the context is ripe for such a development, and—especially—if leaders eager to seize the day emerge at the right time.

In another version of such causal reasoning, scholars have adapted Darwinian evolutionary theory to explain change. Darwin's argument—that all species evolve, that all presently existing species are descendants of previously existing species, and that evolution occurs through a struggle for survival in which only the "fittest" prevail—was quickly adopted by certain nineteenth-century social theorists. The fact that Darwin's evolutionary theory was not intended to describe sociocultural events but instead changes that we now recognize as being genetic did not deter such enthusiasts. Nor did many stop to consider that the "struggle" Darwin described was not head-to-head combat among species, in which the "best" would eliminate or dominate the others, but a process of adaptation to the environment, in which any species survived only so long as it remained perfectly adapted. From these (mis)appropriations of Darwin, however, it was no great leap to argue that the privileges of the elite were just, clear evidence of their superiority. Herbert Spencer's *Social Statistics* (1850) and *The Man versus the State* (1884), for example, objected to any intervention by the state in the economy and sought a society in which individuals could pursue their own private interests unimpeded by any official restraints. William Graham Sumner was another who championed a kind of radical individualism, insisting that in the struggle for existence in the competitive marketplace, the fittest survive, just as in the natural world. The title of his book *What Social Classes Owe to Each Other* (1883) implied a rhetorical question, to which the answer was a resounding "nothing."

Adopting another kind of socially determinist thinking, some historians have sought to show how historical change occurs as one biological generation supersedes another; the new generations have different interests, experiences, needs from their predecessors, and they thus must alter the world. Exactly what this theory means is, however, too often left vague. It is not even entirely clear what constitutes a generation. The French scholar Jean-Louis Soulavie (1752–1813) thought a generation to be fifteen years; others have taken it to be thirty-three and a third, thus making three generations per century. To even the casual observer, such proposals raise questions. How is a generation to be measured, and how determined? If simply by biology, then what kinds of claims are being made about the relationship between biology and history? Does being born fifteen or twenty or thirty-three and one-third years after someone else place one in a different historical epoch? And what about all the people who are between generations? Obviously, this can be a slippery, even an absurd, concept—poor stuff for historical reasoning.

Yet there are, in fact, useful ways of thinking about generations and their role in history. There are moments, short periods of time, when events so encapsulating and so powerful engage so many members of a population at a key time in their lives that they thereafter regard themselves and behave as a group. The generation of the late sixties and early seventies in the United States is one such cohort; the socioeconomic changes of the postwar years, in which this generation was born, along with the civil rights movement, the antiwar movement, and the women's movement which occurred as this cohort reached adulthood, combined to produce a true "historical" generation—a group of women and men who shared political outlook, social ambitions, cultural preferences. The people who experienced World War II—whether by fighting themselves, suffering the losses of loved ones, or enduring the horrors of warfare at home— also constitute a generation in this sense.

Collective experiences of this kind can even create a "generation" out of a group that is not a demographic cohort, that is, people who are not roughly the same age. The people who experienced the changes in the former Soviet Union of the late eighties and early nineties might constitute such a generation; so too might the people—whether then twenty years old, forty, or sixty—who witnessed and took part in the Prague Spring of 1968. Jan Romein (*The Watershed of Two Eras*, 1978) argued that the decade around 1900 was one such period in Europe, for the accumulation of traumatic experiences associated with the waning of European hegemony, the decline of elite bourgeois culture, colonial resistance, and the end of nineteenth-century optimism combined to change forever the lives of many people.

In recent years, there has been considerably more interest among historians in other aspects of social life, a much different, more subtle, and in some sense broader definition of the social (see, in particular, the earlier discussion of the *Annales* school). Norbert Elias's already mentioned *Civilizing Process* was one of the first to make this point a central theme in Western history. His argument is premised on the claim that things once considered almost natural were in fact aspects of social behavior—manners, personal hygiene, sexual practices, notions of personal privacy—and that such practices fundamentally changed with the Renaissance. This insight has prompted work, as we have explained, not only on the codes of given historical cultures and how these are learned, put to use, and preserved, but also on the nature, extent, and possibility of nonconformity. It has also, however, inspired historians to examine how social groups are defined by shared behavior.

c. Biology and "Race"

We have only to look at the civil rights movement of the sixties in the United States or the black power movement that followed, or to look for that matter in France at Le Pen's National Front or the "Touche pas à mon pote" ("Don't hassle my buddy") countermovement, to recognize the historical importance of racism. The hatreds that drive racial politics are not, to be sure, unique to social situations in which "race," as technically defined, is an issue. The situation in northern Ireland makes the point perfectly. What this comparison reveals is that racial struggles are fueled by tensions concerning socioeconomic position—jobs, social place, security, respect.

"Race" is of course a cultural and social and political category, hardly a biological category at all except in trivial and highly unstable ways. Struggles between "races" have, however, created racial stereotypes that then seem to acquire their own life, and themselves become "causes" so that "race" comes to signify a set of attitudes and behaviors. It is thus that a pathology is ascribed to a "race." In Europe, for example, it is often gypsies who are so stigmatized. But is their behavior a result of their "gypsyness" or a consequence of the treatment they have been afforded by hostile governments and dominant groups in society? What logic explains the way gypsies have been ostracized in most of Europe, while since World War II most western European countries have worked hard to make their societies hospitable to Jews—whom they once shunned and racialized with the same intensity?

The roots of racial theory run deep in European history, certainly back to the Enlightenment, which celebrated all created beings but gave pride of place to a Greek ideal of beauty which was equated with Aryanism. It has even deeper roots in the positivism of Hippolyte Taine, and above all in the romanticism of Thomas Carlyle and others who found perfection in the Anglo-Saxon body type. With romanticism came as well the ideal of the *Volksgeist* and with it the potential for a virulent kind of nationalism, irrationalism, the worship of "great men" and "great nations." Social Darwinism and imperialism in the nineteenth century added the crucial element of "scientific" racism, and when these ideologies were combined with race-based slavery in the Americas, the potent form of racism that still infects Western culture took root. It is thus that "race" became a historical category, an issue that has seemed to some historians a crucial element of any equation explaining historical change.

d. Environment

In most of the world, for most of human history, humankind has been subject to nature—to climate and topography, to flora and fauna. Even after the invention of agriculture and the stunning technological advances that accompanied it, people remained nature's prisoners. Particularly in the past century, historians have begun systematically to consider the ways that the environment has determined human history.

Le Roy Ladurie, for example, has shown that for the entire 450 years between about 1300 and 1750, the population of France did not grow because a kind of stasis had been reached between the capacity of the earth to support the population and the population's ability to affect the given rate of productivity. To be sure, between about 1000 and 1300 Europe's population had mushroomed, but growth was abruptly and dramatically stopped at the dawn of the fourteenth century, in large part because new diseases entered the society from abroad (brought in by merchants and soldiers who were the vanguards of the newly expansive European culture). The first major onslaught, the Black Death of 1348–50, wiped out at least one quarter of the population. Europe would not recover, as we have said, for at least two, in some places four, centuries. In short, Western civilization's greatest struggles have not been with other peoples, but with nature—bugs of all kinds, diseases, drought, floods, cold, heat.

Le Roy Ladurie's argument about climate is part of a more general debate about the transformation of the social order at the end of the Middle

Ages. The debate turns on the role of class conflict in ending European serfdom, with marxists generally arguing for the centrality of class in this story and other, what we might call "liberal," historians, insisting on the importance of exogeneous factors such as commerce or—here Le Roy Ladurie enters—disease and climate. Many scholars studying the relationship between climate and social change are not, however, participants in such arguments. Recently, for example, Mary Dobson published a study (*Contours of Death and Disease in Early Modern England*, 1997) rigorously correlating disease with place in early modern England, by a process of carefully mapping the reports of disease and showing the geographical patterns of that distribution. The result was a powerful inferential argument about the effects of environment on health.

e. Science, Technology, and Inventions
Technology has indisputably played a major role in human history. While all historians acknowledge this importance, some have gone further, seeking to explain major structural changes in purely technological terms. These arguments, even in the sophisticated forms presented by scholars such as Lynn White (*Medieval Technology and Social Change*, 1962), go either too far or not far enough. In the first case, they reduce historical complexity to the point of absurdity (the printing press "caused" the Reformation). In the second, they do not consider the sociocultural and political factors that made technological change possible, and those that made technological developments popular. Still, historians do and must take technology's power seriously. Each civilization has produced its own innovations out of an internal dynamic between the people and their environment, but imports from other cultures have also sometimes been the cause of dramatic changes. Until the twelfth century, for example, Europe was a backwater technologically, much outclassed by both China and Islamic civilization. The Crusades introduced Europeans to many agricultural techniques they did not know, so that these conflicts helped propel the spectacular improvements in agricultural productivity that Europe enjoyed between 1000 and 1300. Gunpowder was brought from Mongolia in 1257; paper and clocks came from the Islamic Mediterranean, via Spain. The application of European mining technology to the New World, in Peru and Mexico, flooded Europe with unheard-of amounts of gold and silver, forever changing the European economy. Centuries later, industrialization transformed Europe, and then the world.[1]

Of all the inventions in human history, perhaps none has been more

1. See Arnold Pacey, *Technology in World Civilization* (Cambridge, Mass., 1990).

significant than writing (invented ca. 3000 B.C.E.), but in European history pride of place might well go to the printing press, which was developed in the fifteenth century. It allowed texts to be reproduced and distributed hundreds of times more quickly, and it allowed scholars and scientists to work simultaneously on identical texts. It made reading possible for the masses and played a huge role in preparing Europe's ordinary people for the democratic revolutions that mark the West's modern history. Elizabeth Eisenstein was probably right when she argued in *The Printing Press as an Agent of Change* (1979) that the Renaissance itself is unimaginable without the printing press. The previous "Renaissances" of the ninth and twelfth centuries in Europe had sputtered out, she reasoned, in large part because the textual work at the heart of the "Renaissance" enterprise could not be preserved and widely enough distributed. The effects of printing on the Reformation are as visible, for the evangelism at the heart of the Protestant reform would not have been as effective had preachers and theologians not had the capacity to distribute texts widely and quickly. The scientific revolution, the Enlightenment, even industrialization, are similarly hard to imagine without the printed book.

f. Power

While the story of power relations has been variously thought of as struggles between peoples, or between subjects and rulers, or between individuals, the term "power" has no fixed definition. Political scientists, sociologists, historians, and cultural theorists have spent many pages trying to provide a precise sense of the term. Bertrand Russell (*Political Ideals*, 1917), for example, defined power as the ability to prevent others from doing what they want, and equated it with possession. Harold Laswell and Abraham Kaplan (*Power and Society*, 1952) saw power as a relation between men, which serves to establish social codes and exercise social control. Herbert Alexander Simon (*Models of Men*, 1987) regarded power as a condition of inequality; power is always power *over* someone or something, although there is a reciprocal relationship between the powerful and the dominated. According to Paul Valkenburgh (*Indeiding tot de politicologie*, 1968; Introduction to politicology), power is that relationship which enables one (person) to alter or limit the choices of another. Michel Foucault has, of course, most famously redefined power for the late twentieth century, arguing that power is not a thing, a relationship, a force field; it is not something people "have" or don't "have," "exercise" or don't "exercise." It is an effect, produced less by force or the threat of force than by knowledge—by the ability to set the terms of conversation, understanding, and vision.

Working in a tradition that sees power struggle as primary, many historians have turned their attention to political revolution, necessarily violent revolution, as an inevitable ingredient of fundamental historical change. Consequently, historians have inherited many different interpretations about the nature and importance of these events. Karl Marx thought violent revolution integral to class struggle. Jules Michelet, the great romanticizer of the French Revolution, regarded that historical conflict as the uprising of "anonymous masses" who sought freedom and fulfillment as members of the French nation. A great many scholars have dissected the revolutionary process itself, hoping to develop a model for understanding how it is that societies come to the point of revolution. Crane Brinton's 1938 *The Anatomy of Revolution* treats the revolutionary process as an illness with its typical phases: first signs of corruption, the revolutionary fever, the terror, the healing. The sociologist Vilfredo Pareto (1848–1923) argued that political change is cyclical, reflecting the alternation of different ruling elites. The first are the idealists, the "lions" he called them; they are inevitably followed by a generation whose aims are to further their own interests and who cannot see beyond them.

g. Public Opinion and the Mass Media

Adapting a different approach, some historians, especially those influenced by certain traditions in sociology, have focused on changes in public opinion. These studies have often foregrounded the history of communications media, for such media serve to win over a group or even an entire population to a certain point of view. Analyses of communication media generally approach the study by breaking the communication event into four parts: the source (the sender), the recipient (the public), the medium, and the message. The impact of any message is likely to be enhanced if it emanates from a source of official power, perhaps a dictator, or if it accords, at least in part, with already accepted views. The message can initially have a negative impact if it is significantly at odds with the views of the recipient, but over time the recipient will often change his or her views in conformity with the message. The goal, when one is trying to influence public opinion, is to make the message a generally accepted "fact," a point of view that seems normal. According to some theorists, the cognitive dissonance experienced by a populace when a foreign or unacceptable idea is presented can be overcome by presenting both sides of the issue; in some cases the first version of the facts prevails, in others the second. The message can also play upon fear and other emotions.

Public opinion can also, however, be manipulated more subtly, by means of the rumor. Even if false, rumors can have an enormous impact.

A notorious example is the "rumor of Orléans" (in France) of 1969, a story which would not die and which was eagerly spread by the French press. The story was that Jewish shopkeepers in Orléans were luring girls to work as shop assistants and then selling them off into prostitution. In fact, no girls were ever reported missing. Like this particular rumor, all rumors work best when they build upon already existing suspicions or fears. Researchers studying rumors and their effects frequently find it almost impossible to trace the source of the rumor and must content themselves with analyzing its effect. Here, however, an array of new questions faces the historian. To what extent is the rumor's effect dependent upon its convergence with already widely accepted views within a particular social group or subculture or upon its role as replacement for official information that for some reason is considered unreliable or untrustworthy?

2. The Role of the Individual

A perennially favorite question is whether, to put it simply, (great) men and women make history or history makes (great) men and women. In fact, of course, both statements are to some extent true. It is hard to imagine summer 1991 in Moscow without Yeltsin. But the failure of the coup led by Vladimir Kryuchkov, head of the KGB, is probably not so much explained by any individual failing on Kryuchkov's part—he was a skilled maneuverer—as it is by the refusal of a Russian population, which had by then enjoyed six years of glasnost, to tolerate a return to the old order. That summer is, thus, a story both about "leading actors," even "heroes," and about a self-conscious collectivity.

It is never entirely clear how much of the credit for change should go to the individual versus the "temper of the times." How is that a certain idea will at one moment be eagerly taken up by the public and that another is accepted, if at all, only grudgingly? The explanation cannot rest entirely with the quality of the idea. To be sure, the demagogic talents of the leader pushing the idea may have something to do with the difference, but it is just as likely that technical and material matters are decisive. Consider, for example, the effect of the *Encyclopedia* in eighteenth-century France. Surely it would have had considerably less importance without the distribution capabilities of the powerful firms of international booksellers (in Neuchâtel, Switzerland, in The Hague, in Amsterdam, and elsewhere in Europe) who so aggressively marketed it. In such cases, we have also to consider the receptivity of the audience, its readiness to accept what is being said. Marx's ideas got relatively little hearing in Germany around 1850, while they changed history in Russia in 1917. A lot had happened between the two dates, and the socioeconomic situation in each was entirely different.

Whatever conclusion we might draw about the usefulness of history that focuses on individuals, there is no doubt that historians have long celebrated the dominating personality. And it is no wonder such figures have this appeal; their lives are inherently interesting to most people. In addition, they offer historians readily accessible explanations: they are concrete, active, in some sense knowable, just as "social forces," political "processes," or—still worse—"mentalités" are vague, hard to pin down, slippery. Typically, historians who focus on individuals emphasize psychological characteristics as the "causes" of historical change. For Thucydides, writing in the fifth century B.C.E., war was caused by dominating men. Philippe de Commines attributed the conflict between the fifteenth-century king of France and the duke of Burgundy to aspects of their respective personalities. In 1919 Huizinga sought to explain social changes in terms of ritualized performances stage-managed by princes and courtiers. Thomas Carlyle's *On Heroes, Hero-Worship and the Heroic in History* is perhaps the best example of the genre. Carlyle's subjective biographies represent, to be sure, an extreme; he was one of the great romantics, and his biographies are premier examples of how far that tradition would go in celebrating the individual and ignoring the social circumstances that produced him.

Although work like Carlyle's is surely naive, it is also a mistake to underestimate the effect an individual can have. Imagine what today's world would be like had Mohammed, Confucius, or Christ not lived, if Marx had not written, if there had been no Hitler! Even in political cultures where policy is made and executed collectively, as it is in most parliamentary democracies, the decision-makers and the executives are still an elite group that is often dominated by a single figure. Let us remember, however, that it is not just the elite individual who makes a place in history. Would French history have been the same without Joan of Arc, American history without Martin Luther King?

Historians who wish to focus on the importance of the individual must, at a minimum, be sure to take account of the situation that made it possible for one person to have such an effect. Let us take one example. In world capitals such as Vienna around 1900, Paris in the 1920s, and New York in the 1970s and 1980s, where creative individuals in many fields congregate, perform, discuss, test one another, share ideas—in such places it is much easier for a talented individual to find fellow artists ready to respond to and encourage his or her most outrageous experiments, easier to develop an audience receptive to such experimentation. Without Vienna, would there have been Freud, Klimt, or Schiele? Without Paris, Picasso or Gertrude Stein? Without New York, Martha Graham, Jackson Pollock, Twyla Tharp, George Balanchine, or Woody Allen?

Although it is certainly true that historians today tend to put more emphasis on ordinary people and on anonymous "forces" than on heroes, they are not the first historians to recognize the role of common people in history. Edward Gibbon, who wrote at the end of the eighteenth century, described the fall of the Roman Empire more as a product of social disintegration caused by the clash of two civilizations than as the result of decisions taken by a few people. Some of the romantic historians (although not Carlyle) celebrated the "people" as the repository of the national spirit and as the source of the nation-state's legitimacy. Marx, of course, brusquely dismissed the role of "leaders," seeing them simply as representatives and agents of class interests. And the obvious should never be forgotten: that monarchies and command systems of other kinds, such as armies or the organized church, place individuals in positions of great and visible power. It is folly to ignore this structural fact.

Underlying these larger questions about the ultimate importance of the individual in history is a series of more practical problems. First, how do historians specify the importance of an individual, his or her effect? Herbert Alexander Simon, whom we have already mentioned, has proposed a quantitative measure: the power of an individual is a function of the number of people who are bound by or consider themselves morally or materially bound by the decisions of the person. Second, the sources on which historians rely very often do not tell us just who the decision-makers (or the intellectual authors) were, but ascribe the document or the decision to the juridical or administrative authors, or even to a fictive body in whose name the text was issued. Thus, the historian must go beyond the source, to the history that created it, in order to determine the role any individual played in its creation. It is also often the case, particularly in political matters, that responsibility for a decision is attributed to a single, visible person (for example, the president of the United States) who becomes the object of the opposition's criticism and serves to deflect attention from the real agents in the matter. In modern electoral politics, something similar happens when a cult of personality develops around a single figure, to whom all action is attributed; in fact, that person may be just a figurehead for a powerful group of ideologues.

But it is always dangerous to assume that titular leaders are not making their own decisions. Even President Ronald Reagan, who had a well-deserved reputation for leaving much to his subordinates, took charge on those matters close to his heart. For example, when he was scheduled to make a speech dealing with the Soviet action in shooting down a Korean airliner in September 1983, he set aside the draft his speechwriters provided and rewrote the entire speech in longhand. It was that event that gave Reagan an opportunity to reformulate his famous attack on the Soviet Union as the "evil empire," which he had first voiced in the British Parliament on June 8, 1982. Some of his correspondence with the Soviet leaders he wrote in his own hand as well and on his own initiative, simply informing key cabinet members after he had written the letter. And when letters were drafted by subordinates (as most were), he kept a careful eye on the content, both for style and for matters that he considered important. For instance, during arms control negotiations with Mikhail Gorbachev in 1985, Reagan insisted on offering the Soviets access to any defensive systems the United States might develop (specifically the Strategic Defense Initiative, known as Star Wars). U.S. defense experts advised that there was no concrete way to share SDI technologies without risk to U.S. security and tried several times to persuade Reagan to modify his language in correspondence with Gorbachev. Reagan refused, and finally himself provided the language committing the United States to share technologies. Gorbachev, as it turned out, did not believe he was serious, and thereby missed an opportunity to rapidly negotiate a major reduction of strategic weapons. Although the U.S. bureaucracy would have resisted a commitment to share, Reagan would have overruled his subordinates and made such a commitment if Gorbachev had been willing to reduce strategic weapons substantially.[2]

C. History Today

Although change and causality remain central concerns of historians, serving even to define the profession, historians have always differed in the way they pose questions about these matters and the kinds of causal relations they expect to find. Today scholars approach these issues very differently from their predecessors. The most visible difference from the past is how diverse history writing is today. Historians treat a much greater range of topics, and they do so by employing a much wider variety of theories and methods. Many of these changes reflect the technical and methodological developments we have sketched in this book: history's

2. For this story, see Jack F. Matlock, *Autopsy of an Empire: The American Ambassador's Account of the Collapse of the Soviet Union* (New York, 1995), pp. 78, 81–82, 87–96. Details of this story were also provided by Ambassador Matlock in private correspondence.

encounters with other disciplines, from which scholars have taken tools, method, theory, and subject matter; and history's own internal turmoil, its own examination of its ways of doing things and of the scholarship produced in the past. The political and social upheavals of the twentieth century are an integral part of this story as well, with the two World Wars playing crucial roles in altering the intellectual climate in which historians work. The first war dramatically ended the optimism that had characterized the nineteenth century—optimism about continual progress in human affairs, about the glories of modern science, about the increasing "civility" of the world. The second brought the Holocaust. Reflecting this new pessimism, during the interwar years several historians published bleak analyses of the West and of history's possibility. From 1918 came Oswald Spengler's *Der Untergang des Abendlandes* (*The Decline of the West*, 1926); from 1933 the first volume of Arnold Toynbee's *Study of History*; and from 1936 Johan Huizinga's *In the Shadow of Tomorrow* (orig., *In de schaduwen van morgen*, 1935). In 1919, the French writer Paul Valéry, reacting against the nationalistic historiography that had dominated the previous century, warned that "civilizations are as mortal as any living creation."[3]

The demographic upheavals that have characterized the profession constitute a third, and equally powerful, fuel. The academy itself, and the historical profession with it, are very different places from those they were even twenty or thirty years ago. Today there are a great many more women historians, which helps account for the emergence of women's history as a major field of study. Increasingly, history is also written and taught at the university level by African Americans, Hispanics, and other social groups who once had limited access to the academy, and these scholars have helped develop the fields of African American and ethnic history. These demographic changes have produced more, however, than new subfields. They have also tended to democratize the academy, making it a place that tolerates (even if it does not always welcome) intellectual innovation and experimentation that would have been impossible in days past. One institutional consequence of these changes is that history departments throughout the West, nowhere more so than in the United States, are increasingly allied with sister disciplines in interdisciplinary programs such as American Studies, Ethnic Studies, Asian Studies, or Women's Studies, places which at their best nurture innovation, self-reflection, and risk-taking. Such demographic changes have been even

3. In *P. Valéry: An Anthology*, ed. J. R. Lawler (Princeton, 1977). The original French, *Note et digression*, was published in 1919.

more marked among the student body. Before World War II, only a small percentage of Americans attended college or university, and most of them were socially privileged white males, all but a few of European descent. Today about half the American population spends time in such institutions; more of them are female than male, and a significant portion are of non-European descent. In Europe, a similarly dramatic demographic revolution did not begin until the late 1960s, but it has had as profound an effect on universities there. History curricula reflect these developments. Today, history courses simply can no longer be about what American students sometimes scathingly call "dead white men" or about the West, for students demand to know about what they consider "their" past. No matter how important a white European male may have been in making that past, students insist on learning as well about how other people experienced—and participated in shaping—their history.[4]

While these changes have energized historical studies in countless ways—and, we should also acknowledge, have been possible in part because of the discipline's ability to absorb new intellectual currents—history is undoubtedly not the sure-footed discipline it once seemed to be. All the beliefs that gave our predecessors such confidence seem, today, impossibly naive: that history could teach us lessons and provide us models for living a good and useful life; that by studying history we could discover immutable laws of human behavior; that our objects of study were self-evident, our methods reliable, our skills adequate; that we could securely know how we came to be who we are; that we could, in fact, really *know* what happened in the past. Today, some say, the discipline of history is experiencing a "crisis," a failure of nerve, a loss of direction, a sense of futility. For some, it seems impossible to write useful history at all. For others, the only response to the crisis is resistance, a stubborn refusal to acknowledge the challenges of the present, whether they are social, intellectual, or political. For those scholars, history should be done the way it "always has been" (a dubious notion in any case) and the historian's goal should be to objectively render the truth about the past.

Our own position is more moderate. Although we do not think that the methods of source criticism we have been describing in this book are all passé—in fact we are sure that good history writing today depends more than ever on many of these craft skills—we agree with many of our colleagues that it is not possible in the early twenty-first century to do history as it has been done in the past. We also share many of the uncertainties

4. On this theme, see Edmund E. Jacobitti, *Composing Useful Pasts: History as Contemporary Politics* (Albany, N.Y., 2000).

about method, theory, and the nature of historical knowledge that frustrate so many of our colleagues. Although the crisis has its political and institutional aspects, which should not be ignored—the expansion of subject matter, the erosion of disciplinary boundaries, the democratization of the academy—its nature is fundamentally epistemological. At its heart lie two issues: the problem of objectivity and the status of the fact.

1. The Problem of Objectivity
In detective stories, the ideal investigator is perfectly objective, incorruptible; he or she does not allow outside forces to influence pursuit of the "facts"; he or she gathers evidence dispassionately, evaluates it rigorously, rejects that which does not "fit," and finally finds out the "truth." In some sense, the typical journalist is imagined to pursue a similar mission—the "true" story, the way it "really" happened. And to do so, this journalist too must be free of biases, personal commitments, entanglements—all the paraphernalia of human life.

That no such objectivity is possible, of course, no researcher should know this better than the professional historian. Ironically, however, there is perhaps no scholarly discipline in the humanities or social sciences in which the goal of pure "objectivity" has been more ardently sought, more obsessively worried over. The careful methods of source criticism we have been discussing in this book were in fact developed explicitly to achieve this goal; they were regarded as the historian's route to objectivity, the method by which he or she sifted out the biases, untruths, and limitations of the information available. Today, we are much more aware that there are no foolproof ways to render the historian nonhuman. First, each historian is a distinct individual, with distinct talents, skills, and resources; each will therefore bring different abilities to the work of research and interpretation. Second, all historians approach their work burdened with an array of individual experiences that affect their reaction to events; they have heard different voices, have different memories, lived through different times. Historians have long known that such differences characterize the people they study; in recent years they have become even more aware of how much in this respect they themselves share with their subjects.

More structural factors play an equally important role in making objectivity an unattainable goal. Every historian occupies a social place that influences not only how the world is seen, but even *what* is seen. Class and all that it entails (education, sense of privilege, fears, ambitions, material resources), political location (party allegiances, political system of the historian's home country and that country's place in the world), gender, age, ethnicity—all these factors determine the historian's capacities as much as they determine the history of the people he or she is studying. Moreover, "facts" are themselves rendered "facts" through the lenses such factors create. It is for this reason that historians pay as much attention to the way a document or a TV news program is received as they do to what is actually written or said—and for this reason that they, no less than the average reader or viewer of a TV program, know themselves to be inadequate reporters.

Let us look more systematically at some of the more obvious reasons for the difficulties historians face in trying to be objective. First, there is a group of what we might call conscious factors. Censorship is one such factor. In totalitarian regimes, censorship is clearly visible and attempts to be complete, at least as concerns what are considered matters of state (a definition that can be very broad indeed). Even in countries where speech is supposedly "free," there are limits to anyone's ability to tell all. In many Western countries, the press can be subjected to damage suits for libel if personal affairs are too closely reported; in all, the press has to be careful not to alienate the powerful, irritate possible sources, make too many enemies. More fundamentally, historians are limited by their own ideologies, their own way of understanding the world. In one sense, we can use the term "ideology" simply to mean beliefs consciously held ("I am a political conservative," "I am a Christian"), and it is certainly true that such beliefs shape an individual's interpretation of events. But in some ways these beliefs are easier to hold at bay when one is trying to be objective than is the entire ideological system in which one is embedded.

In the latter sense, ideology is almost unconscious, very difficult—perhaps impossible—to retrieve. It is a system of values which inform action, or which are thought to inform action—ideas about good and bad, about right and wrong, about what is "natural" and "given" and what, in contrast, is "changeable" or "man-made." In this sense, ideology is a product of culture—learned, to be sure, but learned at so deep a level that it is not easily distanced. Medieval people, Lucien Febvre was one of the first to demonstrate, simply could not imagine a world without god. There was, in their ideology, no place, no possibility, for not-god, for atheism. Modern scholars have helped some of us see that fixed categories of gender are also ideological constructions, that in fact there is no coherent, stable "woman" or "man" in human history, that any culture's "woman" or "man" is an ideological product. That so many people in our own age have had such trouble even grasping this argument is testimony to its ideological rootedness.

Given these difficulties, is it possible to achieve anything like objectivity? And if not, then why do history? Many historians (ourselves included) would answer these questions by conceding that "objectivity" is not possible, but they would insist that historical study can, nevertheless, yield useful knowledge. Most of us would explain our position by pointing out that a good historian not only never can but never should achieve the perfectly indifferent stance implied by the word "objectivity." We choose historical topics out of interest, we pursue stories deep into archives because we are fascinated by the event or the people being studied, we privilege some facts over others because we *care*. This does not make us bad historians or make the enterprise of writing history fruitless. It makes us human; and it makes history more art than science, more an act of interpretation than a discovery.

The trick, then, is to construct our interpretations responsibly, with care, and with a high degree of self-consciousness about our disabilities and the disabilities of our sources. First, we must analyze and read our documents meticulously, learning to recognize the kinds of knowledge they produce, learning to see their limits, learning to exploit their possibilities and make use of their biases. These are the skills we have been emphasizing in this book, for they constitute the historian's tool chest; they are the elements of the craft. Second, historians must learn to recognize that they can read sources only from the standpoint of their position—a position, as we have emphasized, that is determined as much by individual attributes as it is by more structural factors. We can never fully escape this standpoint; in some ways we are its prisoners. But we can, nevertheless, write useful histories from that standpoint, if we recognize and scrupulously take account of our likes and dislikes, our biases, and our prejudices. If we can understand or at least acknowledge our ideological position, we can also write histories that self-consciously display those limitations to our readers. We can thus implicate our audiences in the histories we write, making them see *how we see* as well as what we see. If we do so, we can produce useful knowledge about the past, or at least about our access to that past.

2. The Status of the "Fact"

For a Western-trained historian working at the turn of the twenty-first century, there is perhaps no greater threat to the craft than the statement that "there are no facts," that is, no verifiable, indisputable objects of knowledge. Perhaps the only thing that is certain about the arrival of the Pilgrims in New England was that they arrived. Anything else we know about that arrival is filtered through discourses—discourses of discovery, redemption, conquest, civilization, manhood, whiteness, to name just a few—that make it impossible to provide an "objective" account about any aspect of these people's settlement. All we can know about the colony is how the sources that come to us from that time represent the settlement. This is especially true of the documents provided by the settlers: their diaries, letters, official reports; their fiscal accounts, inventories, order forms; their legal rulings, statutes, and broadsheets; their poems, prayers, songs, and sermons. But it is also true even of the archaeological record; the walls and building foundations that survive, the pots and fabrics these people left, all are laden with meanings that historians can analyze, but beyond which it is very hard to go. Scholars can say useful and interesting things, for example, about what people ate and how they sheltered themselves, or how they interpreted their encounter with the Native Americans, but what they can "know" is in some sense internal to the sources that provide that information. Historians' accounts of the Massachusetts Bay Colony are thus interpretations of interpretations, not recitations of "facts."

What is the historian supposed to do with such a statement? First, let us remind readers that historians have long accepted a fairly mild version of this statement. Our entire craft is based precisely on the understanding that our knowledge of any event comes to us through sources which we know are *not* perfect reflections of "reality," which are constructions of reality, and which have to be decoded in order for us to understand what reality they construct. Second, however, it is true that most historians, for most of the long history of our profession, have thought that a reality lay behind these sources and that if we read our sources skillfully enough we could arrive at that reality. Today many of us would disagree, arguing that any reality that lay behind the sources is, finally, inaccessible to us, no matter how skilled we are—and that we have to settle for studying the reality that sources construct rather than "reality" itself.

While this approach acknowledges the critique of empiricism implied by postmodernism, it does not ultimately abandon the idea that history is a craft and that "sources" are the object of our study. To that extent, then, we preserve what our postmodern critics have called the "fetishism of sources." We do not think, however, that to retain this focus on sources is to privilege them as vehicles to truth or to position ourselves as magicians able to reveal those hidden truths. It is to acknowledge, more humbly, that sources are all we have—and to insist that we can learn something by reading them carefully.

Does that mean business as usual? For some, it will. Some historians will, undoubtedly, continue to work under the old presumptions. They may be more tentative about their claims to truth and to objectivity, but they will write, speak, and teach as though their research provides access to a truth that approximates reality. For others, however, it will mean more self-conscious histories, ones which are less about "how it really was" in a given age than about how that age created reality—about how the sources left by the people who then lived constructed their reality and construct for the historian today all of their reality he can know. Readers must ponder for themselves whether this approach offers an adequate solution to the challenge posed by poststructuralism.

Research Bibliography
Contents

Note: This bibliography is intended as a reference guide for students beginning historical research. It does not reproduce secondary literature cited in the body of this text.

A Note on Electronic Media: As this book goes to press, the computer is transforming the world of historical research. Because the range of materials being rendered in electronic form grows daily and because the form of delivery and access is changing rapidly as the Internet takes over from CD-ROMs, any list of reference materials and sources drawn up today would be obsolete once this book were in print. Hence, we have not attempted to provide a comprehensive list of all electronic resources available. We have, however, indicated whether references materials we mention are now on-line, and we have provided the current address, if available (note, however, that addresses change frequently).

For the cautious and thoughtful researcher, electronic resources can be an enormous help. Materials on CD-ROM and on the Internet can often be searched more thoroughly, and certainly more rapidly, than paper sources can. World Wide Web catalogs and bibliographies can be updated constantly and instantaneously. Electronic library catalogs and indexes can allow the researcher quickly to pursue lines of exploration that might have been too time-consuming to investigate using reference books. But this new style of research demands new skills, including mastery of different kinds of electronic searches and new ways of evaluating the validity and reliability of source materials.

Four principal categories of reference materials are today commonly found in electronic form. First, the catalogs of many major library systems are now partially or completely on-line. This means that researchers anywhere in the world can have access, for example, to the Library of Congress catalog or to the holdings of academic research libraries via systems such as MELVYL, which provides access to the book and periodical holdings of the University of California, the California State Library, and the California Historical Society. In addition, two international databases of references materials are accessible on-line: WorldCat and Eureka (the latter is the on-line gateway to the Research Libraries Information Network, known as RLIN and available by subscription). Second, subject bibliographies and guides covering a wide range of topics can also be found in electronic form. *Women's Resources International*, for example, provides listings of journal articles, books, and book chapters published since 1972 in the fields of women's studies, gender studies, and feminist theory. The *International Medieval Bibliography* lists books, periodicals, essays, reviews, and manuscripts on European medieval history and related topics (the present version includes items published between 1976 and 1995; a full copy of the printed version [1968 ff.] is about to go on-line). The *Biography and Genealogy Master Index* provides citations for biographical information from reference works including biographical dictionaries and encyclopedias. Third, primary and secondary sources themselves can be found on-line or on CD-ROM. For example, the Library of Congress's *American Memory* Web site includes a growing collection of text, film, photography, and recordings on a range of topics in American history. The *Historical Statistics of the United States: Bicentennial Edition on CD-ROM* provides extensive statistics on social and economic issues for the years 1790–1970. The *Patrologia Latina Database* includes a full-text electronic version of the Latin portion of *Patrologiae cursus completus*. Fourth, numerous scholarly journals can now be found on the Internet. The public access JSTOR site includes back issues of major print publications such as the *American Historical Review* and *Speculum*. Journals published exclusively on the Internet are listed at a site called *New Jour*.

Although the increasing abundance of electronic materials provides new avenues for the researcher, "on-line" does not mean "free" or easily available. As noted above, most of the resources can be used only by those with access to CD-ROMs or by subscription; in effect, this means only by members of university communities (students and faculty) whose libraries are subscribers to these services or by individuals with rights to use the facilities of such libraries or other research institutions that hold such subscriptions. And it is crucial to keep in mind that the maxim "you get what you pay for" often applies to those Web sites that are free. The information available on the Internet without cost is frequently misleading, incomplete, or just plain wrong. Another crucial point is that the amount of material in electronic form, although huge and growing rapidly, represents only a small part of the material actually in print—whether bibliographic, encyclopedic, or sources themselves. Electronic tools thus should be seen as one component in a research package that includes print sources.

Using electronic source materials can seem deceptively easy. But searching the Web is not the same as using a library, and electronic catalogs and indexes must be navigated with techniques different from those used for their paper counterparts. Internet searching is done with a tool called a search engine. There are many different search engines available, and they work in different ways, often providing varying results for the same search. A guide can be found at the Internet Public Library site http://www.ipl.org/ref/websearching.html. The National Endowment for the Humanities' EDSITEment site (http://edsitement.neh.gov) provides a guide to the best humanities (including history) sites on the Web.

I. BIBLIOGRAPHIES, GUIDES, DICTIONARIES

A. General Bibliographies and Guides to Libraries

1. General Guides to Books and Databases

I. P. Boehm and A. S. Birkos, *Reference Works: History and Related Fields with Research News on the Social Sciences and Humanities*, Santa Barbara, Calif., 1967.

I. Lancashire, *The Humanities Computing Yearbook, 1989–90: A Comprehensive Guide to Software and Other Resources*, Oxford, 1991.

R. Balay, *Guide to Reference Books*, London, 1996, 11th ed.

M. Mullay and P. Schlicke, *Walford's Guide to Reference Material*, London, 1996, 7th ed. (only 1 vol. published).

J. M. Hillard, *Where to Find What: A Handbook to Reference Service*, Lanham, Md., 1998, 4th ed.

[Gale Research Inc., Detroit], *Gale Directory of Databases*, CD-ROM and WWW-subscription, ERL database. Contents: detailed descriptions (addresses, update frequency, subject coverage, time span, rates) of 9600 databases that are publicly available or accessible through subscription (on-line vendor, CD-ROM, other computer-readable storage medium); also includes defunct databases. Subject coverage: databases of all types in all subject areas worldwide, in English and other languages, including humanities, social sciences, news, and general interest.

[H. W. Wilson Company], *Cumulative Book Index*, CD-ROM and WWW-subscrip-

tion, books published since 1982; partial electronic version of *Cumulative Book Index: A World List of Books in the English Language*, New York, 1898–1999.
[Bowker Electronic Publ. Ed.], *Books in Print*, CD-ROM and WWW-subscription, since 1987. Contents: listings of in-print, out-of-print, and forthcoming books from over 44,000 North American publishers. Directory information for publishers also available.
[J. Whitaker and Sons Ltd, London], *British Books in Print*, CD-ROM and WWW-subscription, since 1988. Contents: listings of books in the U.K.
[Ministerio de Cultura de España, Madrid], *Libros españoles en Venta*, CD-ROM and WWW-subscription. Contents: listings of books in print in the Spanish language, from all countries, on all subjects.

2. General Guides to Periodicals

[F. Dietrich Verlag], *Bibliographie der fremdsprachigen Zeitschriftenliteratur. International Index to Periodicals*, Leipzig—Osnabrück, 73 vol. from 1911 to 1964. Contents: index to articles in over 1000 periodicals, published in Europe and the U.S. Keywords in German. For German periodicals: Id., *Bibliographie der deutschen Zeitschriftenliteratur*, 128 vol., 1896–1964. The follow-up to both series is the following item, *Internationale Bibliographie*.
[F. Dietrich Verlag], *Internationale Bibliographie der Zeitschriftenliteratur*, Leipzig—Osnabrück, yearly 1965–. Also available on CD-ROM and on-line with subscription.
[Institute for Scientific Information, Philadelphia], *Arts and Humanities Citation Index*, CD-ROM and WWW-subscription. Contents: bibliographic data from more than 1100 arts and humanities journals, along with relevant items from more than 5800 science and social science journals. Subject coverage: history, archaeology, art, classics, film, language, linguistics, literature, philosophy, religious studies. The CD-ROM is called *Arts and Humanities Citation Index*, the on-line version *Arts and Humanities Search Database*.
[Institute for Scientific Information, Philadelphia], *Web of Science*, WWW-subscription. Contents: combination of the databases of the aforementioned *Arts and Humanities Citation Index*, and of the two other indexes of this Institute, one on *Social Sciences* and the other on *Sciences* (each of them also separately available on CD-ROM). This combined database is superior to the individual ones, because historical studies may be located in all of the three subcollections; another advantage is that the larger database is more frequently updated. Publications from 1988 on.
[R. R. Bowker, Providence, R.I.], *Ulrich's Serials Database*, CD-ROM and WWW-subscription, ERL database. Contents: bibliographic descriptions and subject classification for ca. 210,000 serial publications (journals, magazines, annuals, conference proceedings, yearbooks, monographic series), information on publication cancellations and on former names of publications, addresses for 90,000 publishers in 200 countries. Subject coverage: all types of serials, including scientific and scholarly publications. This guide also mentions the databases in which the periodicals are excerpted.

[H. W. Wilson Company], *Book Review Digest*, WWW-subscription. Contents: index to articles in 100 leading periodicals, published in English in the U.S., Canada, and the U.K.; short abstracts from the reviews.

[Chadwyck-Healey, Cambridge, U.K.], *Periodicals Contents Index*, WWW-subscription. Contents: index to articles in older reviews, and thus a useful addendum to most of the CD-ROMs, which give only recent articles; new product, now incomplete, but very promising.

3. General National Bibliographies

a. General overview

B. Bell, *An Annotated Guide to Current National Bibliographies*, Alexandria, Va., 1986.

b. Books and periodicals published in the U.S.

[Library of Congress, Washington, D.C.], *CDMARC Bibliographic*, CD-ROM, is the catalog of the Library of Congress; covers holdings acquired since 1968; since 1991 updated every three months; complete, because of the automatic cataloging of all publications in the U.S. in this collection; contains in addition numerous books published worldwide, outside the U.S. Specific CD-ROM for serials.

c. Books published in Europe

To find a book published in a European country, consult the following CD-ROMs which contain general bibliographies; produced by several scientific institutions and distributed by Chadwyck-Healey, Cambridge, U.K. (address: http://www.chadwyck.co.uk)

[Buchhändler-Vereinigung GmbH], *Deutsche Nationalbibliographie*, Frankfurt-am-Main, since 1989, covering publications from 1986 on. A retrospective guide for 1945–65 was published in 1995; the years 1966–85 are in preparation.

[British Library], *British National Bibliography*, London, since 1986, covering publications from 1950 on; archival disk for 1950–85, cumulative indexes 1986–.

[Bibliothèque Nationale de France], *Bibliographie nationale française*, Paris, since 1989, covering publications from 1970 on.

[Istituto Centrale per il Catalogo Unico], *Bibliografia nazionale italiana*, Florence, since 1995, covering publications from 1958 on.

[Biblioteca Nacional de España], *Bibliografía nacional española desde 1976*, Madrid, since 1992, covering publications from 1976 on.

[Biblioteca Nacional de Portugal], *Bibliografia nacional portuguesa*, Lisbon, since 1995, covering publications from 1980 on.

4. On-Line Gateways to Academic Libraries

a. Worldwide libraries

WebCATS: Library Catalogues on the World Wide Web, WWW-public access (http://www.lights.com/webcats); links to international on-line library catalogs.

[Univ. of California, Berkeley], *Libweb: Library Servers via WWW,* WWW-public access (http://sunsite.berkeley.edu/Libweb)

[OCLC, On-Line Computer Library Center, Dublin, Ohio], *Worldcat,* WWW-subscription; composite on-line catalog.

[RLIN, Research Libraries Information Network], *Eureka,* WWW-subscription; composite on-line to the catalogs of major research and academic libraries (archives, museums, law, medical, art and music libraries, historical societies, and book clubs).

b. United States libraries

[Library of Congress, Washington, D.C.], *Library of Congress catalog,* WWW-public access (http://catalog.loc.gov).

[Columbia Univ., New York], *Clio: Columbia Libraries Information On-Line homepage,* WWW-public access (http://apthorp.cul.columbia.edu/webpac-bin/wgbroker?new+-access+clio); holdings of Columbia Univ. Libraries since 1981.

[Harvard Univ., Cambridge, Mass.], *Hollis,* WWW-public access (http://lib.harvard.edu); holdings of all libraries at Harvard.

[Univ. of California, Berkeley], California Digital Library, *Melvyl,* WWW-public access (http://www.melvyl.ucop.edu); holdings of Univ. of California, California State Library, California Historical Society. Other address: http://sunsite.berkeley.edu/catalogs.

c. European libraries

[Koninklijke Bibliotheek, The Hague], *Gabriel Gateway to Europe's National Libraries,* WWW-public access (http://www.kb.nl/gabriel); Web site with links to ca. 50 libraries of European universities.

B. Dictionaries, Encyclopedias, and Fact Finders: History, Humanities, Social Sciences

1. Guides

T. Kabdebo and N. Armstrong, *Dictionary of Dictionaries and Eminent Encyclopedias,* London, 1997, 2nd ed.

S. C. Awe, *Arba Guide to Subject Encyclopedias and Dictionaries,* Englewood, Colo., 1997.

2. General Encyclopedias

G. Howat (ed.), *Dictionary of World History*, London, 1973.

J. Bowle, *The Concise Encyclopaedia of World History*, London, 1979.

E. Bayer, *Wörterbuch zur Geschichte. Begriffe und Fachausdrücke*, Berlin, 1985, 2nd ed.

A. Henderson and L. Baker (eds.), *Worldmark Encyclopedia of the Nations*, 5 vol., Detroit, 1998, 5th ed.

[Encyclopedia Britannica], *Britannica Online*, WWW-subscription (http://www. eb.com); over 72,000 articles, including 12,000 illustrations, maps, graphs, photographs, and innumerable links to additional Internet resources. Free access to a reduced database at http://www.britannica.com.

[Electric Library], *Concise Columbia Electronic Encyclopedia*, WWW-public access (http://www.encyclopedia.com); only 17,000 articles but free; links to relevant websites; can be consulted via alphabetical list or by keywords.

3. Chronological Tables of Historical Events

W. L. Langer (ed.), *An Encyclopedia of World History: Ancient, Medieval, and Modern, Chronologically Arranged*, London, 1987, 6th ed.

B. Grun, *The Timetables of History*, New York, 1991, 3rd ed. (adapted from: W. Stein, *Kulturfahrplan*, Munich, 1990).

S. H. Steinberg and J. Paxton, *Historical Tables, 58 B.C.–A.D. 1990*, London, 1991, 12th ed.

N. Williams and H. Mellersh, *Chronology of World History*, 4 vol., Santa Barbara, Calif., 1999. Ed. on CD-ROM: Oxford, 1994 (address: Helicon Publ., Oxford).

J. Paxton and E. Knappman, *The Wilson Calendar of World History*, New York, 1999 (based on Steinberg and Paxton, 1991).

4. Dictionaries and Encyclopedias by Subject

a. Archaeology and material culture

F. Cabrol, a.o. (eds.), *Dictionnaire d'archéologie chrétienne et de liturgie*, 15 vol., Paris, 1907–53.

H. Witthöft, a.o. (eds.), *Sachüberlieferung und Geschichte. Siegener Abhandlungen zur Entwicklung der materiellen Kultur*, 15 vol. to date, Ostfildern—Sankt Katharinen, 1984–95.

L. R. Owen, *Dictionary of Prehistoric Archeology*, Tübingen, 1996.

B. M. Fagan (ed.), *The Oxford Companion to Archaeology*, Oxford, 1996.

I. Shaw and R. Jameson, *A Dictionary of Archeology*, Oxford, 1999.

b. Ancient history

G. Wissowa (ed.), *Pauly's Realencyclopädie der classischen Altertumswissenschaft*, 68 vol. (A–Z), Stuttgart, 1893–1972; 15 supplement vol. (A–Z), Stuttgart, 1903–78.

H. Cancik and H. Schneider (eds.), *Der Neue Pauly. Enzyklopädie der Antike*, 4 vol. published (from A to Gro.), Stuttgart—Weimar, 1996–98. New version of the "Pauly-Wissowa."

A. P. Kazhdan (ed.), *The Oxford Dictionary of Byzantium*, 3 vol. (A–Z), New York—Oxford, 1991.

S. Hornblower and A. Spawforth (eds.), *The Oxford Classical Dictionary*, New York—Oxford, 1996, 3rd ed.

c. Medieval history

J. R. Strayer (ed.), *Dictionary of the Middle Ages*, 12 vol. + 1 vol. index, New York, 1982–91.

N. Angermann, R. H. Bautier, a.o. (eds.), *Lexikon des Mittelalters*, 9 vol. (A–Z), Munich—Zurich, 1977–98.

R. McKitterick, C. Allmand, a.o. (eds.), *The New Cambridge Medieval History*, 5 vol. available (2–3, 5–7 of 7 planned vols.), Cambridge, U.K.—New York, 1995–2000.

M. E. Bunson, *Encyclopedia of the Middle Ages*, New York, 1995.

d. Early modern and modern history

C. Stern, *Lexikon zur Geschichte und Politik im 20. Jahrhundert*, Cologne, 1971.

M. Dunan, *Larousse Encyclopedia of Modern History, from 1500 to the Present Day*, New York, 1981.

I. Gutman (ed.), *Encyclopedia of the Holocaust*, 4 vol., New York—London, 1990.

M. Lee (ed.), *Larousse Dictionary of Twentieth Century History*, New York, 1994.

H. J. Hillerbrand (ed.), *The Oxford Encyclopedia of the Reformation*, 4 vol. (A–Z), New York—Oxford, 1996.

E. Epstein, *Dictionary of the Holocaust*, Westport, Conn., 1997.

[National Textbook Company], *Dictionary of 20th Century World History*, Lincolnwood, Ill., 1997.

J. Palmoski, *A Dictionary of Twentieth-Century World History*, Oxford, 1997.

G. Gallup, *The Gallup Poll Cumulative Index: Public Opinion, 1935–1997*, London, 1999.

e. Church history, religion, canon law

A. Baudrillart, R. Aubert, a.o. (eds.), *Dictionnaire d'histoire et de géographie ecclésiastiques*, 27 vol. (159 fasc.) published, from A to Jérôme, Paris, 1912–99 (Catholic).

A. Vacant (ed.), *Dictionnaire de théologie catholique*, 30 vol. (A–Z), Paris, 1903–50; tables, 3 vol., 1951–72.

R. Naz (ed.), *Dictionnaire de droit canonique*, 7 vol. (A–Z), Paris, 1935–65.

M. Viller (ed.), *Dictionnaire de spiritualité ascétique et mystique. Doctrine et histoire*, 16 vol. (A–Z), Paris, 1937–94; + vol. 17 (Tables générales), Paris, 1995.

M. Buchberger (ed.), *Lexikon für Theologie und Kirche*, 14 vol., Freiburg, 1957–68, 2nd ed. (10 vol.: A–Z, 1957–65; 1 vol.: Register, 1967; 3 vol.: Das Zweite

Vatikanische Konzil, 1966–68); new, 3rd ed.: W. Kasper (ed.), Freiburg-in-Breisgau, 1993– (Catholic).

[Pontificia Universita Lateranense], *Bibliotheca sanctorum*, 13 vol., Rome, 1961–70; vol. 13 is an index. In 1987 a first appendix was published; biographies and iconography.

[The Catholic University of America], *The New Catholic Encyclopedia*, 14 vol. (A–Z), San Francisco— Toronto—London—Sydney, 1967; vol. 15: index to 1–14 (1967); vol. 16, suppl. on 1967–74 (1974); vol. 17, suppl. on 1975–77 (1979); vol. 18, suppl. on 1978–88, with an integrated index to vol. 16–18 (1989). Focuses on the Catholic Church but excellent for other Christian churches.

G. Krause and G. Müller, *Theologische Realenzyklopädie*, Berlin, 1976–; reached vol. 27 (1997); Protestant; see F. Schuman, *Register zu Band 1–17*, Berlin, 1996.

D. H. Farmer, *The Oxford Dictionary of Saints*, Oxford—New York, 1987, 2nd ed.

J. D. N. Kelly, *The Oxford Dictionary of Popes*, Oxford—New York, 1988, 2nd ed.

F. L. Cross, *Oxford Dictionary of the Christian Church*, Oxford, 1997, 3rd ed. Anglican in tone but informative on other Christian churches.

f. Military history

R. E. Dupuy and T. N. Dupuy (eds.), *The Harper Encyclopedia of Military History: From 3500 B.C. to the Present*, New York, 1993, 4th ed. (+ bibliography and indexes).

T. N. Dupuy, a.o. (eds.), *International Military and Defense Encyclopedia*, Washington, D.C., 1993 (+ bibliography and index).

g. History of ideas, history of science

P. P. Wiener (ed.), *Dictionary of the History of Ideas*, 4 vol., New York, 1973; vol. 5, index, 1974.

W. F. Bynum, E. J. Browne, R. Porter, *Dictionary of the History of Science*, Princeton, 1981.

T. Bottomore (ed.), *A Dictionary of Marxist Thought*, Oxford—Cambridge, Mass., 1991, 2nd ed.

R. L. Maddex, *The Illustrated Dictionary of Constitutional Concepts*, Washington, D.C., 1996.

R. Scruton, *A Dictionary of Political Thought*, London, 1996, 2nd ed.

h. Art, film, iconography

G. Schiller, *Ikonographie der christlichen Kunst*, 7 vol., Gütersloh, 1966–80.

E. Kirschbaum (ed.), *Lexikon der Christlichen Ikonographie*, 8 vol. (A–Z), Rome—Freiburg—Basel—Vienna, 1968–76 (hundreds of illustrations).

J. Hall, *Dictionary of Subjects and Symbols in Art*, London, 1979, 2nd ed.

S. Sadie (ed.), *The New Grove Dictionary of Music and Musicians*, 20 vol., London, 1980.

H. C. Ackermann and J. R. Gisler, *Lexicon Iconographicum Mythologiae Classicae*, 16 vol. (A–Z), Zurich—Munich, 1981–97 (hundreds of illustrations); 2 vol. indexes, Munich, 1999.

G. Brown and H. Geduld, *The New York Times Encyclopedia of Film*, 13 vol., index included, New York, 1984 (movies date from 1896 to 1979).
E. Kasten, a.o. (eds.), *Saur Allgemeines Künstlerlexikon: Die bildenden Künstler aller Zeiten und Völker*, 23 vol. to date; 3 vol. index for vols. 1–20, Munich, 1992–99.
J. Chevalier and A. Gheerbrant, *A Dictionary of Symbols*, Oxford, 1994.
E. Katz, *The Film Encyclopedia*, New York, 1994, 2nd ed.
K. Kuiper, *Merriam-Webster's Encyclopedia of Literature*, Springfield, Mass., 1995.
J. Turner (ed.), *The Dictionary of Art*, 34 vol. (A–Z), index included, London—New York, 1996.
D. Gaze, *Dictionary of Women Artists*, 2 vol., London—Chicago, 1997.
I. Königsberg, *The Complete Film Dictionary*, New York, 1997, 2nd ed.
H. E. Roberts, *Encyclopedia of Comparative Iconography: Themes Depicted in Works of Art*, 2 vol., Chicago—London, 1998.
[Department of Art and Archaeology, Princeton University], *Index of Christian Art*; index on cards (copies in Vatican Library and at Univ. of Utrecht).

i. American history

R. H. Ferrell, *Dictionary of American History*, 8 vol., New York, 1976–78; supplement, New York, 1996.
G. Carruth, a.o. (eds.), *Encyclopedia of American Facts and Dates*, New York, 1979.
G. Porter (ed.), *Encyclopedia of American Economic History*, 3 vol., New York, 1980.
M. Kupiec Cayton, E. J. Gorn, P. W. Williams (eds.), *Encyclopedia of American Social History*, 3 vol., New York, 1993.
J. Salzman (ed.), *Encyclopedia of African-American Culture and History*, 5 vol., New York, 1996.
L. Urdang, *The Timetables of American History*, New York, 1996.
S. Altman, *The Encyclopedia of African American Heritage*, New York, 1997.
M. C. Carnes, *American History*, New York, 1998.
[Grolier], *The Encyclopedia Americana*, 30 vol., Danbury, Conn., 1999.
[Encyclopedia Britannica], *Britannica Online*, WWW-subscription (http://www.eb.com); free access to a reduced database at http://www.britannica.com. Guide to black history, with links to the W.E.B. Du Bois Institute, Harvard Univ.; gives alphabetical biographies, bibliography, time line, audio-video clips. Direct Web reference for Du Bois site: http://web-dubois.fas.harvard.edu.

j. Biographies

R. Slocum, *Biographical Dictionaries*, 3 vol., Detroit, 1986, 2nd ed.; international bibliography of more than 16,000 collections.
[Gale Research, Inc., Detroit], *Biography and Genealogy Master Index*, CD-ROM and WWW-subscription, London, 1993: over 11 million citations from 700 biographical dictionaries, who's whos, encyclopedias.
L. Stephen and S. Lee (eds.), *Dictionary of National Biography*, 63 vol., London, 1885–1900; a supplement vol. every ten years. The 10th supplement by C. G. Nicholls covering 1986–90 (Oxford—New York, 1996) contains one alphabetical index covering 1901–90. Bio- and bibliographical information on notable

people in the British Isles and its colonies who died before 1985; also available on CD-ROM, 1995: distribution at http://www.oup.co.uk/newdnb. A *New Dictionary of National Biography* will be released in print and as an electronic publication in 2004.

[American Council of Learned Societies], *Dictionary of American Biography*, CD-ROM. Biographical information concerning 19,000 notable Americans who died before December 31, 1980; references to resources for more information. A printed complete index to the printed version, 9 vol., New York, 1981; supplementary indexes in 1990 and 1996.

[American Council of Learned Societies], *Concise Dictionary of American Biography*, 2 vol., New York, 1997, 5th ed.

R. L. Wick, *Arba Guide to Biographical Resources*, London, 1998.

J. A. Garraty and M. C. Carnes (eds.), *American National Biography*, 24 vol., New York, 1999.

[H. W. Wilson Company], *Biography Index*, CD-ROM and WWW-subscription; from antiquity to the present.

k. Geography, weights and measures, numismatics

N. Cavalli, *Table de comparaison des mesures, poids et monnaies*, Marseille, 1960.

F. von Schrötter, *Wörterbuch der Münzkunde*, Berlin—Leipzig, 1970, 2nd ed.

J. Graesse and F. Benedict, *Orbis Latinus. Lexikon lateinischer geographischer Namen des Mittelalters und der Neuzeit*, 3 vol., Brunswick, 1972, 4th ed.; 120,000 placenames.

R. E. Zupko, *A Dictionary of Weights and Measures for the British Isles: The Middle Ages to the Twentieth Century*, Philadelphia, 1985.

I. Kretschmer, a.o., *Lexikon zur Geschichte der Kartographie*, 2 vol., Vienna, 1986.

H. Hahnt and B. Korr, *Alte Masse, Münze und Gewichte. Ein Lexikon*, Mannheim, 1987.

R. E. Zupko, *Revolution in Measurement: Western European Weights and Measures since the Age of Science*, Philadelphia, 1990. The same author published similar dictionaries for Britain, France, and Italy.

H. Witthöft, *Handbuch der historischen Metrologie*, 4 vol., Sankt Katharinen, 1991–94.

R. S. Carlton, *The International Encyclopaedic Dictionary of Numismatics*, Iola, Wisc., 1996.

A. D. Mills, *A Dictionary of English Placenames*, Oxford, 1998, 2nd new ed.

Note: An extensive international bibliography concerning measures appears in: R. C. Van Caenegem, F. L. Ganshof, L. Jocqué, *Introduction aux sources de l'histoire médiévale*, Turnhout, 1997, pp. 522–32.

l. Philosophy and psychology

R. J. Corsini (ed.), *Encyclopedia of Psychology*, 4 vol., New York, 1994, 2nd ed.

T. Honderich, *The Oxford Companion to Philosophy*, Oxford—New York, 1995.

S. Gall, *The Gale Encyclopedia of Psychology*, Detroit, 1996.

E. Craig (ed.), *Routledge Encyclopedia of Philosophy*, 10 vol., London—New York, 1998.

R. Audi (ed.), *The Cambridge Dictionary of Philosophy*, Cambridge, U.K., 1999, 2nd ed.

m. Social sciences (economics, sociology, physical anthropology, and business)

D. L. Sills (ed.), *International Encyclopedia of the Social Sciences*, 18 vol., New York—London, 1968–79; vol. 19 (New York, 1991): "Social Science Quotations."

J. Eatwell, a.o. (eds.), *The New Palgrave: A Dictionary of Economics*, 4 vol., London—New York, 1987; partial update from 1989 to 1991.

E. F. Borgatta and M. L. Borgatta (eds.), *Encyclopedia of Sociology*, 4 vol., New York—Toronto—Oxford, 1992; extensive bibliography for each item.

F. Magill (ed.), *International Encyclopedia of Sociology*, London—Chicago, 1995.

A. Kuper and J. Kuper, *The Social Science Encyclopedia*, London—New York, 1996, 2nd ed.

M. Warner, *International Encyclopedia of Business and Management*, 6 vol., London—New York, 1996.

F. Spencer, *History of Physical Anthropology*, 2 vol., New York—London, 1997.

G. Bannock, *Dictionary of Economics*, New York, 1998, 6th ed.

P. Newman (ed.), *The New Palgrave: Dictionary of Economics and the Law*, 3 vol., London—New York, 1998.

E. Hann Hastings and Phillip Hastings (eds.), *Index to International Public Opinion*, 14 vol. (covers 1984–98), New York, 1986–99.

n. Political science and politics

V. Bogdanor (ed.), *The Blackwell Encyclopaedia of Political Institutions*, Oxford—New York, 1991, new ed.

G. K. Roberts and A. Edwards, *A New Dictionary of Political Analysis*, London—New York, 1991.

W. J. Raymond, *Dictionary of Politics: Selected American and Foreign Political and Legal Terms*, Lawrence, Va., 1992, 7th ed.

L. D. Eigen and J. P. Siegel, *The Macmillan Dictionary of Political Quotations*, New York—Toronto, 1993.

J. Krieger (ed.), *The Oxford Companion to Politics of the World*, New York—Oxford, 1993; 650 articles, on countries, concepts, forms of government, organizations, and biographies.

J. A. Goldstone (ed.), *The Encyclopedia of Political Revolutions*, Washington, D.C., 1998 (+ bibliography and index).

R. Wuthnow (ed.), *The Encyclopedia of Politics and Religion*, Washington, D.C., 1998 (+ bibliography and index).

P. A. O'Hara (ed.), *Encyclopedia of Political Economy*, New York, 1998.

F. Bealey, *The Blackwell Dictionary of Political Science*, Malden, Mass., 1999.

o. Linguistic works, dictionaries, glossaries

W. Zaunmüller, *Bibliographisches Handbuch der Sprachwörterbücher*, Stuttgart, 1958; bibliography of more than 5600 dictionaries.

R. L. Collison, *Dictionaries of English and Foreign Languages: A Bibliographical Guide to Both General and Technical Dictionaries*, New York, 1971, 2nd ed.

[European Association for Lexicography, Dictionary Society of North America],

Lexicographica: International Annual for Lexicography, Tübingen, annual bibliography from 1985 (covering 1984) on.

W. Bright, *International Encyclopedia of Linguistics*, 4 vol., New York—Oxford, 1992.

R. E. Asher (ed.), *The Encyclopedia of Language and Linguistics*, 10 vol., Oxford, 1994 (includes index).

T. A. Sebeok (ed.), *Encyclopedic Dictionary of Semiotics*, 3 vol., Berlin—New York, 1994, 2nd ed. (includes bibliography).

A. L. DeMiller, *Linguistics: A Guide to the Reference Literature*, Englewood, Colo., 2000.

p. Communications and media

E. Barnouw, a.o. (eds.), *International Encyclopedia of Communication*, 4 vol., New York—Oxford, 1989.

H. Drost, *The World's News Media*, London, 1991; a listing of newspapers and other forms of media, worldwide.

D. Webster Hollis, *The Media in America*, Santa Barbara, Calif., 1995.

R. Weiner (ed.), *Webster's New World Dictionary of Media and Communications*, New York, 1996.

q. Women's history

M. Parry, *Larousse Dictionary of Women*, New York, 1996.

H. Tierney, *Women's Studies Encyclopedia*, 3 vol., Westport, Conn., 1999, rev. ed.

A. Commire (ed.), *Women in World History: A Biographical Encyclopedia*, 6 vol. (covering A to Harp), Detroit, 1999–2000.

r. Non-Western cultures

G. T. Kurian, *Encyclopedia of the Third World*, New York—Oxford, 1992, 4th ed.

5. Historical Atlases

H. Bengtson, a.o., *Grosser Historischer Weltatlas (Bayerischer Schulbuch-Verlag)*, Munich, 1972–81, 5th ed.

W. R. Shepherd, *Historical Atlas*, Totowa, N.J., 1980, rev. 9th ed. (American version of F. W. Putzger, *Historischer Weltatlas*, last German ed.: Bielefeld, 1980, 100th ed.).

G. Franz, *Historische Kartographie. Forschung und Bibliographie*, Hannover, 1980, 3rd ed.; description of 858 atlases.

H. E. Stier, a.o., *Westermanns Grosser Atlas zur Weltgeschichte*, Brunswick, 1985, 11th ed.; the most extensive (530 maps).

H. Middleton, *Atlas of Modern World History*, Oxford, 1989.

H. Kinder and W. Hilgemann, *DTV-Atlas zur Weltgeschichte*, Munich, 1991, 25th ed.

R. Overy, *Atlas of the 20th Century*, London, 1996.

G. Barraclough, *The Times Atlas of World History*, London, 1997, 5th ed.

[University of Texas at Austin], *The Perry-Castañeda Library Map Collection*, WWW-public access (http://www.lib.utexas.edu/Libs/PCL/Map_collection/historical/ history_main.html); collection of historical maps; also links to historical maps in a great number of other Web sites.

C. General Guides and Research Aids for Historians

1. General Guides

W. Wagar, *Books in World History: A Guide for Teachers and Students*, Bloomington, Ind., 1973.

H. J. Poulton, *The Historian's Handbook. A Descriptive Guide to Reference Works*, Norman, Okla., 1974, 3rd ed.

A. J. Walford, *Guide to Reference Material*, 3 vol., London, 1996, 7th ed. (vol. 2: social and historical sciences); vol. 1 of 8th ed. was published in 1999; others in process.

T. P. Slavens, *Sources of Information for Historical Research*, New York, 1994; core works on national histories.

A. Brundage, *Going to the Sources: A Guide to Historical Research and Writing*, Wheeling, Ill., 1997, 2nd ed.

J. Tosh, *The Pursuit of History*, New York, 2000, 3rd ed.

2. Searchable Internet Databases of Interest for Historians

[National Endowment for the Humanities], *EDSITEment*, WWW-public access (http://edsitement.neh.gov/history.html?all); guide to important history and humanities sites on Internet.

[University of Groningen, The Netherlands], *WWW Services for Historians*, WWW-public access (http://odur.let.rug.nl/ahc/; click on "History Links").

D. Guides to Secondary Works

1. General Bibliographies

a. Retrospective bibliographies

Note: Older bibliographies may contain valuable references that are not included in the recent printed and electronic guides.

F. M. Coulter and M. Gersenfeld, *Historical Bibliographies: A Systematic and Annotated Guide*, New York, 1965.

D. S. Berkowitz, *Bibliographies for Historical Researchers*, Waltham, Mass., 1969.

E. H. Boehm, *Bibliographies in History*, 2 vol., Santa Barbara, Calif., 1988; all countries.

R. H. Fritze, B. E. Coutts, L. A. Vyhnanek (eds.), *Reference Sources in History: An Introductory Guide*, Santa Barbara, Calif., 1990; mostly English-language titles in European and American history.

M. B. Norton and P. Gerardi (eds.), *Guide to Historical Literature*, 2 vol., New York: American Historical Association, 1995, 3rd ed.: list of monographs by subject; replaces the *Guide* of G. F. Howe of 1961.

b. Current bibliographies

M. Haverhals, a.o., *Bibliographie*, in: *Revue d'Histoire ecclésiastique*, Louvain, 1900–98. First vol. treats publications of 1899; last published vol. treats publications of 1996–97 (1998). Although focusing on church history, this is in fact a general bibliography; several tables have been published indexing the vols. of the years 1900–26, 1927–40, 1941–60, 1961–75.

[Historical Association], *Annual Bulletin of Historical Literature*, London, 1912–98. First vol. treats publications of 1911 (1912); last published vol. treats 1996 (1998).

[International Committee of Historical Sciences], *International Bibliography of the Historical Sciences*, Paris, 1930–99. First vol. treats publications of 1926 (1930); last published vol., 62, 1997, treats 1993.

c. Databases on-line and on CD-ROM

[Association for History and Computing, in connection with the Queen Mary and Westfield College in London], *Historical Computing Bibliography*, CD-ROM and WWW-subscription, 1993–; address: http://odur.let.rug.nl/ahc.

[ABC-Clio], *America: History and Life*, CD-ROM and WWW-subscription; address: 130 Cremona, P.O. Box 1911, Santa Barbara, CA 93116–1911, or 34A Great Clarendon Street, Oxford, OX2 6AT, England. Contents: citations and abstracts (14,000 records a year) of books, articles (from 2100 journals), dissertations published since 1964; also, since 1988, reviews of films and video products. Subject coverage: history, area studies, current affairs, interdisciplinary studies of historical interest, history-related topics in the social sciences and humanities, *but exclusively* for the U.S. and Canada.

[ABC-Clio], *Historical Abstracts*, CD-ROM and WWW-subscription (same address as *America* . . .). Contents: citations and abstracts of books, articles, dissertations published in forty languages since 1955; on CD-ROM since 1982. Subject coverage: history of the world, *except* the U.S. and Canada. Chronological coverage: part A, Modern History Abstracts (1450–1914), part B, Twentieth Century Abstracts, 1914 to the present. An annual cumulative index (ed. R. W. Davis) is available, covering subjects, authors, titles, and reviewers.

[University Microfilms, Ann Arbor, Mich.], *Dissertation Abstracts*, CD-ROM and WWW-subscription. Contents: dissertations, mostly in the U.S.; covers 1861 to the present, searchable by keywords. Also available via OCLC.

2. Bibliographies of Periodical Literature

[Carrolton Press], *CRIS: The Combined Retrospective Index Set to Journals in History, 1838–1974*, Washington, D.C., 1977–78; contains indexes, by subjects and keywords, to 240 English-language journals in history, through 1974.

E. H. Boehm, a.o., *Historical Periodical Directory*, 5 vol., Santa Barbara, Calif., 1981–86; 8900 journals.

3. Bibliographies of Books and Periodicals, by Topic

a. By country

Austria

Retrospective bibliographies

E. H. Boehm and F. Fellner (eds.), *Oesterreichische Historische Bibliographie, 1945–1964*, 3 vol., Salzburg—Santa Barbara, Calif., 1967–85.

D. Salt, *Austria: World Bibliographical Series*, vol. 66, Oxford—Santa Barbara, Calif., 1986.

Current bibliography

E. H. Boehm, F. Fellner, G. Hödl (eds.), *Oesterreichische Historische Bibliographie*, Santa Barbara, Calif. (from 1977 also Salzburg), yearly, 1st vol. in 1968 treating 1965.

Belgium

Retrospective bibliographies

H. Pirenne, *Bibliographie de l'histoire de Belgique*, Brussels, 1931, 3rd ed.; primary sources and secondary literature for the period from Roman times to 1914, published through 1930.

P. Gérin, a.o. (eds.), *Bibliographie de l'histoire de Belgique*, 4 vol., Louvain—Paris, 1960–86; covers the period 1789–1940.

J. A. Van Houtte (ed.), *Un quart de siècle de recherche historique en Belgique, 1944–1968*, Louvain—Paris, 1970; annotated listings of books and articles.

P. Gérin, *Nouvelle initiation à la documentation écrite de la période contemporaine*, Liège, 1982; covers modern history.

R. C. Riley, *Belgium*, World Bibliographical Series, vol. 104, Oxford—Santa Barbara, Calif., 1989.

L. Genicot (ed.), *Vingt ans de recherche historique en Belgique, 1969–1988*, Brussels, 1990; annotated listings of books and articles.

Current bibliography

J. Dhondt, R. Van Eenoo, a.o. (eds.), *Bibliographie de l'histoire de Belgique*, in: *Revue belge de philologie et d'histoire*; annual current bibliography, first vol. treats publications of 1952 (1953); last vol. published in 1999 treats publications of 1997.

Canada

E. B. Ingles, *Canada*, World Bibliographical Series, vol. 62, Oxford—Santa Barbara, Calif., 1990.

Czechoslovakia (former)

D. Short, *Czechoslovakia*, World Bibliographical Series, vol. 68, Oxford—Santa Barbara, Calif., 1986.

H. Jilek, *Bibliographie der böhmischen Länder von den Anfangen bis 1948*, 3 vol., Cologne, 1986–90.
Bibliografie Ceskoslovenské historie za rok, yearly 1961–.

France

Retrospective bibliographies
J. Glénisson, *La recherche historique en France de 1940 à 1965*, Paris, 1965; Id., *La recherche . . . depuis 1965*, Paris, 1980.
P. Duval, *Les sources de l'histoire de France des origines à la fin du XVe siècle*, t. 1, 2 vol., Paris, 1971 (this 1st tome covers from the beginning to the 5th century).
F. Barbier, *Bibliographie de l'histoire de France*, Paris, 1987.
F. Chambers, *France*, World Bibliographical Series, vol. 13, Oxford—Denver, Colo., 1990, rev. ed.
M. Balard, *Bibliographie de l'histoire médiévale en France (1965–1990)*, Paris, 1992 (= addition to Id., *L'histoire médiévale en France*, Paris, 1991).

Current bibliography
C. Albert-Samuel, a.o. (eds.), *Bibliographie annuelle de l'histoire de France*, Publ. du *CNRS*, vol. 1 treats 1955, Paris, 1956; last published vol. treats 1998 (1999); in 1964 an extra volume was published treating publications of 1953–54.

Germany

Retrospective bibliographies
H. Heimpel and H. Geuss (eds.), *Dahlmann—Waitz, Quellenkunde der deutschen Geschichte. Bibliographie der Quellen und der Literatur zur deutschen Geschichte*, 11 vol., Stuttgart, 1965–98, 10th ed.; contents: sources and secondary literature.
D. S. Detwiler, *West Germany*, World Bibliographical Series, vol. 72, Oxford—Santa Barbara, Calif., 1987.
W. Baumgart, *Bücherverzeichnis zur deutschen Geschichte: Hilfsmittel, Handbücher, Quellen*, Munich, 1988, 7th ed.

Current bibliographies
F. Hartung, a.o. (eds.), *Jahresberichte für deutsche Geschichte*, new series, Berlin, vol. 1, 1952 (treating 1949), last vol. 1997 treating 1996). Biennial, German history from the earliest period through 1945 (continuation of a former series with the same title, 1920–42).
[Arbeitsgemeinschaft ausseruniversitärer historischer Forschungseinrichtungen], *Historische Bibliographie*, Munich, from 1987 (treating 1986) on.
Bibliographie zur Zeitgeschichte, Stuttgart, 1953–.

Great Britain

Retrospective bibliographies
E. B. Graves, a.o. (eds.), *Bibliography of British History*, 7 vol., Oxford, 1951–96; covers the period from Roman times to 1989.

J. J. Hecht and G. R. Elton (eds.), *Bibliographical Handbooks* [Conference on British Studies], 8 vol., Cambridge, U.K., 1968–87; covers the period 1066 to the present; less comprehensive than Graves.

J. Cape (ed.), *Writings on British History, 1901–1933*, 5 vol. (in 7 tomes), London, 1968–70; covers works on the period 450–1914, published between 1901 and 1933.

A. E. Day, *England*, World Bibliographical Series, vol. 160, Oxford—Santa Barbara, Calif., 1993.

J. T. Rosenthal, *Late Medieval England, 1377–1485: A Bibliography of Historical Scholarship, 1975–1989*, Kalamazoo, Mich., 1994.

L. J. Butler and A. Gorst (eds.), *Modern British History: A Guide to Study and Research*, London, 1997.

Current bibliographies

A. T. Milne, D. J. Munro, H. J. Creaton, a.o. (eds.), *Writings on British History*, London, 1937–86; annual; first vol. published in 1937 treating the publications of 1934 (from about 450 to 1914); last vol. published in 1986 treating the publications of 1973–74 (from about 450 to 1939).

G. R. Elton, A. Gee, a.o. (eds.), *Annual Bibliography of British and Irish History*, Royal Historical Society, Hassocks, later Oxford, annually 1976–. First vol. published in Hassocks, 1976, on the publications of 1975; last available vol. published in Oxford, 2000, on the publications of 1999 (from 450 to the present). This series is the follow-up of Milne.

[CD-ROM]: J. Morrill (ed.), *The History of Britain, Ireland and the British Overseas* [Royal Historical Society], Oxford, 1998; first edition in electronic form, includes publications to 1992 (is supplementary to the printed *Annual Bibliography*).

Greece

M. J. Clogg, *Greece*, World Bibliographical Series, vol. 17, Oxford—Santa Barbara, Calif., 1980.

Hungary

T. Kabdebo, *Hungary*, World Bibliographical Series, vol. 15, Oxford—Santa Barbara, Calif., 1980.

Italy

Retrospective bibliography

L. Sponza, *Italy*, World Bibliographical Series, vol. 30, Oxford—Santa Barbara, Calif., 1995.

Current bibliography

[Giunta centrale per gli studi storici], *Bibliografia storica nazionale*, Rome, vol. 1, 1942 (on 1939); index of books and articles published in Italy on Italian history.

The Netherlands

Retrospective bibliographies
H. De Buck, *Bibliografie der geschiedenis van Nederland*, Leiden, 1968 (unchanged reprint in 1979).
P. King, *The Netherlands*, World Bibliographical Series, vol. 88, Oxford—Santa Barbara, Calif., 1988.

Current bibliographies
A. Gast, a.o., *Repertorium van boeken en tijdschriftartikelen betreffende de geschiedenis van Nederland*, Leiden, 1943–95 (on 1940–91).
[Pica, Leiden], *Repertorium van boeken en tijdschriftartikelen betreffende de geschiedenis van Nederland*, WWW-subscription; since 1998 the repertory of Gast is continued by this digital distribution by Pica (Schipholweg, 99, PB 876, 2300 AW Leiden, The Netherlands), for publications from 1992 on.

Poland

Retrospective bibliographies
J. Baumgart and S. Gluszek, *Bibliografia historii polskiej za lata, 1944–47*, Warsaw, 1962.
A. Wyczanski, *La recherche historique en Pologne, 1945–1960*, Warsaw, 1970.
A. G. Kanka, *Poland: An Annotated Bibliography of Books in English* [Garland Reference Library of the Humanities], New York, 1988.
G. Sanford, *Poland*, World Bibliographical Series, vol. 32, Oxford—Santa Barbara, Calif., 1993; rev. ed.

Current bibliography
[Académie des Sciences, Warszawa], *Bibliografia historii polskiej*, yearly, 1st vol. 1952, treating 1948.

Portugal

Retrospective bibliographies
P. T. Unwin, *Portugal*, World Bibliographical Series, vol. 71, Oxford—Santa Barbara, Calif., 1987.
A. H. R. de Oliveira Marques, *Guia de historia da la republica portuguesa*, Lisbon, 1997.

Current bibliographies
A. Machado de Faria (ed.), *Arquivo historico de Portugal*, Lisbon, 1958–.

Romania

Retrospective bibliographies
A. Deletant, *Romania*, World Bibliographical Series, vol. 59, Oxford—Santa Barbara, Calif., 1985.
O. D. Popa, *Ceaucescu's Romania: An Annotated Bibliography*, Westport, Conn., 1994; publications treating 1944–89.

Current bibliography
S. Pascu, a.o., *Bibliografia istorica a Rombniei*, Bucarest, Academia Republicii Social-
iste Rombnia, 1985–.

Soviet Union (former)
P. L. Horecky, *Russia and the Soviet Union: A Guide to Basic Publications*, Chicago,
1965.
A. Thompson, *Russia/USSR*, World Bibliographical Series, Oxford—Santa Bar-
bara, Calif., 1979.
B. Schaffner, *Bibliography of the Soviet Union*, Metuchen, N.J., 1995.
[Inter Documentation Catalogue, Leiden, The Netherlands], *Russia, USSR, East-
ern Europe: Books and Serials*, 1996.

Spain (including some references to scholarly literature on Latin America)
Retrospective bibliographies
A. Palau y Dulcet, *Manual del librero hispano-americano. Bibliografia general española*,
28 vol., Barcelona, 1948–77; index: A. Palau Claveras, *Indice alfabetico . . .* , 7
vol., Oxford, 1981–87.
O. F. Gonzalez, *Manual bibliografico de estudios espanoles*, Pamplona, 1976.
G. J. Shields, *Spain*, World Bibliographical Series, vol. 60, Oxford—Santa Barbara,
Calif., 1985.

Current bibliography
[Centro de estudios historicos internacionales], *Bibliographia historica de España e
Hispanoamérica*, Barcelona, Universidad, from 1955 on (treating publications
of 1953–54); books and articles on Spanish and Latin American history, published in western Europe and the Americas.

Sweden

Retrospective bibliographies
K. Setterwall, a.o., *Svensk historisk bibliografi*, 6 vol., Stockholm—Uppsala,
1881–1978.
L. B. Sather, *Sweden*, World Bibliographical Series, vol. 80, Oxford—Santa Barbara, Calif., 1987.

Current bibliography
Bibliography, in: *Scandinavian Journal of History*, 1984–, in English; before: *Excerpta
historica nordica*, 10 vol., Copenhagen, 1955–80.

Switzerland

Retrospective bibliographies
J. L. Santschy, *Manuel analytique et critique de bibliographie générale de l'histoire suisse*,
Bern, 1961.
H. K. Meier, *Switzerland*, World Bibliographical Series, vol. 114, Oxford—Santa
Barbara, Calif., 1990.

Current bibliography

H. Barth, *Bibliographie der Schweizergeschichte*, 3 vol., Basel, 1914–15; after 1915 annual updates, from 1921 on as an appendix of *Zeitschrift für Schweizerische Geschichte*.

United States

Retrospective bibliographies

N. R. Priess, *American Studies: An Annotated Bibliography of Reference Works for the Study of the United States*, Seattle, Wash., 1978.

[R. R. Bowker Co.], *The American Book Publishing Record cumulative, 1950–1977: An American National Bibliography*, 15 vol., New York, 1978.

[R. R. Bowker Co.], *The American Book Publishing Record cumulative, 1876–1949: An American National Bibliography*, 15 vol., New York, 1980.

F. Freidel, *Harvard Guide to American History*, 2 vol., Cambridge, Mass.—London, 1980.

H. P. Beers, *Bibliographies in American History, 1942–1978*, 2 vol., Woodbridge, Conn., 1982.

S. R. Herstein, *United States of America*, World Bibliographical Series, vol. 16, Oxford—Santa Barbara, Calif., 1982.

G. L. Cole, *Civil War Eyewitnesses: An Annotated Bibliography of Books and Articles, 1955–1986*, Columbia, S.C., 1988.

Current bibliographies

[ABC-Clio], *America: History and Life*, CD-ROM and WWW-subscription; references: see above, Sec. D.1.c. (Databases on-line and on CD-ROM).

[University Publications of America], *Scholarly Book Reviews*, CD-ROM, since 1992 (on publ. from 1991 on), updated every three months, reviews of books published in the U.S. and Canada.

Yugoslavia (former)

J. J. Horton, *Yugoslavia*, World Bibliographical Series, vol. 1, Santa Barbara, Calif., 1990.

b. By region

Africa

Retrospective bibliographies

Y. Scheven, *Bibliography for African Studies, 1970—1986*, London, 1988.

Y. Scheven, *Bibliography for African Studies, 1987–1993*, London, 1994.

J. B. Howell and Y. Scheven, *Guides, Collections and Ancillary Materials to African Archival Resources in the U.S.*, Madison, Wisc., 1996.

A. Kagan and Y. Scheven, *Reference Guide to Africa: A Bibliography of Sources*, Lanham, Md., 1998.

Current bibliographies

M. Mahoney and M. Driskell (eds.), *International Africa Bibliography: Current Books, Articles and Papers in African Studies*, London, yearly, 1970–.

H. Blackhurst, *Africa Bibliography*, Manchester, U.K., yearly, 1985–.

Research Bibliography

Asia

Retrospective bibliographies
G. R. Nunn, *Bibliography of Asian History*, Cambridge, U.K., 1971.
G. R. Nunn, *Asia: Reference Works: A Selected Annotated Guide*, London, 1980.
M. L. P. Patterson, *South Asian Civilization: A Bibliographical Synthesis*, Chicago, 1981.
G. R. Nunn, *Asia and Oceania: A Guide to Archival and Manuscript Sources in the U.S.*,
   5 vol., London—New York, 1985.
H. T. Zurndorfer, *China Bibliography: A Research Guide to Reference Works about China
   Past and Present*, Honolulu, 1999.

Current bibliographies
G. E. Gaskill (ed.), *Far Eastern Bibliography*, in: *The Far Eastern Quarterly*, from 1948
   to 1956 (treating 1955).
H. P. Linton (ed.), *Bibliography of Asian Studies*, in: *The Journal of Asian Studies*, from
   1957 (treating 1956) to 1969 (treating 1968).
R. C. Howard (ed.), *Bibliography of Asian Studies*, Ann Arbor, Mich., from 1970
   (treating 1969) to 1997 (treating 1991).
[University of Leiden], *Bibliotheca Orientalis*, Leiden, annual review from 1944 on.
   Last vol. in 1998.
[Association for Asian Studies, Univ. of Michigan, Ann Arbor], *Bibliography of
   Asian Studies*, WWW-subscription, http://bas.umdl.umich.edu/b/bas; from
   1971 to the present.

Eastern and Southeast Europe

P. L. Horecky, *East Central Europe: A Guide to Basic Publications*, Chicago, 1969.
Idem, *Southeastern Europe: A Guide to Basic Publications*, Chicago, 1969.
M. Croucher, *Slavic Studies: A Guide to Bibliographies, Encyclopedias, and Handbooks*,
   Wilmington, Del., 1993.
S. D. Gyeszly, *Eastern Europe: A Resource Guide: A Selected Bibliography*, San
   Bernardino, Calif., 1994.
R. H. Burger and H. F. Sullivan, *Eastern Europe: A Bibliographic Guide to English Lan-
   guage Publications, 1986–1993*, Englewood, Colo., 1995.

Latin America

Retrospective bibliographies
S. A. Bayitch, *Latin America and the Caribbean. A Bibliographical Guide to Works in Eng-
   lish*, Coral Gables, Fla., 1967.
C. Griffin and J. R. Warren, *Latin America: A Guide to the Historical Literature*, Austin,
   Tex.—London, 1971.
R. A. McNeil, *Latin American Studies: A Basic Guide to Sources*, Metuchen, N.J., 1990.
P. H. Carrington, a.o., *Latin America and the Caribbean: A Critical Guide to Research
   Sources*, New York, 1992.
J. M. Perez, *Latin American Bibliography*, Lanham, Md., 1998.

Current bibliographies
M. Burgin, a.o. (eds.), *Handbook of Latin American Studies (Humanities)*, Cambridge,

Mass., 1947, treating publications of 1944; until 1976, then continued by the following series.

D. M. Martin, a.o. (eds.), *Handbook of Latin American Studies (Humanities)*, Austin, Tex., from 1977 on, last vol. in 1997. Now also available on Internet, WWW-public access: *Handbook of Latin American Studies*, (http://lcweb2.loc.gov/hlas). Contents: citations and abstracts of books, book chapters, articles, conference papers.

[Duke University], *Hispanic American Historical Review*, Washington, D.C., 1918–25; Durham, N.C., 1926–; yearly bibliography; indexes: C. Gibson, *Guide to the HAHR, 1946–1955*, Millwood, N.Y., 1976; S. Ross, *Guide to the HAHR, 1956–1975*, Durham, 1980.

Near and Middle East—Islam

J. D. Pearson, *Index Islamicus, 1906–1955*, London—Cambridge, U.K., 1958; *1956–60*, 1962; *1961–65*, 1967; *1966–70*, 1972; *1971–75*, 1977; *1976–80*, 1983; also available on CD-ROM, 1998.

G. N. Atiyeh, *The Contemporary Middle East, 1948–1973: A Selective and Annotated Bibliography*, Boston, 1975.

D. Grimwood-Jones, *Middle-East and Islam: A Bibliographical Introduction*, New York, 1979; supplement: P. Auchterlomie, *Middle-East and Islam*, Zug, 1986, treating 1977–83.

Catalogue of English Language Books and Periodicals on the Arab and Islamic World, New York, 1981.

W. Behn, *Index Islamicus, 1665–1905*, Millersville, Pa., 1989.

S. R. Silverburg, *Middle East Bibliography*, Metuchen, N.J., 1992.

G. J. Roper, *Index Islamicus, 1981–1985*, London—Cambridge, U.K., 1991; *1986–93*, 1995; *1994–97*, 1999; also available on CD-ROM.

Southern Europe

J. Loughlin (ed.), *Southern European Studies Guide*, London, 1993; bibliography on Cyprus, Greece, Italy, Malta, Portugal, and Spain.

c. By period

Classical

Retrospective bibliographies

T. P. Halton and S. O'Leary, *Classical Scholarship: An Annotated Bibliography*, White Plains, N.Y., 1986.

K. Hopwood, *Ancient Greece and Rome: A Bibliographical Guide*, Manchester, U.K.—New York, 1995.

G. Whitaker, *A Bibliographical Guide to Classical Studies*, 2 vol., Hildesheim—New York, 1997.

Current bibliography

Bibliographie critique et analytique de l'Antiquité gréco-latine, in: *L'année philologique*, from 1928 on (treating 1927). Contents: Greek and Roman history, literature, philosophy, art, archaeology, religion, mythology, science, Greek and Latin language, early Christian history, numismatics, papyrology, and epigraphy. Period from the 2nd millennium B.C. through the early middle ages (ca. 500–800 A.D.). Now also available on CD-ROM: *The Database of Classical Bibliography*; electronic form of the printed volumes 45–60 (1976–90) of *L'année philologique*, covering 248,399 items (books and articles) published on classical subjects, in any language, from 1974 to 1989. Address: ScholComm@aol.com.

Medieval

Retrospective bibliographies and general guides
L. J. Paetow, *A Guide to the Study of Medieval History*, London, 1931, 2nd ed. (rpt., 1980).
C. P. Farrar and A. P. Evans, *Bibliography of English Translations from Medieval Sources*, New York—London, 1964, 3rd ed.
R. C. Van Caenegem and F. L. Ganshof, *Guide to the Sources of Medieval History*, Amsterdam, 1978.
G. C. Boyce, *Literature of Medieval History*, 5 vol., New York, 1981; publications from 1930 to 1975; update of Paetow.
E. U. Crosby, a.o. (eds.), *Medieval Studies: A Bibliographical Guide*, New York—London, 1983; 9000 entries, in 138 subdivisions (countries, themes).
J. M. Powell (ed.), *Medieval Studies: An Introduction*, Syracuse, 1992, 2nd ed.; esp. overview of various auxiliary sciences useful for medieval history.
R. C. Van Caenegem, F. L. Ganshof, L. Jocqué, *Introduction aux sources de l'histoire médiévale* [Corpus Christianorum. Continuatio Mediaevalis], Turnhout, 1997 (update of the English version of 1978).
O. Guyotjeannin, *Les sources de l'histoire médiévale*, Paris, 1998.
[Georgetown University, Washington, D.C.], *Labyrinth*, WWW-public access (http://www.georgetown.edu/labyrinth); research guides and primary source materials in medieval history.

Current bibliographies
[International Medieval Institute, Leeds], *International Medieval Bibliography*, Leeds, printed version, 1968–. Contents: books, articles from 900 journals and Festschriften, essays, reviews, and manuscripts. Subject coverage: history, archaeology, literature, and theology. See next item.
[University of Leeds], *International Medieval Bibliography, 1972–1996*, CD-ROM, 1997; address: www.brepols.com/publishers; items from 1976–95 included.
C. Leonardi (ed.), *Medioevo latino. Bolletino bibliografico della cultura europea dal secolo VI al XIII*, Spoleto, Società Internazionale per lo Studio del Medioevo Latino, 1980–. On-line and CD-ROM version: http://sismel.meri.unifi.it.

Renaissance

[Fédération internationale des sociétés et instituts pour l'étude de la Renaissance], *Bibliographie internationale de l'Humanisme et de la Renaissance*, Geneva, yearly from 1966 on.

Modern

J. Roach, *A Bibliography of Modern History*, Cambridge, U.K., 1968.

J. P. Halstead and S. Porcari, *Modern European Imperialism: A Bibliography of Books and Articles, 1818–1972*, 2 vol., Boston, 1974.

H. Kehr and J. Langmaid, *The Nazi Era, 1919–1945: A Select Bibliography*, London, 1982.

T. Vogelsang, a.o., *Bibliographie zur Zeitgeschichte: 1953–1980. Geschichte des 20. Jahrhunderts bis 1945*, Munich—New York, 1982; *Supplement 1981–1989*, Munich—New York, 1991.

P. Ross, *Fascism and Pre-Fascism in Europe, 1890–1945: A Bibliography of the Extreme Right*, Brighton, U.K. 1984.

R. J. Caldwell, *Era of the French Revolution: A Bibliography of the History of Western Civilization, 1789–1799*, 2 vol., New York, 1985.

A. J. Edelheit, *Bibliography on Holocaust Literature*, Boulder, Colo., 1986.

A. G. S. Enser, *A Subject Bibliography of the First World War: Books in English, 1914–1987*, London, 1990.

A. G. S. Enser, *A Subject Bibliography of the Second World War and Aftermath: Books in English, 1939–1974*, London, 1977; Id., *1975–1987*, Brookfield, Vt., 1990.

C. Lehmann, *Der Zweite Weltkrieg. Auswahlbibliographie*, Dresden, 1995.

J. F. Higbee, *Western Europe since 1945*, Lanham, Md., 1996; listing of primarily English language sources on Europe in the humanities and social sciences, since World War II.

d. By subject

African American history

L. D. Smith, *Afro-American History: A Bibliography*, Clio Bibliography Series, 2 and 8, 2 vol., New York—Oxford, 1974–80.

H. Aptheker, *Afro-American History*, New York, 1992.

P. T. Murray, *The Civil Rights Movement: References and Resources*, New York, 1993.

Art

E. Arntzen and R. Rainwater, *Guide to the Literature of Art History*, Chicago—London, 1980.

[Getty Information Institute], *Bibliography of the History of Art*, WWW-public access, since 1991 (www.getty.edu/gateway/index; click on "databases"). Contents: several bibliographic databases; the *Bibliography* is an English-French database (as a follow up to the former *Répertoire d'art et d'archéologie*, published from 1910 on, by the Société des amis de la bibliothèque d'art et d'archeologie, Paris), providing up-to-date bibliography on all aspects of Western art (144,000 records, in 1999). The *Avery Index* is the only American index giving current literature in architecture and design; by subscription via http://www.getty.edu/publications. *Witt Computer Index* contains more than one million photographic reproductions.

[H. W. Wilson Company], *Art Index*, CD-ROM and WWW-subscription, since

1984. Contents: ca. 257,000 citations to books and articles in ca. 225 periodicals in the U.S. and Europe. Subject coverage: art history, archaeology, film, photography, etc.

Diaries

P. P. Havlice, *And So to Bed: A Bibliography of Diaries published in English*, Metuchen, N.J., 1987.
B. Klibanski, *Collection of Testimonies: Memoirs and Diaries. 1. Guide to the Yad Vashem Archives, Catalogue 12*, Jerusalem, 1990.
L. Arksey, a.o. (eds.), *American Diaries*, 2 vol., Detroit, 1983–97.

Film

[Univ. of California, Berkeley], *The American Film Institute Catalog of Motion Pictures*, 14 vol., New York, 1971–88, on 45,000 movies from 1893 to 1970. Now also on CD-ROM and on-line at http://afi.chadwyck.com.
P. Cowie (ed.), *World Filmography*, London, yearly, 1977–98.
[International Federation of Film Archives], *International Film Archive*, CD-ROM; address: 6, Nottingham St., London, W1M 3RB; bibliography of holdings of 125 institutions worldwide. Includes: *International Index to Film Periodicals, International Index to Television Periodicals*, 1983–.
[British Film Institute], *Film Index International*, CD-ROM; address: Chadwyck-Healey, Cambridge, U.K.; 90,000 films, yearly updated.

Legal History

J. Gilissen (ed.), *Bibliographical Introduction to Legal History and Ethnology*, 9 vol., Brussels, 1963–88; mostly on secondary literature but also on primary sources.

Military history

[Commission Internationale d'histoire militaire comparée], *Bibliographie internationale d'histoire militaire*, Bern, annual, 1977–98.

Religion and history of religion

[American Theological Library Association], *Religion Index (ATLA)*, CD-ROM and WWW-subscription (http://www.atla.com/products/products.html; click on "Atla Print"), since 1975. Contents: 1,000,000 citations to ca. 500 journals and 450 works, 1949–. Subject coverage: all aspects of world religions, history of religion, theology, church history, biblical studies, church and state, archaeology.
Tze-chung Li, *Social Science Reference Sources: A Practical Guide*, New York, 1990, 2nd ed.

Urban history

Retrospective bibliography
H. Stoob, *Bibliographie zur deutschen historischen Städteforschung*, 2 vol., Cologne, 1986–92.

H. J. Teuteberg and C. Schütte, *Vergleichende geschichtliche Städteforschung. Annotierte Gesamtbibliographie, 1976–1988*, Münster, 1989.

R. Rodger, *A Consolidated Bibliography of Urban History*, Aldershot, 1996.

W. Prevenier and P. Stabel (eds.), *Bibliographies on European Urban History* [Studia Historica Gandensia, 282], Ghent, 1996; Belgium, Ireland, Spain.

Current bibliography

R. Rodger, *Urban History*, Cambridge, U.K., from 1987; last vol., n. 26, 1999. Contents: ca. 1000 items, from monographs and 560 periodicals.

Women's history

P. K. Ballou, *Women: A Bibliography of Bibliographies*, Boston, 1986, 2nd ed.

S. M. Stuard (ed.), *Women in Medieval History and Historiography*, Philadelphia, 1987 (paperback rpt., 1991).

[National Information Services Corporation, NISC], *Women's Resources International*, CD-ROM: Wyman Towers, 3100, St Paul St., Baltimore, Md., 21218. Contents: 116,000 listings of books and articles since 1972, on women's studies, gender studies, feminist theory and literary criticism; nonprint resources.

[Haverford College, Pa.], *Medieval Feminist Index*, WWW-public access (http://www.haverford.edu/library/reference/mschaus/mfi.html).

E. Primary Sources

1. Guides to Published (and Unpublished) Sources

Note: Most of the guides mentioned above, especially in Sections D.1 (Guides to Secondary Works: General Bibliographies) and D.3 (Guides to Secondary Works: Bibliographies of Books and Periodicals, by Topic), also provide references to printed and unprinted primary sources and text editions. This is especially the case for the works of Heimpel and Geuss, Powell, Pirenne, and Van Caenegem, Ganshof, and Jocqué.

a. General

A. W. Pollard and G. R. Redgrave, *A Short-Title Catalogue of Books Printed in England, Scotland, and Ireland, 1475–1640*, London, 1991, 2nd ed.

D. Wing, *A Short-Title Catalogue of Books Printed in England, Scotland, Ireland, Wales, and the British Americas, 1641–1700*, New York, 1994, 2nd ed.

[British Library], *English Short Title Catalogue (ESTC)*, CD-ROM and WWW-subscription; address: Great Russell Street, London, WC1B 3DG (http://www.bl.uk/collections/epc/cdflier.html). Contents: 400,000 full descriptions for every item printed in England and in England's dependencies throughout the world, from 1473 to 1800 (books but also songs, pamphlets, etc.). Resumes the just-mentioned printed versions but extends the chronological range. Another CD-ROM and WWW-subscription exists for the incunabula in the British Isles: [British Library and Gale Group, Farmington Hills, Mich.], *Incunable Short Title*

Catalogue. For the 19th and 20th centuries an edition has been started: *Nineteenth Century Short Title Catalogue*, Newcastle upon Tyne, from 1984 on, for the years 1801–1918.

[St John's University, Collegeville, Minn.], *The Hill Monastic Manuscript Library*, CD-ROM and WWW-subscription; copies of ca. 90,000 vol. of manuscripts (25 million pages), from libraries in Europe and the Middle East; address: http://www.hmml.org.

[Univ. of California, Berkeley], *Online Medieval and Classical Library*, WWW-public access (http://sunsite.berkeley.edu/OMACL). Contents: hundreds of major classical and medieval works, in original language and in English translation.

b. Middle Ages

A. Potthast, *Bibliotheca historica medii aevi. Wegweiser durch die Geschichtswerke des europäischen Mittelalters bis 1500*, Berlin, 1896, 2nd ed.; partly (A–N) replaced by the following item.

[Istituto Storico Italiano, Rome], *Repertorium fontium historiae medii aevi*, Rome, 1962–98. Contents: analysis and bibliography of medieval authors of chronicles, annals, etc., 400–1500, arranged alphabetically; now reached vol. 8, letter N; O–P is in progress. An index is available on WWW-public access (http://rm-cisadu.let.uniroma1.it/isime [note the numeric after "uniroma"]).

[Institut de Recherche et d'Histoire des Textes], *Répertoire bio-bibliographique des auteurs latins, patristiques et médiévaux*, Paris—Cambridge, U.K., 1987; 492 microfiches: 210,000 cards, 18,000 medieval authors.

J. Berlioz, a.o. (eds.), *Identifier sources et citations* [L'atelier du médiéviste], Turnhout, 1994.

A. J. Andra, *The Medieval Record: Sources of Medieval History*, Boston, 1997.

P. Tombeur, a.o. *Thesaurus Diplomaticus. Guide de l'utilisateur. CD-ROM* [Cetedoc. Comité national du Latin médiéval. Commission royale d'Histoire], Turnhout (Brepols), 1997. Contents: CD-ROM with analyses, full text, and photographs of all printed and unprinted charters before 1200, made by or granted to institutions and individuals in the southern Netherlands; update until 1225 is ready; program intends to reach 1350, and to be constantly updated for new archival findings and new editions. This first electronic charter edition will be extended to other European countries.

c. Modern history

Y. Bauer, a.o., *Guide to Unpublished Materials of the Holocaust*, 5 vol., Jerusalem, 1970–79.

J. Robinson and P. Friedman, *The Holocaust and After: Sources and Literature in English*, Jerusalem, 1973.

d. Latin America

M. Grow (ed.), *Scholars' Guide to Washington, D.C., for Latin American and Caribbean Studies*, Washington, D.C., 1992, 2nd ed.

e. Women's history

American Women's History: A Research Guide, WWW-public access (http://frank.mtsu.edu/~kmiddlet/history/women.html).

A Guide to Uncovering Women's History in Archival Collections, WWW-public access (http://www.lib.utsa.edu/Archives/links.htm).

2. Selected Published Source Collections

a. Church, hagiography, and religion

Acta sanctorum [= AA.SS], 67 vol., Antwerp, Brussels, Tongerloo, 1643–1940. Contents: edition, by the Jesuit community in the Spanish Netherlands, the Bollandists, of the *Vitae* (= lives) of the saints, grouped under the date of their feast, reaching November 10. Additional editions and studies in the Bollandist periodical *Analecta Bollandiana*; index: F. Halkin, *Inventaire hagiographique des t. 1 (1882) à 100 (1982)*, Brussels, 1983; full ed. on CD-ROM and on-line (subscription) is planned, to be published from 1999 to 2002 by Chadwyck-Healey, Cambridge, U.K.: http://acta.chadwyck.co.uk. The first part, covering January–April, was released in 2000.

J. P. Migne, *Patrologiae cursus completus* [= Patrologia Latina], 222 vol., Paris, 1844–64; CD-ROM and Internet in progress by Chadwyck-Healy, Cambridge, U.K, 1993–: http://pld.chadwyck.co.uk.

E. Dekkers, a.o. (eds.), *Corpus christianorum. Series latina*, 147 vol., Turnhout, 1954–96. Contents: critical edition of old Christian authors, to 735; continued for Christian authors from 735 to the 12th century by the series *Continuatio mediaevalis*, 146 vol., 1966–96.

P. Tombeur, *Cetedoc Library of Christian Latin Texts*, Turnhout, 1991–; edition on microfiches and on CD-ROM, of the *Corpus christianorum*, of Migne, *Patrologiae*, and other editions, with wordlists and many other indexes. Contents: 34 million forms from 1900 texts (e.g., the Vulgate, the Old Testament) from 400 authors (Augustine, Bernard of Clairvaux, Thomas à Kempis).

Note: Information on available collections, Internet and CD-ROM: www.brepols.com/publishers; http://www.chadwyck.co.uk.

b. Editions of sources on national history

Note: The best overview is R. C. Van Caenegem, F. L. Ganshof, L. Jocqué, *Introduction aux sources de l'histoire médiévale*, Turnhout, 1997, 295–322.

France

Chartes et diplômes relatifs à l'histoire de France, 25 vol., Paris, 1908–.

Germany

Monumenta Germaniae Historica, Hannover, 1826–. Contents: editions of sources from 500 to 1500; [CD-ROM], ed. Brepols, from 1996 on (project covers the whole collection).

W. Heinemeyer, *Gesamtverein der deutschen Geschichts- und Altertumsvereine*, Cologne, 1986, 2nd ed.

Great Britain

Rerum Britannicarum Medii Aevi Scriptores (Rolls Series), 253 vol., London, 1858–1911. Listings in: M. D. Knowles, *Great Historical Enterprises*, London, 1963, 98–134.

E. L. C. Mullins, *Texts and Calendars: An Analytical Guide to Serial Publications [to 1957]*, London, Royal Historical Society, 1958; Id., *Texts . . . 1957–1982*, London, 1983.

United States

[Library of Congress, Washington, D.C.], *American Memory*, WWW-public access (http://lcweb2.loc.gov/ammem). Contents: texts, films, photographs, recordings, on all possible topics of American history.

[Bureau of the Census, Washington, D.C.], *Historical Statistics of the United States*, WWW-public access (http://www.census.gov/mp/www/pub/gen/msgen11b.html). Contents: statistics on a large number of social and economic issues for the years 1790–1970. Now also available on a CD-ROM edition by Cambridge University Press: S. Carter, a.o. (eds.), *Historical Statistics of the United States*, Cambridge, U.K., 1997; see http://uk.cambridge.org/reference/catalogue/0521585414.

[University of Chicago], *Center for Research Libraries*, WWW-public access (http://wwwcrl.uchicago.edu/info/crlcat.htm); access to U.S. and foreign documents of the most varied kinds.

W. B. Dickinson, a.o., *Historic Documents*, 27 vol., Washington, D.C. 1973–99 (includes cumulative indexes; a global index covering 1972–95 appeared in 1997).

[U.S. Department of Health], *Vital Statistics of the U.S., 1992–93*, 3 vol., Hyattsville, Md., 1996–99.

c. Medieval

Memdb: an online searchable database of information concerning the medieval and early modern periods of European history: http://scco1.rutgers.edu/memdb.

3. Newspapers

[Lexis-Nexis ed., Dayton], *Lexis-Nexis Academic Universe*, WWW-subscription: 9443, Springboro Pike, PO Box 933, Dayton, OH 45401–0933. Contents: a searchable archive of full-text articles and transcripts from over 18,000 publications (newspapers, journals) and media broadcasts (wire services, newsletters, government documents, transcripts of broadcasts), going back to the mid-1980s.

The New York Times Index, New York, 1913–.

[Chadwyck-Healey, Cambridge, U.K.], *The Times (London) Index*, CD-ROM and WWW-subscription, Reading, U.K., 1973–.

[Chadwyck-Healey, Cambridge, U.K.], *Financial Times* (U.K. ed.), CD-ROM and WWW-subscription (tables not included).

Le Monde (Paris), on CD-ROM: full text 1987–, selection of the archives of the journal for 1939–96; http://archives.lemonde.fr; also check a more general French Web site: http://www.ocd.fr.

4. On-line Periodicals

[Univ. of California, San Diego], *New Jour*, WWW-public access (http://gort.ucsd. edu/newjour). Contents: guide to scholarly journals published exclusively on the Internet.

[University of Michigan, Ann Arbor], *JSTOR*, WWW-public access (http://www. jstor.org). Contents: free access to the full text of articles in some 117 scholarly journals (mostly from the start of the journal to a cut-off point of 3 to 5 years ago): e.g., *American Historical Review, Journal of Modern History, Journal of American History, Speculum.*

F. Inventories of Archives and Libraries in Europe and the United States

1. General

D. H. Thomas and L. M. Case, *The New Guide to the Diplomatic Archives of Western Europe*, Philadelphia, 1975.

G. E. Weil, *The International Directory of Manuscripts, Collections, Libraries, Repositories and Archives, I, Europe. The Manuscript Collections*, Paris, 1978.

R. Wedgeworth (ed.), *A.L.A. World Encyclopedia of Library and Information Services*, Chicago, 1986, 2nd ed.

A. Vanrie (ed.), *International Directory of Archives*, in: *Archivum. International Review on Archives*, vol. 38, Munich—New York—London—Paris, 1992, 4th ed.; lists, addresses, and practical information on archives in the whole world; see also vol. 36, 1991, for an *International Bibliography of Directories and Guides to Archival Repositories.*

P. O. Kristeller and S. Krämer, *Latin Manuscript Books before 1600: A List of the Printed Catalogues and Unpublished Inventories*, Munich, 1993, 4th ed.

B. Bartz, *World Guide to Special Libraries*, Munich, 1995, 3rd ed.

J. R. Fang, *World Guide to Library, Archive, and Information Science*, Munich, 1995, 2nd ed.

W. van der Meer (ed.), *World Guide to Libraries*, New York—Munich, 1998, 13th ed.; addresses and brief description of collections.

http://www.uidaho.edu/special_collections/Other.Repositories.html (gives links to thousands of Web sites of archives and document collections throughout the world).

2. Belgium and the Netherlands

J. Nicodème, *Répertoire des inventaires d'archives conservées en Belgique*, Brussels, 1970.

W. J. Formsma, *Gids voor de Nederlandse archieven*, Haarlem, 1985, 4th ed.

L. M. T. L. Hustinx (ed.), *Overzicht van de archieven . . . in Nederland*, 14 vol., Alphen aan de Rijn, 1979–92.

3. Central and Eastern Europe

M. Hughes, *Guide to Libraries in Central and Eastern Europe*, London, British Library, 1992.

4. France

J. Favier, *Les Archives Nationales. Etat général des fonds*, 5 vol., Paris, Archives Nationales, 1978–88.

[Archives Nationales], *Etat des inventaires des archives départementales, communales et hospitalières*, 2 vol., Paris, 1984.

J. Favier, *Les Archives Nationales. Etat des inventaires*, 3 vol., Paris, Archives Nationales, 1985–91.

E. K. Welsch, *Archives and Libraries in France*, New York, Council for European Studies, 1991.

5. Germany, Austria, and Switzerland

Archive im deutschsprachigen Raum, 2 vol., Berlin—New York, 1974; revision of the 1932 ed. by P. Wentzke and G. Lüdtke. Contents: on 8000 archives in Germany, Switzerland, and Austria.

E. Welsch, a.o., *Archives and Libraries in a New Germany*, New York, Council for European Studies, 1994.

6. Great Britain

H. Jenkinson, *Guide to the Public Records, I. Introductory*, London, 1949.

Guide to the Contents of the Public Record Office, 3 vol., London, 1963–69.

J. Foster and J. Sheppard, British Archives. *A Guide to Archive Resources in the United Kingdom*, New York, 1995, 3rd ed.

7. Italy and the Vatican

G. Battelli, a.o., *Bibliografia dell'Archivio Vaticano*, 6 vol., Città del Vaticano, 1962–95; description of collections, editions.

L. E. Boyle, *A Survey of the Vatican Archive*, Toronto, 1972.

R. J. Lewanski, *Guide to Italian Libraries and Archives*, New York, Council for European Studies, 1979.

C. Pavone, a.o., *Guida generale degli Archivi di Stato italiani*, 4 vol., Rome, 1981–94.

I. Zanni Rosiello, *Andare in archivio*, Bologna, 1996.

8. Poland

R. C. Lewanski, *Guide to Polish Libraries and Archives*, New York, 1974.
M. Konopka, *Archiwa w Polsce*, Warsaw, 1998.

9. Soviet Union (former)

R. C. Lewanski, *Eastern Europe and Russia/Soviet Union: A Handbook of Western European Archival and Library Resources*, New York, 1980.
P. K. Grimsted, *A Handbook for Archival Research in the USSR*, New York, 1989.
L. V. Repulo, *Arkhivy Rossii*, Moscow, 1997 (English version: *Archives of Russia*, Armonk, N.Y., 2000).
P. K. Grimsted, *A Directory and Bibliographic Guide to Holdings in Moscow and St. Petersburg*, London, 1998.

10. Spain

Guia de los archivos estatales españoles, Madrid, 1984, 2nd ed.
[Asociacion Española de Archiveros Eclesiasticos], *Guia de los archivos y las bibliotecas de la Iglesia en España*, 2 vol., León, 1985.
[Ministry of Culture], *Spanish Ministry of Culture*, WWW-public access (http://www.mcu.es/lab/index.html). Contents: guide to the state libraries and archives.

11. United States

P. M. Hamer, *A Guide to Archives and Manuscripts in the U.S.*, New Haven, Conn., 1961.
F. B. Evans (ed.), *Guide to the National Archives of the United States*, Washington, D.C., 1988.
F. P. Prucha, *Handbook for Research in American History: A Guide to Bibliographies and Other Reference Works*, Lincoln, Nebr., 1994.
[National Archives and Records Administration, Washington, D.C.], *NARA Archival Information Locator, Guide to Federal Records in the National Archives of the U.S.*, WWW-public access (http://www.nara.gov). Contents: information on holdings of the National Archives of the U.S., on the Regional Records Services, on presidential libraries, on publications, locations, and hours.
[Library of Congress, Washington, D.C.], *The RLIN Archives and Manuscript Collections (AMC) File*, WWW-public access (http://www.lcweb.loc.gov/z3950/rli-namc.html). Search tool for locating archives and manuscripts (including oral history collections and personal collections). Includes former inventories and guides; more specifically: the National Union Catalog of Manuscript Collections, 1959–95; the National Inventory of Documentary Sources in the U.S.; the Directory of Archives and Manuscript Repositories in the U.S., 1996.
[National Association of Government Archives and Records Administrators], *Nagara*, WWW-public access (http://www.nagara.org/websites.html). Contents: links to catalogs of National, Provincial, and State Archives of the U.S. and Canada.

J. W. Raimo, *A Guide to Manuscripts relating to America in Great Britain and Ireland*, Westport, Conn., 1979, 2nd ed.

II. Additional Readings on Selected Technical Topics

A. Library Science

F. Milkau and G. Leyh, *Handbuch der Bibliothekswissenschaft*, Wiesbaden, 1952–65.
S. L. Jackson, *Libraries and Librarianship in the West*, New York, 1974.
P. Dain and J. Y. Cole (eds.), *Libraries and Scholarly Communications in the United States: The Historical Dimension*, New York, 1990.

B. Archival Science

A. H. Leavitt, *Manual for the Arrangement and Description of Archives*, New York, 1940; still useful.
P. Marot, R.H. Bautier, M. Duchein (eds.), *Manuel d'archivistique*, Paris, 1970.
J. Papritz, *Archivwissenschaft*, 4 vol., Marburg, 1983, 2nd ed.
F. Hildesheimer, *Les archives*, Paris, 1984.
P. Walne (ed.), *Dictionary of archival terminology*, Munich—New York, 1988, 2nd ed.; English, French, Spanish, German, Italian, Russian, Dutch.
B. Delmas, *Dictionnaire des archives, français-anglais-allemand*, Paris, 1991.
J. Favier and D. Neirinck (eds.), *La pratique archivistique française*, Paris, 1993.
E. Franz, *Einführung in die Archivkunde*, Darmstadt, 1994.
Archivum: review with practical information and yearly current bibliography, 1951–.

C. Text Editing

J. Hamesse (ed.), *Les problèmes posés par l'édition critique des textes anciens et médiévaux*, Louvain-la-Neuve, 1992.
T. W. Machan, *Textual Criticism and Middle English Texts*, Charlottesville, Va., 1994; mostly on literary texts.
A. J. Veenendaal and J. Roelevink, *Unlocking Government Archives of the Early Modern Period*, The Hague, 1995.
V.P. McCarren and D. Moffat (eds.), *A Guide to Editing Middle English*, Ann Arbor, Mich., 1998; on editing literary and scientific writings; on the use of computer software.

D. Guides to Source Analysis

1. General

L. Genicot (ed.), *Typologie des sources du moyen âge*, 86 fascicules to date, Turnhout, 1972—2000 (from 1993 directed by R. Noël). Tables on fascs. 1–50 published in 1992 (ed. L. Genicot).

2. Personal Narratives

J. Vansina, *Oral Tradition: A Study in Historical Methodology*, Chicago, 1965.
P. P. Hovlice, *Oral History: A Reference Guide*, Jefferson, N.C., 1985.
J. Vansina, *Oral Tradition as History*, Madison, Wisc., 1985 (rpt., 1997).
R. Parks and A. Thomson (eds.), *The Oral History Reader*, New York, 1988.
P. R. Thomson, *The Voice of the Past: Oral History*, Oxford—New York, 1988, 2nd ed.
M. Frisch, *A Shared Authority: Essays on the Craft and Meaning of Oral and Public History*, Albany, N.Y., 1990.
R. J. Grele, *Envelopes of Sound*, New York, 1991.
D. K. Dunaway, *Oral History: An Interdisciplinary Anthology*, Walnut Creek, Calif., 1996.
Oral Histories Online, WWW-public access (http://sunsite.berkeley.edu:2020/dynaweb/teiproj/oh), Web site on oral history from the University of California at Berkeley.

E. Technical Aids and Auxiliary Sciences

In general: R. C. Van Caenegem, F. L. Ganshof, L. Jocqué, *Introduction aux sources de l'histoire médiévale*, Turnhout, 1997, pp. 443–550.

1. Paleography

L. E. Boyle, *Medieval Latin Palaeography. A Bibliographical Introduction*, Toronto, 1984 (2207 items).
B. Bischoff, *Latin Palaeography: Antiquity and the Middle Ages*, Cambridge, U.K., 1991 (rpt., 1993), translated from German.
J. Stiennon, *Paléographie du moyen âge*, Paris, 1991, 2nd ed.
F. Gasparri, *Introduction à l'histoire de l'écriture*, Louvain-la-Neuve, 1994.
J. Stiennon, *L'écriture [Typologie des Sources du Moyen Age occidental]*, Turnhout, 1995.
The Digital Scriptorium, WWW-public access (http://sunsite.berkeley.edu/Scriptorium), a visual catalog of dated and datable manuscripts from American collections, useful for paleographers and art historians.
A. Cappelli, *Lexicon abbreviaturarum. Dizionario di abbreviature latine ed italiane*, Milan, 1979, 6th. ed. Thousands of solutions for abbreviations. English translation: D. Heimann and R. Key, *The Elements of Abbreviation in Medieval Latin Palaeography*, Lawrence, Kans., 1982. The 1961 ed. of Cappelli is in fact a reprint of the 3rd ed. of 1929, revised by the author after the original of 1899. New research done since 1929 may be found in two more recent repertories, giving additions, but not replacing Cappelli: K. Siefert, *Abbreviaturen. 2000 deutsche und lateinische Abkürzungen aus alten Urkunden*, Beerfelden, 1995, 7th ed.; A. Pelzer, *Abbréviations latines médiévales*, Louvain—Paris, 1995, 3rd ed. For abbreviations in English charters: C. T. Martin, *The Record Interpreter: A Collection of Abbreviations*, London, 1910, 2nd ed.
O. Pluta (ed.), *Abbreviationes*, CD-ROM; Bochum, in progress since 1993. Address:

http://www.ruhr-uni-bochum.de/ philosophy/projects/abbrev.htm. Present volume: 60,000 medieval Latin abbreviations; available at a cost of 48 Euros. When finished, this database will replace Cappelli.

2. Diplomatics

H. Bresslau, *Handbuch für Urkundenlehre*, 2 vol., Leipzig, 1912–31 (rpt., 1968–69; index by H. Schulze in 1960).

L. E. Boyle, *Diplomatics*, Syracuse, N.Y., 1992, 2nd ed.

O. Guyotjeannin, J. Pycke, B. M. Tock, *Diplomatique médiévale*, Turnhout, 1995, 2nd ed. (with addenda).

M. M. Carcel Orti, R. H. Bautier, W. Prevenier, a.o., *Vocabulaire International de la Diplomatique* [Commission Internationale de Diplomatique], Valencia, 1997, 2nd ed. A most useful handbook, giving definitions of all possible terms of diplomatics in several languages (English, French, German, Latin, Spanish, Dutch, etc.; 13 indexes).

3. Codicology, Miniatures, and Rare Books

A. Dain, *Les manuscrits*, Paris, 1964.

L. Gilissen, *Prolégomènes à la codicologie*, Ghent, 1977.

D. Muzerelle, *Vocabulaire codicologique. Répertoire méthodique des termes français relatifs aux manuscrits*, Paris, 1985.

J. Lemaire, *Introduction à la codicologie*, Louvain-la-Neuve, 1989.

M. P. Brown, *Understanding Illuminated Manuscripts: A Guide to Technical Terms*, London, 1994 (a dictionary with a bibliography).

D. H. Steinberg, *Five Hundred Years of Printing*, New Castle, Del.—London, 1996 (overview and bibliography of printed books).

Scriptorium. Revue internationale des études relatives aux manuscrits, Antwerp (now Brussels), 1946–.

4. Chronology

a. Handbooks for deciphering old dating systems

H. Grotefend, *Taschenbuch der Zeitrechnung*, Hannover, 1982, 12th ed.; the most practical handbook for translating dates according to the present-day Western calendar (see also the long version: *Zeitrechnung* . . . , Hannover, 1891–98, rpt., 1970–84).

C. R. Cheney, *Handbook of Dates for Students of English History*, London, 2000, 2nd ed., rev. M. Jones; practical guide to techniques for deciphering old dating systems.

M. Gervers, *Dating Undated Medieval Charters*, Rochester, N.Y., 2000.

b. Time scales and lists of rulers

C. G. Allen (ed.), *Rulers and Governments of the World*, 3 vol., London—New York, 1977–78.

W. Conze, a.o., *Epochen und Daten der deutschen Geschichte*, Freiburg i. Breisgau, 1983, 3rd ed.

E. Fryde, a.o., *Handbook of British Chronology*, London, 1986, 3rd ed.

T. Charmasson, a.o., *Chronologie de l'histoire de France*, Paris, 1994.

5. Papyrology

N. Lewis, *Papyrus in Classical Antiquity*, Oxford, 1989.

P. W. Pestman, *The New Papyrological Primer*, Leiden—New York, 1994, 6th ed. This is a revised version of the study by D. Martin (1965).

H. A. Rupprecht, *Kleine Einführung in die Papyruskunde*, Darmstadt, 1994 (gives a full bibliography).

R. S. Bagnall, *Reading Papyri, Writing Ancient History*, London—New York, 1995.

6. Heraldry and Genealogy

L. G. Pine, *Your Family Tree: A Guide to Genealogical Sources*, London, 1962; handsome bibliography.

J. Franklyn and J. Tanner, *An Encyclopaedic Dictionary of Heraldry*, Oxford, 1970; terminolgy in 7 languages.

O. Neubecker, *A Guide to Heraldry*, New York, 1980.

C. A. Von Volborth, *Heraldry*, New York, 1981.

O. Neubecker, *Deutsch und Französisch für Heraldiker*, Munich, 1983.

E. Zieber, *Heraldry in America*, New York, 1984.

T. FitzHugh, *The Dictionary of Genealogy*, London, 1991, 3rd ed.

S. Friar, *Heraldry for the Local Historian and Genealogist*, Stroud, Gloucestershire, 1997.

M. Pastoureau, *Heraldry*, New York, 1997.

Archivum Heraldicum, Lausanne, 1954– (before, from 1887: *Archives héraldiques suisses*); excellent periodical.

7. Numismatics

R. Carson, *Coins: Ancient, Medieval, and Modern*, London, 1970.

P. Grierson, *Bibliographie numismatique*, Brussels, 1979, 2nd ed.

R. G. Doty, *The Macmillan Encyclopedic Dictionary of Numismatics*, New York—London, 1982.

E. Clain-Stefanelli, *Numismatic Bibliography*, Munich, 1985.

P. Spufford, *Handbook of Medieval Exchange*, London, 1986.

Idem, *Money and Its Use in Medieval Europe*, Cambridge, U.K., 1988.

P. Grierson, *The Coins of Medieval Europe*, London, 1991.

[International Numismatic Commission], *A Survey of Numismatic Research, 1966–71*, New York, 1973; *1972–77*, 1979; *1978–84*, 1986; *1985–90*, 1991; *1990–95*, 1997.

8. Epigraphy

A. Deman, *Epigraphie latine*, Brussels, 1977, 2nd ed.
J. S. Allen and I. Sevcenko, *Literature in various Byzantine Disciplines, 1892–1977*, vol. 1, *Epigraphy*, Washington, D.C., 1981.
W. Koch, *Literaturbericht zur mittelalterlichen und neuzeitlichen Epigraphik (1976–1984)*, Munich, 1987; Id., *(1985–1991)*, Munich, 1994.
R. Favreau (ed.), *Epigraphie et iconographie*, Poitiers, 1996.
R. Favreau, *Epigraphie médiévale* [L'atelier du médiéviste, n. 5], Turnhout, 1997.

9. Sigillography

G. C. Bascapé, *Sigillografia*, 3 vol., Milan, 1969–84.
M. Pastoureau, *Les sceaux*, Turnhout, 1981.
R. H. Bautier, *Vocabulaire international de sigillographie*, Rome, 1990.

10. Archaeology

M. Joukowsky, *A Complete Manual of Field Archaeology*, Englewood Cliffs, N.J., 1980.
M. J. Aitken, *Science-based Dating in Archeology*, London—New York, 1990.
I. Hodder, *Reading the Past*, Cambridge, U.K., 1991, 2nd ed.
A. Clark, *Seeing beneath the Soil: Prospecting Methods in Archaeology*, London, 1996.
C. Renfrew and P. Bahn, *Archaeology: Theories, Methods, and Practice*, [London—New York], 1996, 2nd ed.
J.-M. Pesez, *L'archéologie*, Paris, 1997.

11. Auxiliary Sciences of Art History

L. F. Genicot, *Introduction aux sciences auxiliaires traditionelles de l'histoire de l'art*, Louvain-la-Neuve, 1984.

12. Statistics

S. Kotz and N.L. Johnson (eds.), *Encyclopedia of Statistical Sciences*, 9 vol. (A–Z), New York, 1982–88; 3 vol. with updates, 1989–99.
K. H. Jarausch and K. A. Hardy, *Quantitative Methods for Historians*, Chapel Hill, N.C., 1991.
R. Darcy and R. C. Rohrs, *A Guide to Quantitative History*, Westport, Conn., 1995.
R. D. Drennan, *Statistics for Archeologists*, New York, 1996.
A. Aron and E. Aron, *Statistics for the Behavioral and Social Sciences*, Upper Saddle River, N.J., 1997.
J. Jaccard and M. A. Becker, *Statistics for the Behavioral Sciences*, Pacific Grove, Calif., 1997, 3rd ed.
L. Madrigal, *Statistics for Anthropology*, Cambridge, U.K.—New York, 1998.
B. Thorne and S. Slane, *Statistics for the Behavioral Sciences*, Mountain View, Calif., 2000, 3rd ed.

13. Computers and History

E. Shorter, *The Historian and the Computer: A Practical Guide*, Englewood Cliffs, N.J., 1971.
A. Gilmour-Bryson (ed.), *Computer Applications to Medieval Studies*, Kalamazoo, Mich., 1984.
D. I. Greenstein, *A Historian's Guide to Computing*, Oxford—New York, 1994 (extensive bibliography of 24 pp.).
G. Jaritz, a.o. (eds.), *The Art of Communication: Proceedings of the Eighth International Conference of the Association for History and Computing*, Graz, 1995.
J. L. Pinol and A. Zysberg, *Métier d'historien avec un ordinateur*, Paris, 1995.
C. Harvey and J. Press, *Databases in Historical Research*, New York, 1996.
M. J. Lewis, *Using Computers in History*, London—New York, 1996.

III. Basic Readings on Historiography and Theory

Note: This list is limited to books in English that focus on traditions of Western historiography or on major social and cultural theorists whose work has deeply affected Western historiography. It is necessarily a very selective list, emphasizing recent commentaries or surveys. Readers will find references to the principal works of major theorists, to non-English sources, and to article literature in those sources. In particular, readers may wish to consult M. B. Norton (ed.), *A Guide to Historical Literature* (3rd ed.), American Historical Association and Oxford University Press, 1995.

A. Historiography

1. Classics

T. Carlyle, *On Heroes and Hero-Worship and the Heroic in History*, London, 1840.
G. W. F. Hegel, *Reason in History*, London, 1892; orig. Ger., Berlin, 1842.
F. Nietzsche, *The Use and Abuse of History*, New York, 1914; orig. Ger., Leipzig, 1893.
J. Burckhardt, *Force and Freedom: Reflections on History*, New York, 1943; orig. Ger., Berlin, 1905.
J. Burckhardt, *On History and Historians*, New York, 1958; orig. Ger., Berlin, 1929.
C. L. Becker, *The Heavenly City of the Eighteenth Century Philosophers*, New Haven, Conn., 1932.
Idem, *Everyman His Own Historian*, New York, 1935.
P. Geyl and A. J. Toynbee, *Can We Know the Pattern of the Past?*, Bussum, The Netherlands, 1948.
M. Bloch, *The Historian's Craft*, New York, 1953; orig. Fr., Paris, 1949.
H. Butterfield, *The Whig Interpretation of History*, London, 1950.
I. Berlin, *The Hedgehog and the Fox*, New York, 1953.
I. Berlin, *Historical Inevitability*, New York, 1954.

J. B. Bury, *The Idea of Progress*, New York, 1955.
J. Huizinga, *Men and Ideas: History, the Middle Ages, and the Renaissance*, New York, 1959; 2nd ed., Princeton, 1984.
E. H. Carr, *What Is History?* New York, 1961.
P. Geyl, *Encounters in History*, New York, 1961.

2. *Histories of Historiography*

F. Stern (ed.), *Varieties of History*, New York, 1956.
W. Wagar (ed.), *The Idea of Progress since the Renaissance*, New York, 1969.
G. Mazour, *The Writing of History in the Soviet Union*, Stanford, Calif., 1971.
G. G. Iggers, *New Directions in Historiography*, Middletown, Conn., 1975.
D. Hay, *Annalists and Historians: Western Historiography from the 8th to the 18th Centuries*, London, 1977.
E. Breisach, *Historiography: Ancient, Medieval, and Modern*, Chicago, 1983; Chicago, 1994, 2nd ed.
W. Fornara, *The Nature of History in Ancient Greece and Rome*, Berkeley, Calif., 1983.
E. B. Fryde, *Humanism and Renaissance Historiography*, London, 1983.
C. Crossley, *French Historians and Romanticism: Thierry, Guizot, the Saint Simonians, Quinet, Michelet*, London, 1993.
S. Bann, *Romanticism and the Rise of History*, New York, 1994.
M. Bentley (ed.), *Companion to Historiography*, London, 1997.
G. G. Iggers, *Historiography in the Twentieth Century: From Scientific Objectivity to the Postmodern Challenge*, Hanover, N.H., 1997.
D. R. Kelley, *Faces of History: Historical Inquiry from Herodotus to Herder*, New Haven, Conn., 1998.

3. *Theory/Method in History*

R. G. Collingwood, *The Idea of History*, Oxford, 1946.
A. O. Lovejoy, *Essays in the History of Ideas*, Baltimore, 1948.
K. Löwith, *Meaning in History*, Chicago, 1949.
P. Gardiner, *The Nature of Historical Explanation*, Oxford, 1961.
W. H. Dray, *Philosophy of History*, Englewood Cliffs, N.J., 1964.
H. Stuart Hughes, *History as Art and as Science*, New York, 1964.
A. Danto, *Analytical Philosophy of History*, Cambridge, U.K., 1965.
W. H. Dray (ed.), *Philosophical Analysis and History*, New York, 1966.
G. R. Elton, *The Practice of History*, London, 1967.
I. Topolski, *Methodology of History*, Boston, 1976; orig. Pol., Warsaw, 1968.
R. A. Nisbet, *Social Change and History*, New York, 1969.
R. Berkhofer, *A Behavorial Approach to Historical Analysis*, New York, 1971.
H. Fleischer, *Marxism and History*, New York, 1973.
M. Mandelbaum, *The Anatomy of Historical Knowledge*, Baltimore, 1977.
C. Cohen, *Karl Marx's Theory of History*, Oxford, 1978.
P. Burke, *Sociology and History*, London, 1980.
C. Tilly, *As Sociology Meets History*, New York, 1981.

D. C. North, *Structure and Change in Economic History*, New York, 1981.

C. Ginzburg, *Clues, Myths, and the Historical Method*, Baltimore, 1989; orig. Ital., Turin, 1986.

P. Novick, *That Noble Dream: The "Objectivity Question" and the American Historical Profession*, Cambridge, U.K., 1988.

L. Krieger, *Ideas and Events: Professing History*, ed. M. L. Brick, Chicago, 1992.

J. Owensby, *Dilthey and the Narrative of History*, Ithaca, N.Y., 1994.

W. H. Dray, *History as Re-enactment: R. G. Collingwood's Idea of History*, Oxford, 1995.

G. L. Gaddis, *On Contemporary History*, Oxford, 1995.

M. Sheehan, *The Balance of Power: History and Theory*, London, 1996.

B. G. Smith, *The Gender of History: Men, Women, and Historical Practice*, Cambridge, Mass., 1998.

4. On the New Histories

L. de Mause, *The New Psychohistory*, New York, 1975.

T. Stoianovich, *French Historical Method: The Annales Paradigm*, Ithaca, N.Y., 1976.

T. K. Rabb and R. Rotberg, *The New History*, Princeton, 1982.

G. Himmelfarb, *New History and the Old*, Cambridge, Mass., 1987.

W. McK. Runyan, *Psychology and Historical Interpretation*, New York 1988.

J. W. Scott, *Gender and the Politics of History*, New York, 1988.

L. Hunt (ed.), *The New Cultural History*, Berkeley, Calif., 1989.

P. Burke, *The French Historical Revolution: The Annales School, 1929–89*, Cambridge, U.K., 1990.

H. Kaye and K. McClelland (eds.), *E. P. Thompson: Critical Perspectives*, Cambridge, U.K., 1990.

B. Mazlish, *The Leader, the Led and the Psyche: Essays in Psychohistory*, Hanover, N.H., 1990.

P. Burke, *New Perspectives on Historical Writing*, Oxford, 1991.

P. Carrard, *Poetics of the New History: French Historical Discourse from Braudel to Chartier*, Baltimore, 1992.

G. Eley, a.o., *Culture, Power, History*, Princeton, 1993.

A. Wilson (ed.), *Re-thinking Social History*, Manchester, U.K., 1993.

J. Appleby, a.o., *Telling the Truth about History*, New York 1994.

R. Gildea, *The Past in French History*, London—New Haven, Conn., 1994.

D. LaCapra, *Representing the Holocaust: History, Theory, Trauma*, Ithaca, N.Y., 1994.

D. Dworkin, *Cultural Marxism in Postwar Britain: History, the New Left, and the Origins of Cultural Studies*, Durham, N.C., 1997.

5. History and Postmodernism

H. White, *Metahistory: The Historical Imagination in Nineteenth-Century Europe*, Baltimore, 1973.

M. de Certeau, *The Writing of History*, New York, 1988; orig. Fr., Paris, 1975.

F. R. Ankersmit, *History and Tropology*, Berkeley, Calif., 1994.

J. Goldstein, *Foucault and the Writing of History*, Oxford, 1994.
R. F. Berkhofer, *Beyond the Great Story*, Princeton, 1995.
H. Kellner and F. R. Ankersmit (eds.), *A New Philosophy of History*, London, 1995.
K. Jenkins (ed.), *The Postmodern History Reader*, London, 1996.
J. Appleby et al., *Knowledge and Postmodernism in Historical Perspective*, Cambridge, Mass., 1996.
G. Noiriel, *Sur la "crise" de l'histoire*, Paris, 1996. Also see Joan W. Scott, "Border Patrol" and Lloyd Kramer, "Gérard Noiriel's Pragmatic Quest for Paradigms," in *French Historical Studies* 21, 3 (Summer 1998).

B. On Theory from the Social Sciences and Humanities

1. The Traditional Social Sciences: Sociology, Marxism, Anthropology

H. Alpert, *Emile Durkheim and His Sociology*, New York, 1939.
W. Mommsen, *The Political and Social Theory of Max Weber*, Oxford, 1989.
R. Harker, C. Mahar, and C. Wilkes, *An Introduction to the Work of Pierre Bourdieu*, Houndmills, U.K., 1990.
H. Lehmann and G. Roth, *Weber's Protestant Ethic, Origins, Evidence, Contexts*, Cambridge, U.K., 1993.
S. Kalberg, *Max Weber's Comparative-historical Sociology*, Chicago, 1994.
S. W. Friedman, *Marc Bloch, Sociology and Geography: Encountering Changing Disciplines*, New York 1996.
S. Ortner (ed.), *The Fate of "Culture": Geertz and Beyond*, special issue of *Representations* 59 (Summer 1997).

2. Feminist Theory

T. Moi, *Sexual/Textual Politics*, London, 1985.
P. H. Collins, *Black Feminist Thought*, New York, 1990.
J. Butler and J. Scott (eds.), *Feminists Theorize the Political*, New York, 1992.
L. Alcoff and E. Potter (eds.), *Feminist Epistemologies*, London, 1993.
R. Hennessy, *Materialist Feminism and the Politics of Discourse*, New York, 1993.

3. Linguistics, Semiotics, Iconocology, and Hermeneutics

N. Chomsky, *Aspects of the Theory of Syntax*, Cambridge, Mass., 1965.
N. Goodman, *Languages of Art*, Indianapolis, 1968.
R. E. Palmer, *Hermeneutics: Interpretation Theory in Scheiermacher, Dilthey, Heidegger, and Gadamer*, Evanston, Ill., 1969.
J. D. Culler, *Ferdinand de Saussure*, New York, 1977.
J. Bleicher, *Contemporary Hermeneutics: Hermeneutics as Method, Philosophy, and Critique*, London, 1980.
F. R. Ankersmit, *Narrative Logic*, The Hague, 1983.

K. Mueller-Vollmer, *The Hermeneutics Reader*, New York, 1985.
W. J. T. Mitchell, *Iconocology*, Chicago, 1986.
H. P. Rickman, *Dilthey Today: A Critical Appraisal of the Contemporary Relevance of His Work*, New York, 1988.
Y. Lotman, *Universe of the Mind: A Semiotic Theory of Culture*, Bloomington, Ind., 1990.
F. Haskell, *History and Its Images*, New Haven, Conn., 1993.
M. A. Cheetham, a.o. (eds.), *The Subject of Art History: Historical Objects in Contemporary Perspectives*, New York, 1998.

4. Structuralism, Poststructuralism, and Cultural Studies

T. S. Kuhn, *The Structure of Scientific Revolutions*, Chicago, 1962.
J. Culler, *Structuralist Poetics*, New York, 1975.
T. Eagleton, *Literary Theory*, Oxford, 1983.
P. Burke and R. Porter, *The Social History of Language*, Cambridge, U.K., 1987.
R. Rorty, *Contingency, Irony, and Solidarity*, Cambridge, U.K., 1989.
H. A. Veeser, *The New Historicism*, New York, 1989.
U. Eco, *The Limits of Interpretation*, Bloomington, Ind., 1991; orig. Ital., Milan, 1990.
H. Bhabha, *The Location of Culture*, London, 1993.
K. P. Moxey et al., *Visual Culture: Images and Interpretations*, Hanover, N.H., 1993.
N. Royle, *After Derrida*, Manchester, U.K., 1995.

Index